God Without Violence

SECOND EDITION

God Without Violence

A Theology of the God Revealed in Jesus

SECOND EDITION

J. Denny Weaver

CASCADE *Books* • Eugene, Oregon

GOD WITHOUT VIOLENCE
A Theology of the God Revealed in Jesus. Second Edition

Copyright © 2020 J. Denny Weaver. All rights reserved. Except for brief quotations in critical publications or reviews, no part of this book may be reproduced in any manner without prior written permission from the publisher. Write: Permissions, Wipf and Stock Publishers, 199 W. 8th Ave., Suite 3, Eugene, OR 97401.

Cascade Books
An Imprint of Wipf and Stock Publishers
199 W. 8th Ave., Suite 3
Eugene, OR 97401

www.wipfandstock.com

PAPERBACK ISBN: 978-1-5326-9280-2
HARDCOVER ISBN: 978-1-5326-9281-9
EBOOK ISBN: 978-1-5326-9282-6

Cataloguing-in-Publication data:

Names: Weaver, J. Denny, 1941–, author.

Title: God without violence : a theology of God revealed in Jesus, second edition / J. Denny Weaver.

Description: Eugene, OR: Cascade Books, 2020 | Includes bibliographical references and index.

Identifiers: ISBN 978-1-5326-9280-2 (paperback) | ISBN 978-1-5326-9281-9 (hardcover) | ISBN 978-1-5326-9282-6 (ebook)

Subjects: LCSH: 1. Nonviolence—Religious aspects—Christianity. 2. Atonement. 3. Violence in the Bible. 4. God (Christianity). 5. Jesus Christ.

Classification: BT265.3 W44 2020 (print) | BT265.3 (ebook)

Manufactured in the U.S.A.   JUNE 4, 2020

For Zach,

Intuitive Theologian

Table of Contents

Preface to Second, Revised and Expanded Edition ix

Preface to 2016 Edition xi

Introduction 1

Ch. 1: The Story of Jesus 19

Ch. 2: The Story of Jesus and Atonement 33

Ch. 3: Atonement and God 42

Ch. 4: New Testament Teaching and Nonviolence 53

Ch. 5: Active Nonviolence 63

Ch. 6: Atonement, Forgiveness, Restorative Justice 76

Ch. 7: Jesus and Economics 84

Ch. 8: Racism, Ethnicity, and Gender 93

Ch. 9: The Omnipotence of God 101

Ch. 10: The Nonviolence of God's Creation 115

Ch. 11: God of the Biblical Narrative: Violent? 125

Ch. 12: God of the Biblical Narrative: Nonviolent? 132

Ch. 13: God of the Biblical Narrative: A Resolution 146

Ch. 14: Reading the Bible Again 154

Ch. 15: Interpreting Revelation 163

Ch. 16: Looking at the Past in Revelation 171

Ch. 17: Looking Ahead in Revelation? 184

Ch. 18: Does Theology Change? Christology 193

Ch. 19: Does Theology Change? Atonement 206

Open-ended Conclusion 217

Discussion Questions 221

Bibliography 229

Subject Index 235

Scripture Index 241

Preface to the Second, Revised and Expanded Edition

I DESCRIBED THE FIRST edition of *God Without Violence* as a summary for a lay audience of earlier academic writings, and the book was advertised as such. It was and still is a lay-oriented summary. However, in a moment of clarity soon after it appeared, I realized that it was more than a summary. Placing the chapters on change in Christology and atonement at the end of the book was not simply a random variation in the outline. Although I did not realize it at the time, their placement was in fact a reflection of the evolution of my approach to the development of theology. I have come to understand that theology emerges as the words that give meaning to and extend the story of Jesus as given in the New Testament. This process is ongoing, never truly finished. Thus, in addition to its stated purpose of serving lay readers, the book actually represented a new stage in my career-long efforts to understand how nonviolence impacted Christian theology. It is a book-length statement that theology (and ethics) are extensions of or give meaning to the story of Jesus. If theology emerges from the narrative of Jesus, then Jesus' rejection of violence becomes an intrinsic element of theology, and the book is an extended demonstration of that fact. Making explicit what was implicit in the first edition constituted the first reason for producing this revised edition.

Further, producing a revised edition allowed other changes as well. I expanded the discussion of nonviolence in a number of areas—in a new chapter, and with additional paragraphs throughout the book. With those additions, I also took the opportunity to make more visible the claim that Jesus' rejection of violence reflects the character of the Creator God, and the grain of the universe created by that God. The revised subtitle signals this approach to theology.

There have been a number of earlier statements of my understanding of theology, beginning with a forgettable essay published in 1984 that was my first venture into systematic theology after graduate study in Reformation theology. Each of these statements portrayed an answer to my original question about displaying nonviolence in theology, and each statement was stimulated by a development or advance in my understanding beyond the previous one. Given the rather advanced stage of my writing career, this version in hand may well be the last one. It is designed for non-specialists, for congregational study groups or college student classes. It is nonetheless a serious statement of my latest understanding of what theology should look like for Christians who believe that God's truth is revealed in Jesus Christ. It will also serve allies outside of Christian circles who want to know how Christian faith can mean peace.

A number of factors stimulated and facilitated the production of this second, expanded edition. I am grateful to my editor Robin Perry and the folks at Wipf & Stock for authorizing a second edition. In these past years I addressed many people in speaking engagements. Their questions and ensuing conversations revealed material that would expand the book's scope. The contributions of two individuals merit specific thanks. Bethany Johnson, a reservist with Christian Peacemaker Teams who has visited the village of At-Tuwani in the West Bank, read and commented on chapter 5. Valerie Showalter, pastor of Madison Mennonite church where I worship and theologian in her own right, read and provided much valuable commentary on the entire manuscript. Finally, I am continually blessed that my wife Mary accepts the presence of writing in my life.

J. Denny Weaver
Winter 2019–20

Preface to the 2016 Edition

Many people are responsible for planting the seeds that grew into this book. These stimulating folks include the individuals who said that they understood a presentation I had given, but doubted that they would make it through a long book with footnotes. They expressed a wish that I would write a popular version for lay people. Pastors told me that they would appreciate a book that would be accessible to lay readers for Sunday school classes and church study groups. And I was always aware that *The Nonviolent Atonement* and *The Nonviolent God* were not suitable for the college classes that I taught for thirty-one years. The product in hand is the result of these expressed wishes for a popular version of the arguments for nonviolent atonement and nonviolent God.

I need to comment on the fact that this book is supposed to be a popular theology. When friends asked what I was working on, I replied, "a popular theology." Then I routinely explained that "popular" is a technical term. In the academic world, popular does not mean that everyone likes it. It means rather that the end result is accessible to readers who are not specialists in theology. Readers will judge the extent to which this particular product succeeds as popular theology. And of course, I still hope that everyone likes it!

Even though this work intends to be popular theology, I hasten to add that it is nonetheless serious theology. The book deals with real theological and ethical issues, and I hope that readers will learn from and be stimulated and perhaps changed by their study and discussion of these issues.

The book is serious in another way as well. It represents my current thinking on the issues presented. Since learning and doing theology are ongoing tasks, I have wondered if any of the positions argued in this book are different from what I have written previously. I await the findings of future astute analysts to let me know if the views herein have gone beyond or veered away from or perhaps have reaffirmed my earlier writings.

Many people contributed to the writing of this book. Early on, breakfast or coffee shop interviews with Samuel Weaver, Katherine Weaver, Simon Weaver, and Seth Weaver helped me understand what teenagers knew about theology and the kind of arguments they could understand. Further, I needed lay readers to tell me if the manuscript was truly accessible to people who are not specialists in theology. I solicited readers from Madison Mennonite Church, the congregation where I worship. People who volunteered and read parts or all of the first draft of the manuscript are Alison Brookins, Norris Glick, Sandra Glick, Susan Horein, Mo Lancaster, Sally Schmidt, Annali Smucker, and Kent Sweitzer. Each of these folks offered comments and suggestions that I implemented in later revisions. I appreciate their assistance more than I can say. In addition, I am grateful to Michael Shank and Mark Ediger, who read and corrected parts of the manuscript that dealt with science, and to Tyler Nussbaum, whose Sunday sermon provided a reference that I used. Kent Sweitzer did double duty. After reading the first draft, he volunteered to read the entire second draft. He then discussed the manuscript with me over breakfast. Lisa Weaver helped me to conceptualize what it means to write a so-called popular manuscript, critiqued the final draft, and most importantly, provided the discussion questions at the end of the book. Lastly, I am grateful to Hannah Sandvold for creating "Elisha's Feast," the original artwork that graces the front cover.

It is more than gratifying that Wipf and Stock Publishers and editor Robin Parry were interested in my work. I am blessed that my wife Mary continues to respect the fact that I still have a need to produce manuscripts. And last of all, I am grateful to Zach Kaufman, intuitive theologian, whose question frames this book. And to your other question, Zach, when God holds the world in his hands, I don't think that God ever drops the ball.

J. Denny Weaver,
Winter, 2015–16

Introduction

A Seemingly Innocent Inquiry

A FEW YEARS AGO, a young mother sent me an email report on a conversation she had with her five-year-old son following Sunday school. He came home with questions about what God is allowed to do and what parents are allowed to do. After several rounds of queries, his real concern surfaced when he asked, "A parent would never put their child to death on the cross, right?" Many people will have little difficulty realizing that the question reflects the inherited understanding that "God sent Jesus to die on the cross for our sins."

This little boy's question—let's call him Zach—has stayed with me. It implies that he is somewhat skeptical—even fearful—of this inherited theology. It places God behind Jesus' death, orchestrating it. And if God did this to God's son, Zach wondered, would human parents perhaps do it to their son? The unstated implication is that God can and does employ violence. And through Zach's question, we arrive at the conclusion that the Christian God is a violent God, a God who employs violence, a God who would have the Son, Jesus, killed for God's purposes.

In this book readers will discover an understanding of God that will reassure Zach and put his mind at ease. I hope that adults will also appreciate this God as well. They will discover that the Christian God, the God revealed in Jesus, is a God who does not employ violence, a God who would not send Jesus in order to have him cruelly killed on a cross. The Christian God is a nonviolent God. This profession of faith stands at the heart of this book and the questions it addresses.

Much, but not all, of the discussion in this book concerning violence and nonviolence in theology is drawn from my earlier books on nonviolent atonement and nonviolent God.[1] However, the book in hand is more than a popular summary of that material. Beyond the earlier works, the different outline of this book demonstrates a methodology and an important characteristic of theology, namely that Christian theology consists of the words that extend or draw meaning from the story of Jesus as told in the New Testament. Theology is obviously much more than a repetition of that story, but the following pages make clear that it begins with that story.

The seemingly innocent query by a five-year-old boy actually raises a number of significant questions about our inherited theology. For one, it implies that the most important thing Jesus did was to die. But if his most important act was dying, why do the four Gospels spend so much time on his life and teaching, and why do the Gospels end with Jesus' resurrection as the climax of his life?

Apart from the question about imitating God, Zach's query poses a question about our response to this image of the God who would have the Son killed. We hear frequently that "God is love," and that we should worship and adore the God who loves us. But would a God described as "love" really arrange specifically for the killing of God's Son in order to satisfy God's purpose? And pointedly, can we worship and adore a God who would have the Son killed for God's purposes? Do we even want to worship such a God?

The latent fear behind Zach's question points to a link between Christian theology and Christian practice. Zach wanted reassurance that parents would not imitate God's treatment of Jesus. More widely, if God, who is deemed good and called "love," can employ violence for God's purposes, does that authorize God's followers to follow the divine example and employ violence for their purposes? Or at least to employ violence to assist what they believe to be God's purposes? In other words, as God's people, to what extent are we called to imitate and participate in the violence of a violent God?

The idea of a link between theology and actions also concerns the image of Jesus in the inherited idea that God needed Jesus to die for our sins. It is clearly understood that Jesus was innocent and did not deserve to die. Yet Jesus accepted an undeserved death for the good of others.

---

1. Weaver, *Nonviolent Atonement* and Weaver, *Nonviolent God*.

With the manner of his death, Jesus models passive submission to undeserved suffering because a higher authority, namely God, needed it. When I was Zach's age, in Sunday school I learned that I was supposed to "be a Jesus boy." Jesus boys were taught to follow the example of Jesus' actions. But is the model of Jesus, who passively submitted to undeserved suffering or punishment, a good model for five-year-olds like Zach and my boyhood self or for a little girl abused by a father or other male relative? Doesn't this model run counter to the advice responsible parents give their children, namely to run away from abuse and report it? Or what does this model of Jesus mean for a woman who is being abused by a spouse? Should she passively submit to the abuse in the hope that good may come of it, following the example of Jesus who submitted to abuse for the benefit of humankind? Should people who experience discrimination because of their race or gender or sexual orientation just follow the example of Jesus and submit passively to this abuse? Then a different kind of question arises. Given these harmful images, can we understand the life, death, and resurrection of Jesus in such a way that his death is not arranged by God to meet a divine need? Keep reading to discover a resounding "yes" answer to this last question.

Further, any discussion about a God of love and skepticism about God's use of violence leads quickly to questions about the Old Testament. What about the many stories in the Old Testament in which God commanded massacres or caused the deaths of thousands of people? How does the image of this God correspond to the God of love? And what do these stories of God's resort to violence mean for followers of God who seek to obey the commandments of God? And at the other end of the Bible is the book of Revelation. The images of Revelation are often interpreted to say that both God and Jesus will exercise overwhelming violence in final judgment. A claim that God is nonviolent will therefore have to deal with both the Old Testament and with Revelation.

Finally, the worst destruction that people experience from nature is called an "act of God." People buy insurance against an "act of God," that is, against the destruction caused by a tornado or an earthquake or a hurricane. Claiming that the God revealed in Jesus is a nonviolent God will require some comments on the violence that people experience in nature.

Five-year-old Zach is not the only person to contemplate and be disturbed by the implications of a violent God. This book is written for these questioners. I envision two closely related groups of such readers. One group has already left the church and has perhaps even abandoned faith in the Christian God. They can no longer worship a God who would require the death of God's Son and who would kill thousands of people at one blow with an earthquake or a hurricane. Even if they do not return to Christian faith, I trust that such readers will at least discover that there is another way to understand the God of Jesus and what it means to follow the Jesus who reveals God.

The second group of questioning readers are still in the church but are disturbed by the same kind of questions that troubled those who have left. My hope is that the message of these pages will encourage these doubting Christians to stay with the faith and with the church and to assist in spreading the word about a nonviolent God. These readers are represented by two people who spoke to me after I had given presentations in widely separated and distinct venues. A young woman and a young man each said, "After I have heard you talk about a nonviolent God, I decided to give the church another chance." In line with those expressions of faith, the following pages develop an understanding of Jesus and of the God of Jesus that will reassure Zach about the goodness of the God that his parents worship. We will see that the Christian understanding of God, the God revealed in Jesus, is nothing like the violent God so often portrayed in Christian history and in popular imagination.

But even those who have never thought of or been troubled by the implications of Zach's query should read this book as well, and become part of the conversation. After all, Zach's question concerns our understanding of Jesus, and the God of Jesus, and every *Christ*ian is identified by Jesus *Christ*.

But to discuss these issues, let's get familiar with the meaning of "theology."

What Is "Theology"?

This book deals with theology. Stated very simply, "theology" is the words we use to talk about the subject of our ultimate commitment. For many people, the word used to identity that ultimate commitment is "god." For Christians, this god is the God of the Bible. For Christians, then, most generally, theology is the words used to talk about the God of the Bible. In this book, readers will explore what we can say about the God who is revealed in the Bible, and what it means to believe in this God.

But talking about God involves many other ideas as well. In the Bible, God has a people. They were called the children of Israel or the Israelites. The Old Testament tells the story of that people from their beginnings. Their story continues in the New Testament. Jesus was an Israelite. Some of the Israelites accepted Jesus as God's Chosen One, the Messiah. The hope was that the Chosen One would save Israel from their oppressors, which Jesus did, but not in the military way that many had expected. In Hebrew, the original language of the Old Testament, God's Chosen One was called the Messiah. In Greek, the original language of the New Testament, Messiah was translated Christ. Eventually, the Israelites who accepted Jesus as the Christ were called Christians and their continuation as a people was called the church. For those who recognized Jesus as the Messiah, Christ became part of Jesus' name. He is often referred to as Jesus Christ. The Christian church, which takes its identity from Jesus Christ, thus continues a story that began in the Old Testament and continues today. In a wide sense, Christian theology is the words used to extract and draw meaning for today from this long-running story and the God of this story who is ultimately revealed in the life of Jesus.

The story of Jesus is one kind of continuation from the Israelites. Believing that Jesus was the Christ was not a break from the children of Israel. It was rather a continuation, with the addition of the belief that Jesus was the long-awaited Messiah. Since the story of Jesus is a continuation of a story that began in the Old Testament, the theology presented in this book ranges across the Old Testament as well as the New Testament.

It is also important to understand that Israelites who did not recognize Jesus as the Messiah did not thereby cease being God's people. This line of Israelite descendants continues today in the several streams of Judaism. Christians and Jews should see themselves as religious siblings, members of the same family. Members of a family may disagree on issues, but in spite of the disagreements they remain members of the family. Within the religious family descended from the Israelites, Christians and Jews share a belief in the God of the Israelites. This belief means that without either side surrendering its cherished tradition, they can have a disagreement within the family on whether Jesus was the Messiah.[2] This book deals with understandings on the Christian side of this family disagreement.

2. On the idea that the disagreement between Christians and Jews on whether Jesus is the Messiah should not result in mutual exclusion, see Yoder, *Jewish-Christian Schism Revisited* and Boyarin, *Border Lines*.

When Jesus is accepted as God's Chosen One, the Messiah or the Christ, Christian belief follows the story of Jesus as God's story. It means that God is in that story and that God is revealed in Jesus. Words about Jesus are then an important and central part of Christian theology. How Jesus is identified, how God relates to Jesus, and how Jesus is connected to God, are perhaps the most important parts of Christian theology. Since Christians are committed to Jesus, theology that expresses their ultimate commitment concerns Jesus Christ. The discussion of this book will make clear this connection between God and Jesus in dealing with the implication that concerned five-year-old Zach.

The concept of theology can cover a wide range of issues and subjects. There are subcategories and particular foci within the broad range of issues that constitute theology. This book will explore two broad categories. These are the nature of God, and the words that theology uses to talk about Jesus and his work. The broad category that covers Jesus Christ and his work is called Christology. Within Christology is atonement, which is sometimes called the work of Christ. Atonement concerns how Jesus is Savior. The most common inherited atonement motif is the idea that Jesus' death was necessary in order to pay the penalty for the sins of humankind. Zach's question that opened this introduction reflected the roles of God and of Jesus in this understanding. *Theos* is the Greek term for God. If "theology" is used with a narrow definition, properly speaking it concerns what we say about the nature and the attributes of God. However, since the term "theology" is also commonly used as a word that includes the entire range of topics about God and Christ and many other topics as well, here in this book we will use the term theology with this broader meaning, and use terms such as the nature and attributes of God when the focus is specifically on God.

Theology and Ethics

The words we use to express a Christian's understanding of God and our ultimate commitment to God constitutes theology. But there is also another way to express that ultimate commitment. It is the way we live, which is called ethics. Since theology and ethics are different expressions of the same ultimate commitment, they are related. At least they *should* be related. The expression in words—theology—of the Jesus to whom we are committed should correspond to the lived version—ethics—of commitment to Jesus.

If the commitment in words does not match the lived expression, there is an unresolved problem or a disjuncture. This book works with the idea that theology and ethics should agree. In particular, if there is a commitment to Jesus, then other parts of theology should reflect what is learned from the story of Jesus, and the lived expression of that commitment should reflect the teaching and life of Jesus. In this way, living in the story means to continue Jesus's mission to make the reign of God visible in the world. In the chapters of this book, readers are invited to explore a number of issues for which there might be a disjuncture between common practices, and theology about Jesus and his mission to witness to the reign of God. These areas include social and economic questions, and most importantly, issues of the use of violence. Said another way, living in the story of Jesus makes that story present in the world today.

Violence and Nonviolence in Theology

Mention of Jesus' rejection of violence brings to the foreground another of the important issues of this book. Jesus' rejection of violence is an integral part of this discussion. Although Jesus rejected violence, much of standard, inherited, or traditional theology either accommodates the exercise of violence or actually models it in some way. That modeling is reflected in the five-year-old Zach's question reported at the head of this introduction. The narrative of Jesus makes clear that he rejected opportunities for violence. Thus the theology in this book, which is derived from the narrative of Jesus, will be theology in which rejection of violence or nonviolence is visible.

I need to clarify how I understand violence and nonviolence. An essay by Stassen and Westmoreland-White provides a useful definition of violence: "destruction to a victim by means that overpower the victim's consent."[3] This definition covers a range of actions and practices. I use it to include not only total destruction and death but also other levels and kinds of harm as well. Thus, it obviously includes the harm done to people with weapons such as bombs, guns, knives, clubs, or even fists. Use of these weapons includes the harm done in war, but also covers the one-on-one violence of street fighting and spousal abuse and beating of

---

3. Stassen and Westmoreland-White, "Defining Violence and Nonviolence," 18.

children. Words can also cause harm. When a child is continually put down, humiliated, or declared stupid or ugly, great psychological harm can occur. Similar psychological harm occurs when people of a minority group are labeled with derogatory and harmful names.

Some violence is structural or systemic; that is, the systems and structures of the way society is organized can cause harm. Practices, whether legislated or informal, that reflect racist attitudes exert harm on ethnic minorities. Similarly, policies that make it difficult for people to escape poverty do damage to numbers of poor people. Practices that discourage women from entering certain professions or limit their advancement in others do harm to women.

The definition of violence as "destruction to a victim by means that overpower the victim's consent" covers all such instances of violence and more, whether direct or indirect. Some readers may object to including this variety of harmful practices under the category of "violence." Some might argue that labeling the humiliation of a child as violence cheapens the term "violence" for killing or the massive destruction of war. While I understand that argument, this book will include all the practices described here under the category of violence, but will also distinguish among kinds of violence—physical violence from systemic or structural violence, and by labeling the various kinds of structural or systemic violence.

Nonviolence is the absence of these numerous kinds of violence. It is a term of negation, expressing what is not present. But that negation does not really say very much. It does not indicate what the opposite of violence looks like, and it gives no suggestion for action. How much would we know about maintaining a successful marriage, for example, if the only term we had to describe or define a healthy marriage was "non-adultery." I use nonviolence to cover situations in which there is a refusal to use violence, including nonretaliation, as well as to include a variety of kinds of peaceful intervention and active peacemaking strategies. Since there is no action-oriented term that covers all these cases, this book continues to use the term nonviolence to cover this variety of actions and involvements and situations that aim to counter violence or refuse to use violence. Following chapters fill out this introduction to issues of violence and nonviolence and place them in theological context.

With this understanding of violence and nonviolence in mind, the pages of this book will pursue a theology shaped by the narrative of Jesus, who rejected violence and engaged in nonviolent actions that confronted injustice. We will see that the practice of active nonviolence is derived from the story of Jesus. Theology derived from that story underscores and encourages the pursuit of nonviolent ways to counter the many forms of violence that abound in the world today. Comparing this theology with classic or traditional theology will highlight the significance of the nonviolence-shaped theology presented in this book.

Why Jesus?

As her mother reported to me, four-year-old Rachel asked, "Since we have God, why do we need Jesus?" Answering Rachel's question brings us to a point that Christians have always professed to believe, namely that God was revealed in Jesus. When this book begins its discussion about the character of God with a summary of the life and teaching of Jesus, it is not a random decision. In one form or another, the church or Christians have always professed that Jesus revealed God. In the New Testament, the book of Hebrews says, "Long ago God spoke to our ancestors in many and various ways by the prophets, but in these last days he has spoken to us by a Son" (1:1). The belief that God was revealed in Jesus has been expressed in a number of ways. The import of these many statements is the belief that the fullest revelation of God is in Jesus. To learn about God, look at Jesus. Thus it is with specific intent that this book's chase after the image of the God of the biblical story turns to the narrative of the life and teaching of Jesus as the starting point for discovering the character of God.

Some, even many, readers may be surprised that a book about God does not begin with the discussion of God. These readers may have anticipated a discussion of how God is all-powerful (omnipotent) or present everywhere (omnipresent) or all-knowing (omniscient). Or perhaps a discussion of the Trinity and how God is simultaneously one and three. Others may have been expecting to see a discussion of what the Bible says about God—a listing of all the names and characteristics of God found throughout the Bible.

Developing an understanding of God from the narrative of Jesus does not negate or discard such inherited statements about God. Rather, it is a different way to arrive at such discussions. And at some important junctures, beginning from the narrative brings out dimensions of the character of God that are neglected in the inherited understandings.

Thus, starting with the narrative of Jesus actually enriches and expands what we can say about God.

How to Prove Jesus?

A frequent question concerns proof that the story of Jesus is true or proof that Jesus truly represents God. How can we prove that God is revealed in Jesus? How can we prove that Jesus is the place to look to see the character of God? The quick answer is that we cannot prove those claims. That is, we cannot develop an argument that forces a person to believe these claims against his or her will.

Behind the questions is an assumption that there ought to be some kind of universal reference point to appeal to in order to prove in any context that God is revealed in Jesus, and not, for example, in the scriptures of Hinduism. But if such a universal reference point existed, it would actually be a higher authority than the god it would supposedly prove—and then that god would not be an ultimate authority after all. In actuality, all religions make a claim to ultimate authority, and there simply is no higher authority to which we can appeal to decide which among them is true or the most true. What recent philosophers have helped us understand is that every claim to truth comes from and reflects a particular context. Competing truth claims are actually the claims about universal truth from within one particular context pitted against claims about universal truth from another particular context.

Sometimes there is an appeal to "common sense" as a way to demonstrate what is universally true. When everyone sees or knows something, it is claimed, then that product of common sense ought to be universally true. But what constitutes common sense? What everyone agrees is true is itself a product of a given culture, and what constitutes common sense can change from one context to another. Here I cite only one easy-to-understand example. At one time in human history, people thought that the world was flat with one or more domes over it that contained the sun, moon, planets, and stars. People standing on the earth looked up and saw these heavenly entities over head and assumed that they were moving back and forth above the flat earth. This movement of the heavens and the shape and centrality of the earth seemed to be common sense. Our everyday language still reflects those observations, when we speak of the sun "coming up" in the east, being "up above" during the day, and "going down" in the west. But as early as the fourth century before Christ, ancient natural philosophers such as Aristotle had figured out that the earth was round. It was, however, still assumed to be stationary. To account for the several movements of planets, the sun, moon, and stars, ancient celestial observers developed the idea that a number of concentric spheres moved in varying patterns around the stationary earth. With this model, it was still common sense that the earth was at the center of the universe and the sun came up in the morning and set in the evening.

Then in 1543, less than five hundred years ago, the Renaissance astronomer Nicolaus Copernicus developed a model in which the sun was in the center of the universe and the earth revolved around it while rotating on its axis. This was the beginning of astronomy as we know it today. Although not without some early opposition, Copernicus's suggestion overturned what was long assumed to be common sense. We now take Copernicus's view to be common sense, even though astronomers nowadays tell us that neither the sun nor even our galaxy are anything close to the center of the universe. Yet our language still reflects what seemed like common sense for millennia before Copernicus, even though we have long abandoned the idea that it actually reflects the way the sun and earth relate to each other. The point here is to understand that widely accepted "common sense" does not identify universal truth.

If there is no norm of universal appeal and no resort to common sense, does that leave Christians without any means of asserting the truth of Jesus and the belief that God is revealed in Jesus? Not quite. There is still the possibility of testifying or giving a living witness to these truths.

Earlier it was said that one relates to God by living in the story of Jesus. Thus, in our modern context where we recognize that there is no norm of appeal that is universally accepted, the way to testify to the truth of Jesus is to live by that story or in that story when it is not required, and when it might even be costly or dangerous.

When Christians are killed for their beliefs rather than renounce them, they become martyrs for the faith. Being willing to die for the truth of Jesus is a costly witness to the belief that God is in the story of Jesus. Early Christian history praises such martyrs, and throughout the two millennia since Jesus many such martyrs have died as a witness to their faith in the God of Jesus.

The witness to the truth of Jesus can be costly in another sense as well. If Christians follow Jesus' words and are generous with their wealth, they may choose to practice careers not based primarily on the amount of money or prestige that can accrue but on the quality of service the career offers to others. For example, a doctor might decide to leave a comfortable family practice to open a clinic that will serve uninsured people. Or perhaps rather than attempting to climb the corporate ladder, an individual with managerial skills becomes chief operating officer of a church agency or a nonprofit organization. A lawyer might do a lot of pro-bono work for immigrants and poor people rather than seeking high-paying clients in the corporate world. Rather than trying to stack up as many overtime hours as possible, a father or mother might put in time working on a project with Habitat for Humanity or volunteering at a food pantry. Rather than spending money on a vacation cruise, a family might spend the money and use the vacation time to help clean up after a flood or tornado or to serve with a delegation of Witness for Peace or Christian Peacemaker Teams.[4]

This testimony to the truth that God is in the story of Jesus is intrinsically a nonviolent witness. For a witness to be received, the hearer cannot be coerced into accepting. If the witness is to be genuinely received, the hearer must be as free to reject as to accept it. Thus, in principle, the witness that God is in the story of Jesus is a testimony to the nonviolence of the God that is revealed in Jesus. When a witness is made to that story, it is testimony to a gracious gift from God, namely the truth that Jesus' story is God's story.

Why Story?

It is important to see that Jesus is identified by a story that locates him in human history. A story, call it a history, gives a person or institution an identity. No two stories are alike. Thus, to tell a story or stories is the way to identify a person as a unique individual. Stories may also explain or give meaning to current events.

The inherited way of identifying Jesus is to say that he was both God and man or God and human. When understood within their context, those claims about Jesus are not false, but they do not actually say very

---

4. Witness for Peace and Christian Peacemaker Teams are violence-reduction programs that send delegates to trouble spots around the world for fact-finding and nonviolent activism. For Witness for Peace, see http://www.witnessforpeace.org/ and for Christian Peacemaker Teams go to http://cpt.org/. Mennonite Central Committee is the relief and service agency of Mennonite churches. For more information, see http://mcc.org/.

much about Jesus. These terms put Jesus in the categories of God and humanity, but do not identify how he was unique in those categories. When this book uses the New Testament stories to identify Jesus, it goes far beyond identifying him as God and human. It is the stories that make clear how God was present in his life and teaching, and put on display what the reign of God looks like in human form.

Actually seeing and feeling the clarity brought by a story—historical understanding—changed the course of my career as a teacher and scholar. I like to say that French president Charles de Gaulle changed my life. It happened during the term my wife and I spent in Algeria as Mennonite Central Committee personnel from 1966–68. I taught English in a lycée (high school), which had several French people on the faculty. Along with Algerian news, I listened to French news on the radio. In 1968 French President de Gaulle was enacting a number of policies that had many people confused. These actions included vetoing British entry into the Common Market, refusing to sign a nuclear test ban treaty, expelling NATO from Paris, boycotting Israel after the Six-Day War, supporting an independent Quebec, attacking the US dollar as international currency, and instituting university reforms that had students rioting in the streets for a month. When I asked my French colleagues what de Gaulle was doing, the majority said, "the old man is crazy." But my friend Jacques had a different answer. Jacques' father happened to be a member of de Gaulle's party in the French parliament. Charles de Gaulle had prepared a limited edition, three-volume, embossed, leather-bound, profusely illustrated edition of his memoirs as a gift for each Gaullist in parliament. Jacques had his father's copy and loaned it to me. I spent several spellbound weeks reading about the experiences of *le grand Charles* in two world wars. His story was quite revealing. I learned that de Gaulle believed that in World War II, the United States and Britain had failed to accord him the role and the respect that he deserved. Thus, he simply did not trust them. As I read his story, it became clear to me that his policies in 1968 were all designed to counter British and American influence and raise the profile of France at their expense. We might even say that he was getting even with Britain and France for their earlier treatment of him. Rather than being the chaotic policies of a crazy old man, as most of my colleagues said, the policies of 1968 reflected a coherent strategy shaped by de Gaulle's experiences more than two decades earlier. One certainly did not have to agree with his actions, but the story brought clarity to them, and would give insight to those who sought to counter the policies.

Before reading de Gaulle's memoirs, upon return to the United States I had planned to study the Old Testament and become a Bible professor. After seeing how a bit of history—a story—clarified events in France, I decided to change my field of study to church history as the path to understanding the modern church. Reading the memoirs of Charles de Gaulle was the beginning of my understanding of the role of story, and in particular the story of Jesus, in writing Christian theology.

The terms "God" and "humanity" put Jesus in a category, but they say nothing about his particular way of acting in that category. Putting him in those categories does not distinguish him from any other beings identified as God or human. Just as some stories helped me understand the policies of Charles de Gaulle, we need to read the stories given in the New Testament to grasp the uniqueness of Jesus. These narratives locate Jesus in human history. Locating Jesus in a particular time and place gives reality to the claim that he was a human being and how he acted as a human being. And accompanied by the claim that God was revealed in this story, we have a picture of what the reign of God looks like on earth in a particular time and place. Thus, this story tells us a lot about the character of God and what God cares about. And the culmination of that story, namely the resurrection, shows that God truly did enter human history in the life of Jesus. *Since God was in Jesus, his life was not allowed to end.*

It is thus of vital importance to identify Jesus by means of the New Testament story.

Living in the Story

The fact that Jesus is identified by a story is important for Christians, and those who want to understand Christianity. The story supplies the necessary data for living today according to the reign of God as it was made visible in the life and teaching of Jesus.

Over the centuries, people have joined the story of Jesus in many ways. Some people were baptized as babies and grew up in the Christian story and never felt themselves outside of the story. Others were raised in Christian homes in which it was understood that baptism followed a conscious awareness that an individual identified with Jesus as Savior. For people in these families, identifying with Jesus and with the God revealed in Jesus was a growth process, and they may never have sensed themselves separated from God.

Other people came to the story of Jesus as a new learning, entirely separate from their previous experience. For these people, identifying with the story may be a highly emotional experience, what has sometimes been called a crisis conversion. The typical image of a crisis conversation is of a dramatic change in a person's life in response to a preacher's invitation in church or at a revival crusade. People converted in this manner often find great meaning in recounting their previous wicked life, the time of their conversion, and the joy they experience from a new life in the story of Jesus.

Still others may come to a less dramatic, more rational decision that life in the story of Jesus makes more sense or goes better than their previous life path. Such a realization may develop gradually, over a period of time, until the individual realizes that he or she does indeed want to live in the story of Jesus.

But it is not the image of growth versus a crisis experience versus a rational decision that is important. What is significant is that one lives now in the story of Jesus. Primary evidence that one is a Christian is measured not by the kind of conversion but by the way one leads life now.

Living in the story is much more than attempting to copy Jesus. It is a way to bring the story into the present and give it life today. Living in the story means to continue Jesus' mission today of witnessing to the reign of God. Living in the story is a continuation of Jesus' presence in the world.

Issues

A well-known theologian once said that theology is the discipline where if you do not say everything all the time, then you will be accused of leaving something out. The book in your hands certainly does not say everything. Nonetheless, in spite of the warning about potential omissions, the following pages do attempt to provide a well-founded, beginning introduction to what in many ways is a new understanding of God, and the way that such an understanding shapes the way Christians will live. The introduction has mentioned a number of issues that belong to this understanding of God. In order to bring some focus to this many-sided discussion, the introduction concludes with a list of questions that the book attempts to answer.

1) *What is the source of "theology"?*

We will observe how theology is derived from the narrative of Jesus as it is told in the Gospels. Many points of discussion follow from understanding this story as the source of theology.

2) *What does the narrative of Jesus—his life, deeds, death, and resurrection—say for how he is Savior?*

This answer deals with atonement theology. The discussion will expose the violence of the inherited views, such as the one that worried Zach, and display a nonviolent alternative.

3) *How do the life and teaching of Jesus respond to or counter the violence in the world that is both structural and direct?*

We will observe Jesus' response to multiple kinds of violence and social injustice and the implications of his life and teaching for Christians today.

4) *What does the narrative of Jesus say about God?*

The belief that God is revealed in Jesus leads to the conclusion that God is nonviolent. The atonement analysis provides one aspect of this discussion. Others immediately follow from it.

5) *How does all the violence attributed to God in the Old Testament square with the claim that God is nonviolent?*

This question arises immediately from the claim that God is nonviolent.

6) *How do the violent images in the book of Revelation square with the claim that God is nonviolent?*

This question also arises immediately from the claim that God is nonviolent.

7) *What is the significance for the life of Christians today of the belief that God is nonviolent?*

From the life of Jesus who reveals God, we can see what the rule of God looks like on earth, in human form. Thus, living in the life of Jesus is the way to be in contact with God.

8) *What is the character of the Bible and how can a lay person without specialized training expect to read and understand it?*

The theology presented in this book does offer alternatives to much of inherited theology. We will see how understanding that theology begins with a narrative influences our understanding of the nature of the Bible itself, and then provide guidance for the concerned, lay reader.

9) *Has theology changed over time?*

We will see that theology has changed over time, and that changes began already in the Bible.

And now, to the story of Jesus, from which both theology and the Christian life are derived.

1

The Story of Jesus

THE DESIGNATION "CHRISTIAN" COMES from Jesus Christ. Stated most generally, a Christian is anyone who recognizes Jesus Christ as a primary source of truth. This definition encompasses numerous kinds of Christians. It includes understandings of "Christian" that focus primarily on beliefs as well as those that would be oriented around actions. In general, anyone who claims the identity of "Christian" is a Christian. The more telling designation would be to identify the kind of Christian identity the speaker claims. With this general definition of "Christian" in mind. I will use representative events from Jesus' life as found in the New Testament narrative to sketch the story of Jesus from whom all Christians take their name.

The interpretations of the individual elements of the story of Jesus in this chapter are not particularly original. However, their integration into a comprehensive story is my particular synthesis. It is done in a way to emphasize that Jesus and the reign of God witness against injustice in the world.

This book demonstrates the integral relationship of Christian theology and Christian ethics, namely the link between what Christians believe about God and about Jesus, and how Christians should act. Stated with a different focus, living in the story of Jesus means that Christians today continue his presence in the world, and extend his mission to testify to the reign or the rule of God on earth. In this way, the story of Jesus becomes a contemporary story.

Jesus' Birth

What we know about the life of Jesus comes from the New Testament. The Gospels of Matthew and Luke each have a story about the birth of Jesus. Matthew's version contains the familiar story of the wise men who came to visit the baby, born in Bethlehem. King Herod learned about the purpose of their visit, and asked them to inform him where the baby was located. Herod felt threatened by the announcement of another king, and wanted to kill the baby. The wise men were warned about Herod in a dream and left the country without reporting to him. When he heard nothing from the wise men, to eliminate the possibility of a new king coming to power, Herod commanded that all male children around Bethlehem under two years of age should be killed. Meanwhile, the story says that an angel warned Joseph about the threat to the baby Jesus. Joseph took Mary and Jesus to Egypt where they hid until Herod died. When they returned to Palestine two years later, Joseph settled the family in Nazareth.

Luke's Gospel contains the well-known story of the visit by shepherds who came to see the baby Jesus, newly born in Bethlehem. Joseph lived in Nazareth, but went with Mary to the home of his ancestors in Bethlehem when the emperor decreed universal registration. With the heavy travel to Bethlehem at this time, Joseph could not get a room in the inn. The baby was born in a stable, wrapped in blankets, and placed in a manger. Meanwhile, an angel, accompanied by a heavenly choir, announced the birth to the shepherds tending to their flocks outside of Bethlehem. The shepherds went to find the baby, worshipped him as the new king, and returned to the fields with their flocks. Eight days later, it was time to circumcise the baby and he was given the name Jesus. Mary and Joseph took him to Jerusalem for a ceremony of dedication in the temple, where he was recognized and worshipped by Simeon and Anna, two devout visitors to the temple. Following these experiences in the temple, Joseph took the family back to his hometown of Nazareth.

Many popular paintings and manger scenes show both shepherds and wise men gathered around the manger with Mary and Joseph. However, the wise men are only in Matthew's story and the shepherds appear only in Luke's version. It is not possible to harmonize Matthew's account of the family's stay in Egypt for two years with Luke's story of a brief stop in Jerusalem and then taking eight-day-old Jesus to live in Nazareth.

However, we do not need to probe these differing details in order to see that the two accounts agree on elements that are significant for the development of theology. Both stories locate the baby Jesus in the real world of first-century Palestine. He is born at an identifiable time in the history of the Roman empire and the history of Roman occupation of Palestine. Both stories situate his birth in Bethlehem, and both place his growing-up years in Nazareth, whereby he was eventually called a Nazarene. Both versions identify Jesus as a descendant of King David. These items affirm that Jesus belonged to the real world that we live in. And most importantly, they identify Jesus as a Jew, a man who was heir to and a continuation of the story of Israel, the people whose beginning the Bible links to the patriarch Abraham.

Both elements are important—that Jesus was human and in the real world, and that he was identifiably a Jew, who inherited the traditions of Israel. For the moment it is sufficient to say that locating Jesus in our historical world is necessary in order for Christians to see how to identify with and to live in Jesus' story. Stated another way, the link between Christian theology and Christian ethics begins with understanding that Jesus lived in our historical world.

Jesus' Life

Beginning His Ministry

In Luke's Gospel, Jesus began his public ministry with a rather dramatic reading and statement in the synagogue at Nazareth (Luke 4:16–39). He was given the scroll containing the writings of the prophet Isaiah, and he read the section listed in our Bibles as the first one and a half verses of chapter 61:

> The Spirit of the Lord is upon me,
> because he has anointed me
>   to bring good news to the poor.
> He has sent me to proclaim release to the captives
> and recovery of sight to the blind,
>   to let the oppressed go free,
> to proclaim the year of the Lord's favor.

When Jesus had finished the reading, he announced, "Today this scripture has been fulfilled in your hearing."

At first, the audience was enthralled with how well he spoke. However, his additional comments, about a prophet not being accepted in his own country, made them angry, and they attempted to throw him off a cliff to kill him. He escaped. The response of Jesus' audience to his announcement, swinging from adulation to an attempt to kill him, foreshadows the reception of his entire career, which did in fact end with his death.

Jesus used these words from Isaiah to signal that his mission was to proclaim the presence of the reign of God on earth. Speaking about good news for the poor, releasing captives, healing the blind, and freeing the oppressed, all signal that the focus of his mission has a clear social component, which would challenge the status quo of his society. This challenge had a clear economic component as well as aiming at political and social injustice.

Where he stopped reading from Isaiah also signaled something important. He broke off the reading just before Isaiah wrote of proclaiming "the day of vengeance of our God" (61:2b). I read Jesus' stopping place as an indication that the rejection of violence was an intrinsic characteristic of his career and thus of the reign of God.

Jesus' message was that the reign of God had come. Jesus preached that message himself. And when he sent out his followers to preach, sometimes the twelve and another time seventy, their message was that the "kingdom of God has come near" (Luke 10:1–16; 8:1; Matt 9:35—10:15). In his teaching and in his person, Jesus was making the reign of God present to people. Incidents reported about Jesus portray what the reign of God looks like—calling followers, healing, restoring.

Jesus called disciples. We might say that he was creating a new community to carry on the mission of making the reign of God visible, as when he sent out the twelve and the seventy. The church today, and followers of Jesus wherever they are, are the continuation of this community created by Jesus. As the church, we make Jesus' mission our own mission and we continue the presence of Jesus in our world.

The following section continues the discussion of how Jesus witnessed to or made visible the reign of God.

Healings and Restorations

The Gospels contain many stories of people that Jesus healed. Healing gives visibility to the restorative power of God's reign. These healings inspired the common people, but raised opposition among the religious leaders. When Jesus forgave the sins of a paralyzed man whom he also healed, the scribes and Pharisees accused Jesus of blasphemy. Only God can forgive sins, they claimed (Luke 5:17–26). In actuality, Jesus was threatening the temple establishment, through which the priestly class made a lot of money from the sacrifices in the temple. If people could find forgiveness from Jesus without paying for a sacrifice in the temple, that threatened the sacrificial system itself, and its demise would cost the rulers a lot of income.

In addition to healings, the Gospels also contain stories in which Jesus restored people to life who had died. One time he was on his way to the village of Nain, followed by a large crowd. As he neared the city gate, a crowd from the city was taking the body of a dead man for burial. He was the only son of a widow, who was weeping. Jesus felt sorry for her. He approached the bier and said, "Young man, I say to you, rise." The man sat up and was restored to his mother (Luke 7:11–17). Another time a synagogue leader came and begged Jesus to come and heal his twelve-year-old daughter who was dying. But Jesus got delayed by another healing. Before he arrived at the leader's house, word came that the little girl had died, and thus Jesus need not be bothered. But Jesus said, "Only believe, and she will be saved," and he continued on to her house. There he found mourners weeping. Because they knew that the girl was dead, they laughed when he said that she was only sleeping. Then he took her by the hand and said, "Child, get up." She got up, and he suggested that they feed her (Luke 8:40–56).

The stories of healing make an important point about God. The God of Jesus does not kill and take life. God is a giver of life and a restorer of life.

That Jesus restores life and that the God of Jesus restores rather than taking life is an important point for Christians who live in the story of Jesus. This restoration of life is one dimension of the nonviolence of God who is revealed in Jesus. This means that followers of Jesus will likewise refuse to take life and to do harm and will live in ways that restore and heal. Readers should reflect on ways to bring Jesus' mission of healing and restoration into our world today.

Another time Jesus healed in direct defiance of the purity code practiced by the scribes and Pharisees. In the synagogue where he was teaching on the Sabbath was a man with a "withered hand." If Jesus healed on the Sabbath, it would be a violation of the provision against unnecessary labor on the Sabbath. But the scribes and Pharisees knew what Jesus might do and were watching, hoping to catch him in a violation. Jesus knew their plan, but instead of avoiding a confrontation, he called the man to come and stand by him where everyone could see what would transpire. Then Jesus asked those watching, "Is it lawful to do good or to do harm on the Sabbath, to save life or to destroy it?" Then he looked around at them, making eye contact so that he had their attention. And with every eye on him, Jesus commanded the man, "Stretch out your hand." He did, and was healed. The religious leaders were furious (Luke 6:6–11). The original purpose of the Sabbath was for healing and restoration. Laws that prevented healing actually promoted harm. By healing on the Sabbath, Jesus defied those laws, but he was returning the day to its original intent of healing and restoration.

Along with the rules about Sabbath observance, Jesus challenged other purity rules as well. His crossing of racial and ethnic boundaries with Samaritans and gentiles violated several purity rules at once. His interactions with women also violated purity rules and challenged the secondary status of women in his society. In these interactions, Jesus' breaking of the rules of the purity code were akin to practices today that might be called civil disobedience. Jesus was not a passive observer of his society. He performed actions that challenged discrimination against women and against racial and ethnic groups. Following these examples, Jesus' followers today should confront the discrimination that exists in our society. Readers should reflect on ways to continue Jesus' confrontation of discrimination in our contemporary world.

Cleansing the Temple

Perhaps Jesus' most dramatic confrontation of the priestly system was what has been called the cleansing of the temple. This event precipitated the final plot to have him killed.

Jesus had traveled to Jerusalem with his disciples at the time of the Passover. He entered the temple, where animals and pigeons were on sale for sacrifices. He overturned the tables of the money changers and the salespeople, and chased out the animals. In John's account, Jesus used a "whip of cords" (2:15). Combining phrases from Isaiah 56:7 and Jeremiah 7:11, Luke has Jesus say, "My house shall be a house of prayer, but you have made it a den of robbers" (Luke 19:46).

When Jesus forgave sins, there would be no need to offer sacrifices in the temple as the basis of forgiveness. His demonstration in the temple was thus an acting out of the fact that temple sacrifices were not necessary in order to receive God's forgiveness. Not surprisingly, such an act was perceived as a major threat by the priestly establishment and their allies, and they started to develop a plot to have Jesus killed.

Some commentators have used this account, particularly the mention of the whip, to justify violence and revolution. It is in fact nothing of the sort. Recall that healing on the Sabbath was returning the day to its proper intention of healing and restoration. Now, with this action, Jesus was reasserting the rightful purpose of the temple. The whip is not used to injure. A cracking whip makes noise, and it is used to herd animals in the desired direction—in this case, out of the temple.

Teachings and Sayings

Following this demonstrative act of temple cleansing, Jesus went to the temple daily to teach. The religious leaders were looking for a way to kill him, but for a time the support of the people protected him. Because the crowds were hanging on his every word, the leaders feared a riot and were afraid to act (Luke 19:47–48; Mark 1:18).

This time of teaching contains some of Jesus' most well-known sayings and sharpest confrontations of the religious leadership. When shown a coin with Caesar's image on it and asked whether it was lawful to pay taxes to Caesar, Jesus said, "Render to Caesar the things that are Caesar's and to God the things that are God's" (Luke 20:25). They had hoped to trick Jesus into a dangerous admission, but his answer was not one with which they could find fault.

A lawyer from among the Pharisees asked Jesus which commandment was the greatest. Jesus' answer quoted from Deuteronomy 6:5 and Leviticus 19:18.

> You shall love the Lord your God with all your heart, and with all your soul, and with all your mind. This is the great and first

commandment. And a second is like it. You shall love your neighbor as yourself.

On these two commands depend all the law and the prophets, Jesus added (Matt 22:36–38). In another version of this story, a lawyer asked Jesus what he needed to do to inherit eternal life. Jesus asked him what the law said, and the lawyer repeated these two commandments. Jesus replied that he was correct, that eternal life depended on these two commandments (Luke 10:25–28).

The scribes and Pharisees provide hard requirements of the law, Jesus said, but do not follow those laws themselves. Proclaiming "woe" on the scribes and Pharisees, he called them hypocrites and said that they go to great lengths to make a proselyte, but "then you make him twice as much a child of hell as yourselves." They make themselves appear very pious by tithing small things, such as herbs from the garden, but neglect more important parts of the law, such as "justice and mercy and faith." In their teaching of the law, they are like "Blind guides! You strain out a gnat but swallow a camel!" This duplicity makes them like tombs, "whitewashed" on the outside to look beautiful, "but inside they are full of the bones of the dead and of all kinds of filth." Jesus had very sharp words about their references to the earlier prophets, who were persecuted. Although the scribes and Pharisees claimed that they would not have shed the blood of the prophets, Jesus accused them of doing exactly that in their own time. "You snakes, you brood of vipers! How can you escape being sentenced to hell?" Since such behavior invites retribution, Jesus laments the fate of the city. "O Jerusalem, Jerusalem, killing the prophets and stoning those who are sent to you. How often would I have gathered your children together as a hen gathers her brood under her wings, and you would not!" (quotes from Matt 23).

This account of Jesus' actions and his confrontational teaching makes clear that the reign of God that Jesus represented was different from the society in which he lived. Stated differently, the reign of God challenged injustices in Jesus' world, or the reign of God posed a positive alternative to the way things were. In a context that prevented doing good on the Sabbath, Jesus returned the Sabbath to a day of healing and restoration. In a society where rules discriminated against ethnic minorities and identified women as second-class people, Jesus raised the status of women and racial and ethnic minorities. Followers of Jesus today will thus examine their host society in order to find ways to bring his story into the present, continuing his practices to bring healing and restoration and to witness against injustice and discrimination.

This selection of stories and sayings identifies Jesus as one whose life made the reign of God visible. His death also says something about the character of his mission.

Jesus' Death

The way that Jesus faced his death makes visible the nonviolent character of the reign of God that was the focus of his mission.

The cleansing of the temple, along with his confrontational teaching, angered the religious leadership. They met in the home of the high priest to work out a secret plan to have Jesus arrested and killed. Judas, one of Jesus' twelve disciples, went to them and asked how much money they would pay him to betray Jesus. They offered thirty pieces of silver, and Judas agreed (Matt 26:3–5, 14–16).

Jesus arranged to celebrate a Passover supper with his disciples. He knew that he did not have much longer to live. As they were sitting around the table, he told them that he knew one of them would betray him. This announcement disturbed them greatly, and each began to ask if he was the one. Judas also asked, and Jesus said, "You have said so." In the account of this story in the Gospel of John, Jesus knew what Judas was planning. He told him, "Do quickly what you are going to do." Judas left, but the other disciples did not understand what Jesus had meant (John 13:26–30).

At this meal, Jesus performed a ceremony with the disciples using bread and wine. He told them that as often as they were eating together, they should use this ceremony to remember him. Christians still follow the practice of taking bread and wine together to remember Jesus, his death and his resurrection.

From this supper, Jesus went out to pray in the Garden of Gethsemane. It was here that Jesus was arrested. Judas came out at the head of a mob inspired by the religious leadership, and perhaps including Roman soldiers (Matt 26:47; John 18:3). Although Jesus had been teaching daily in the temple, this mob did not recognize him. Judas had arranged to identify him by giving Jesus a kiss of greeting. And Jesus was then arrested.

This arrest provoked one of the disciples, identified in the Gospel of John as Peter (18:10), who drew his sword to defend Jesus. He flailed away and cut off the ear of the high priest's slave. But Jesus healed the man's ear. Jesus explained to Peter that violence was not the way of the reign of God. "Put your sword back into its place; for all who take the sword will perish by the sword. Do you think that I cannot appeal to my Father, and he will at once send me more than twelve legions of angels?" For emphasis, Jesus sarcastically scolded the crowd. "Have you come out with swords and clubs to arrest me as though I were a bandit? Day after day I sat in the temple teaching, and you did not arrest me." If you really understood me, Jesus means to say, you would know that you would not need weapons to arrest me, for violence is not my way. Besides you could easily have arrested me in the temple.

Jesus' principled refusal to use violence becomes most clear during his trial appearance before Pilate. The chief priests and religious leaders accused Jesus of blasphemy as a reason to have him killed. However, the Israelite leaders lacked permission to execute anyone; that authority belonged alone to the Roman occupiers of Palestine. Thus, when lying witnesses were found to implicate Jesus, the chief priests and other leaders brought Jesus to Pilate, the Roman governor of the province.

Pilate asked Jesus if he was a king, and Jesus turned the question back on him, asking whether Pilate was asking on his own, or had others told him. Pilate said that he was not a Jew, meaning that he had no reason to answer. Then Pilate asked why Jesus' own countrymen condemned him. "What have you done?" And Jesus replied, "My kingdom is not from this world. If my kingdom were from this world, my followers would be fighting to keep me from being handed over to the Jews.[1] But as it is, my kingdom is not from here" (John 18:36). The values and practices of the kingdom Jesus represented were different from the values and practices of Pilate's kingdom. Therefore Jesus' followers did not use violence in an attempt to protect him.

Pilate proclaimed that he found no reason to condemn Jesus. He offered the religious leaders and the mob a choice of releasing Jesus or

---

1. "The Jews" in the account of the trial is not a reference to Jews or Judaism as a whole. In Jesus' time, "the Jews" was one of the identifiable religious parties. It might be parallel to the situation today, in which in the public mind "Christian" means so-called conservative views (six-day creation, Great Flood as historic event, rejection of evolution, opposition to gay marriage, and more), but there are actually many parties and denominations of "Christians" who hold quite different perspectives on these issues.

Barabbas. The chief priests and other leaders persuaded the crowd to call for Barabbas. As the mob howled for the death of Jesus, Pilate washed his hands as a public sign that he found Jesus innocent. Nonetheless, Pilate handed Jesus over to be crucified.

Jesus was beaten and otherwise tortured and taken outside the city to a place called Golgotha. Here he was crucified, that is, nailed to a cross, which resulted in a long and painful death. For the Romans, this kind of death served to intimidate the population about the danger of rebellion against the occupation.

Joseph from Arimathea, a wealthy disciple of Jesus, was a God-fearing member of the council who had not consented to the actions against Jesus. Joseph went to Pilate and asked for Jesus' body. Pilate consented. Joseph took Jesus' body, wrapped it in a shroud, and laid the body in a new tomb that he had prepared for himself. A great stone was placed over the entrance to the tomb. Mary Magdalene and Jesus' mother Mary watched to identify the location of the tomb and prepared spices to use in anointing the body.

Two additional observations are important concerning the description of Jesus death. First, notice that the account of Jesus' death has nothing in it about God needing the death of Jesus or sending Jesus to die as some kind of payment for salvation, nor anything about Jesus' death being part of a divine plan. Rather than being needed by God, the killing of Jesus is entirely the work of forces that *opposed* the reign of God. This observation is extremely important for the discussion to follow in Chapter 2.

The second observation has immediate importance. The story of Jesus' death makes very clear that in the reign of God violence is not used. The kingdom Jesus represented is a nonviolent kingdom.

Jesus' Resurrection

On the third day after Jesus' crucifixion, two women, "Mary Magdalene and the other Mary," who was likely his mother, went to visit the tomb. They carried the spices that they had prepared, intending to anoint the dead body.

The problem the women faced was how to remove the heavy stone from the tomb's opening. When they arrived, however, the stone had been rolled back and the tomb was empty. A young man in shining clothes, or perhaps two, identified in one account as an angel, told the women that Jesus was risen from the dead. The visitor instructed them to go and inform his disciples that he was risen, and that they would see him in Galilee. The women left and went quickly to tell the disciples.

The accounts of the resurrection in the four Gospels differ from each other in their details. However, all Gospels agree that Jesus was raised from the dead.[2]

Theologically, resurrection is why Christians proclaim Jesus to be Lord, the highest name for Jesus in the New Testament. Paul wrote to the Romans that Jesus was "declared Son of God with power by resurrection from the dead" (1:4).

"Lord" is a name that implies deity. In classic theological language, this is a statement of the deity of Jesus, or that God was present in the flesh. The resurrection of Jesus means that God was present in the life of Jesus.

When resurrection indicates that God was present in the life of Jesus, then the life of Jesus becomes important for our theology and our practices. It is in Jesus' life, his acts and his teaching, that we see what the reign of God looks like on earth. It concerns people without power, whether due to poverty or because they lack the property ownership that confers political clout. His life involves people such as Samaritans, whose ethnicity attracted discrimination. Looking at the life of Jesus makes visible the fact that the reign of God involves relationships among people, relationships based on equality and respect.

When resurrection testifies that God was present in the life of Jesus, we learn something about the character of God. If Jesus reveals God, then Jesus' rejection of violence displays the character of God, that God is nonviolent; God should be described with nonviolent images. This learning is counter to the many, longstanding images of a God who uses violence or who sanctions violence.

Putting all these things together results in seeing that the resurrection is an invitation to every person. It is an invitation to live in the reign of God made visible in Jesus. Living in the reign of God is where we encounter the reign of God. And this means that the resurrection is the supreme evidence that the story of Jesus, which makes visible the reign of God, is a saving story. It is in this story that people experience God

---

2. For an extended analysis of the resurrection as a historical event, see Wright, *Resurrection of the Son of God*. My discussion to follow of the meaning of resurrection is in harmony with Wright's account on pages 723–36.

and the beginning of salvation in their lives in the present. One day in the future, the reign of God will be here in its fullness. Meanwhile, it has already begun for those who live in the life of Jesus. Those who live in this story—that is, Christians—participate in that future reign of God breaking into the present. And those who participate in the reign of God now will be part of it in the future culmination, whatever that is and whenever it happens.

Lastly, the invitation of the resurrection to live in Jesus' story returns us to the link between Christian theology and Christian ethics. Experiencing the beginning of salvation in the present is to live in Jesus who is identified by the story of the one whom God raised from the dead. To tell the story is to identify Jesus. And to tell the story provides the basis for living in the story, for meeting God in the story, and for bringing the story into the world today. Resurrection, the climax of the earthly dimension of that story, invites all people to identify with Jesus and to live in his story. In theological language, theology (the words about Jesus) and ethics (the way we live as Christians together) are two dimensions of that one story.

The Grain of the Universe

The God revealed in Jesus and described with nonviolent images is the Creator God. With eyes of faith, one can discover evidence of that nonviolent character of God in the universe that God created. That comment leads to a contemporary image, namely the "grain of the universe." As the grain does much to identify the character of a piece of wood, the image of the grain of the universe suggests that the character of God appears in the universe that God created. Those who then live in the life of Jesus are working with the grain of the universe.[3] The pages of this book will indicate a number of areas where this grain becomes visible

This grain is made visible by the life of Jesus and in the actions of those who live in his life. However, beyond the specifically theological appearances, there are areas in which independent or empirical data also points to this grain. On occasion, actions from people outside the Christian community–such as Muslims–have also sensed the grain of the universe. Examples of these several instances will appear in the chapters to follow.

---

3. The idea of the "grain of the universe" is from Yoder, "Armaments and Eschatology," 58.

Conclusion

This chapter has identified Jesus. Jesus' mission was to live as a witness to God and to the reign of God. His life made visible what God's rule looks like on earth. It cares for all people, particularly the marginalized. It is not passive; it confronts injustice, but without resorting to violence. The resurrection put on full display that the life of Jesus was the life of God and a living presence of the reign of God on earth. In other words, it is the conclusion to the story, namely the resurrection, that makes clear the importance of the story. Christology is the part of theology that identifies Jesus. We can say that since this chapter has identified Jesus with a narrative, it is a narrative-based Christology.

It is from this story that Christian theology and ethics develop. The remainder of the book extends this story or draws meaning from it for both theological understanding and practice. The following chapter begins that development by deriving an atonement image from the story of Jesus. Stated differently, the following chapter develops the theology that identifies the story of Jesus as a saving story.

2

The Story of Jesus and Atonement

A SMALL BOY'S MOTHER reminded him that it was time to get ready for church to celebrate Easter. The boy replied, his mother told me with a smile, "Oh Mommy, do we have to kill Jesus again?" This little boy may have missed the idea of yearly celebrations, but he had certainly absorbed the inherited way of explaining how Jesus brings salvation, namely by being killed.

The most common, inherited understanding of atonement is that Jesus made salvation available by dying for our sins. Since atonement theology talks about how Jesus saves, it is often said that atonement theology answers the question, "Why did Jesus have to die?" Or stated another way, "How did Jesus' death bring salvation?" As the little boy's comment so accurately reflected, the conventional way to talk about Jesus as savior is to focus on his death.

I want to shift the focus away from Jesus' death. When we outlined his teaching and life, the climax of the story did not occur with Jesus' death. The culmination came with Jesus' resurrection from the dead, which testified that God was truly in the life of Jesus. Thus we begin this chapter by using the *entire* story of Jesus to discuss how he is Savior. By using the entire story, the emphasis shifts from Jesus' death to his life and resurrection, and the question of atonement becomes, "How does Jesus' life, teaching, death, and resurrection bring salvation?"

The Narrative as Atonement

We have already seen how Jesus' actions confronted injustices. He healed on the Sabbath when that violated the purity code enforced by the religious leaders. This kind of defiance of authority earned him great animosity. In stories that we will consider later in more detail, Jesus used a Samaritan as a good example, when Samaritans were the despised ethnic group. He treated a Samaritan woman as an equal, when according to the purity code, women should be considered unclean. And he was also willing to revise his mission of bringing the reign of God only to Israelites when he was confronted by a gentile woman. That revision also demonstrates respect for women. These incidents display that the reign of God made visible in Jesus confronted or witnessed against various kinds of social injustice of his day. These injustices would be instances of structural violence, and Jesus confronted them with active nonviolence.

Jesus' most assertive and confrontational act was the cleansing of the temple. As we saw, he chased out the animals and overturned the tables of the money changers. This action reflected the fact that one could find forgiveness from God without going through the sacramental system, by which the priestly class made a lot of money. Jesus was a threat to the entire religious system, and those who ran the system wanted him removed.

The act of cleansing the temple was certainly confrontational and revolutionary. That is, it signaled the beginning of a different way of relating to God. It was revolutionary, but it was most certainly not violent. Jesus did not kill anyone, and neither did his followers. This act did not set off a violent revolution. It was rather a prophetic act that symbolically restored the temple to its true purpose, a place where people could worship God and find forgiveness. Today we would call this action active nonviolence or nonviolent resistance.

The violence in the story of Jesus came from elsewhere, from those who wanted to eliminate Jesus. The temple incident posed a threat to the religious authorities in Jerusalem. Ultimately, they developed a plot to have Jesus arrested and then taken before Pilate. They wanted to have Jesus condemned to death and executed by Rome. And Rome's officials and soldiers carried out their request. They crucified him. And three days later he was resurrected.

The question is, in this account, how is Jesus a savior? Or, how does Jesus in this account bring salvation?

The Narrative as Saving Story: Nonviolent Atonement

To find an answer to these questions, we need to start with the culmination of the story, which is the resurrection of Jesus. Since God raised Jesus, one of several meanings of resurrection is that it displays that God was truly in the story of Jesus.

The apostle Paul added an additional element to the meaning of resurrection, which explains how Jesus' story is a saving story. In 1 Corinthians 15 Paul argued with believers in Corinth who accepted Jesus' resurrection but denied a future, general resurrection of the dead. In a well-known argument, Paul said that they could not have one without the other. "If there is no resurrection of the dead, then Christ has not been raised." And if Christ has not been raised, there is a very serious consequence, namely that "your faith is futile and you are still in your sins." Paul explains that death came through a human being, Adam, and now "the resurrection of the dead has also come through a human being," namely Jesus Christ. "For as all die in Adam, so all will be made alive in Christ."

Paul's argument means that those people who identify with Jesus Christ will one day be raised just as Jesus was raised. Jesus is Savior because it is in him that death has been overcome. Jesus confronted the powers of evil with the reign of God in which salvation is found. Evil men who represented the powers of evil tried to eliminate Jesus. They failed. God raised Jesus from the dead, showing where real power resides. When we identify with Jesus by living in his story, we are already participating now in the salvation of the reign of God.

The resurrection of Jesus displays that the ultimate power in the universe lies with God. Jesus shows where the reign of God exists. Then when we join ourselves to Jesus and live in his life, we are joining with the salvation of the reign of God. When we identify with the reign of God made visible in Jesus, we are living now in the salvation that God has worked and is still working in the world. And further, whenever the reign of God comes in its fullness, we will be raised just as Jesus was raised. At least that is true, if we can believe the apostle Paul, the most important theologian of the New Testament.

In identifying the story of Jesus as a saving story, we are following the model of the early church, which is on display in the book of Acts. Six times in Acts the disciples are asked to identify Jesus, the one in whose name they are acting (2:14–39; 3:13–26; 4:10–12; 5:30–32; 10:36–43;

13:17–41). On each occasion, the apostles' response used a narrative outline. In some cases the outline is filled out more than in others, but in every case the minimum comment is that the people in Jerusalem killed Jesus but God raised him. Additional prominent elements include the presence of witnesses to these events and the response of hearers. After Pentecost, for example, those who heard the story were moved to repent, to be baptized, and to join the new movement around Jesus that began to live in this story (Acts 2). This response portrays the story of Jesus as a story of salvation, a salvation that is lived. And the outline is the same one used by Paul in 1 Corinthians 15 as the lead-in to his discussion of resurrection. Thus, in these biblical accounts, participation in the story of Jesus is to participate in the salvation that is intrinsic to the reign of God that was present with Jesus.

To summarize, I have told the story of Jesus in a way that showed the character of the reign of God as it confronted evil forces in the world. These evil powers were threatened and therefore killed Jesus. But in response to this killing, God raised Jesus from the dead. Those who hear and join in this story, that is, those who live in the story of Jesus, experience salvation in the reign of God now, and will one day share in resurrection with Jesus and participate in the reign of God in its fullness. Told in this way, this story answers the question, "How does Jesus' life, teaching, death, and resurrection bring salvation?" In this way, the story is an atonement image.

In this atonement image, with the resurrection Jesus has triumphed over the death-dealing forces of evil, and the reign of God is displayed as the ultimate power in the cosmos. God does not employ violence or take life in this motif; instead, God actually restores life. Because of this nonviolent image of God, in this book I call this image nonviolent atonement.

The significance of nonviolent atonement as an atonement image, and above all as a nonviolent image, becomes apparent when it is compared with the major inherited atonement images.

Atonement Images in History

In the history of the Christian church, there has never been a definitive ruling accepted by all Christians on the one correct understanding of atonement. Theologians have nonetheless offered a variety of answers to the questions concerning how Jesus' death brought salvation to sinful humankind. Historians have then collected these suggestions and have organized them into categories or families of doctrines. Each of these families of answers has a name that indicates something about that family of answers. Because there has never been a universally accepted answer, each answer has sometimes been called a "theory" of atonement. Each can also be called an atonement "motif" or an atonement "image." In this book, I will use the language of theory, motif, and image interchangeably.

Classic Christus Victor

The oldest atonement motif appears in several versions in the writings of the church fathers in the early Christian centuries. One version of this motif pictured a great cosmic battle for control of the universe between the forces of God, commanded by the angel Gabriel, and the forces of Satan. In this battle the forces of evil have captured the souls of humankind. God sent God's Son, namely Jesus Christ, into this battle, and the forces of evil killed Jesus, leading Satan to believe that with God's ultimate "weapon" dead, Satan had won. But Satan did not recognize the deity of Jesus hidden under his human flesh, and three days later, God resurrected Jesus from the dead. The souls of humankind were thus rescued from the clutches of Satan, and Satan was defeated by the resurrection of Jesus. There is here a victorious Christ, which produces the name Christus Victor for this motif.[1]

Another version of Christus Victor also features the souls of sinful humankind captured by Satan. In a desire to save humankind from the clutches of Satan, God offered God's Son as a ransom payment to Satan in exchange for release of the souls of humankind. Satan agreed to the exchange, but did not recognize that it was a trick. Beneath the flesh of Jesus as a human being is his deity, hidden the way bait covers the hook that catches a fish or lures the mouse into a trap. Satan was indeed caught and defeated, and the souls of humankind are saved, making this a ransom version of Christus Victor.

With the triumph through resurrection in view, it is clear that nonviolent atonement fits within the category called Christus Victor. However, the narrative basis of nonviolent atonement, which locates the

---

1. The classic treatment of atonement that brought real visibility to the idea of Christus Victor and of three main types of images was Aulén, *Christus Victor*. Other notable historical descriptions are Paul, *Atonement and the Sacraments* and McDonald, *Atonement*.

confrontation with evil on earth in the life of Jesus, clearly distinguishes nonviolent atonement from the inherited Christus Victor images that picture only a cosmic conflict or a celestial ransom. In other writing I have used the name "narrative Christus Victor" for nonviolent atonement. For purposes of clarity, in this book I use only the term nonviolent atonement.

Satisfaction

Much later, at the end of the eleventh century, Anselm (ca. 1033–1109), Archbishop of Canterbury, articulated what is called the satisfaction theory of atonement. It appeared in his classic book *Cur Deus homo*, published in 1098. Its title in English is *Why God Became Man*.

In Anselm's understanding, human sin has offended the honor of God and thus has disturbed the order of the universe. To reestablish order, the offended honor of God had to be satisfied or placated. That which satisfied God and restored order in the universe was the death of Jesus. Since it was human sin that had offended God's honor, it had to be a human death in payment to God's honor, hence the need for Jesus to be fully human. But to cover the sins of all humankind, the death had to be infinite, and thus the need for the deity of Jesus. Thus God sent Jesus as the God-man to die as a loving sacrifice that would satisfy the offended honor of God on behalf of sinful humans. Sinners who then avail themselves of the benefits of this sacrifice receive salvation from Jesus the savior who died for them. Some recent formulations of the satisfaction motif may fit five-year-old Zach's question about parents putting a son to death on the cross, but the question more nearly belongs to the idea of penal substitution described below.

Anselm posed this image specifically as a rejection of the ransom version of Christus Victor. He argued that it was beneath the dignity of God to make a deal with Satan. Besides, Satan had no rights that God would need to honor even if a deal were made. And further, even if sinful humankind deserved punishment, Satan had no right to administer that punishment. Thus Anselm rejected the ransom theory out of hand, removing Satan from the picture. Only God and sinful humankind remained in the salvation equation. In place of the ransom theory, Anselm posed the satisfaction motif.

Moral Influence

A couple generations after Anselm, Peter Abelard (1079–1142) offered an alternative to the satisfaction theory. Abelard agreed with Anselm that Satan had no rights that God needed to respect and that God would not make a deal with Satan. Thus Abelard also removed Satan from the equation, leaving only God and sinful humankind.

But Abelard also rejected the idea that God had to be placated or satisfied. Since God was always complete and perfect, God did not need such satisfaction. Instead Abelard said that the death of Jesus was God's offering or message to sinful humankind. Sinners fear a punishing God, Abelard said, and thus they rebel and run away from God. In order to show that God was not a harsh, fearful, and demanding judge, but was actually loving and accepting of sinful humankind, God offered the death of the Son. By giving up God's most precious possession, namely God's Son, to die for sinful humankind, God was demonstrating great, infinite love to sinners. The idea was that when sinners saw the great love of God displayed in offering God's Son to die, sinners would then cease fearing God and return to God as a loving father, certain of their acceptance and forgiveness. Abelard's suggestion has been called the moral influence theory of atonement because the loving death of Jesus impacts the psychological or moral feelings of humankind.

Penal Substitution

In the sixteenth century, Martin Luther and John Calvin put forward a major variation of satisfaction theory. In this revised motif, it was not God's honor that was offended. These reformers suggested instead that human sin had violated God's law. Thus it was the penalty of the law that had to be satisfied, and Jesus' death satisfied the penalty of death that was demanded for violation of God's law. In this version, it is often said that when Jesus paid the penalty demanded by the law; as a human being he bore the punishment that we deserve. Being punished in our place meant that Jesus was a substitute for us to satisfy God's law. This version of satisfaction atonement is called substitutionary atonement. To emphasize the idea of punishment for sin, it is called penal substitutionary atonement. Five-year-old Zach's question certainly fits the substitutionary atonement motif.

Initial Comparisons

Each of these motifs, with one exception, speaks to the question of the purpose of the death of Jesus. The exception is the cosmic battle version of Christus Victor, in which the death serves no clear role, other than to constitute a momentary victory for Satan. For the remaining images, however, each features a clear role for Jesus' death. For the ransom version of Christus Victor, the death is offered to Satan to seal God's part of the bargain. For Anselm's satisfaction theory, the death satisfies the offended honor of God, and without that satisfaction the order of the universe remains distorted. For substitutionary atonement, the death pays the penalty demanded by God's law. Finally, for Abelard's moral influence theory, the death of Jesus is directed at sinful humankind; it was God's effort to demonstrate ultimate love to sinners.

A visual image is helpful to distinguish these three families of atonement motifs and the role that each has for the death of Jesus. Visualize a big triangle, with God at the peak, and Satan and humankind at the two points of the base. Then imagine the death of Jesus as an arrow traveling toward one of the three points of the triangle where it accomplishes its intended purpose. For the ransom version of Christus Victor, since the death fulfilled God's part of the bargain with Satan, the arrow travels from God to Satan as the payment for the release of human souls. For the other two images, delete Satan, which leaves only God and sinners in the diagram. With the satisfaction motif, since Jesus as a human being satisfies the offended honor of God on behalf of humans, the arrow flies from humankind toward God. Penal substitution alters the image only slightly. Rather than flying toward God, the arrow flies toward divine law or God's law, but in spite of the alteration it is nonetheless an arrow aimed Godward from the side of sinful humankind. Finally, for the moral influence motif, the target of the death is humankind, which means that the arrow representing Jesus' death flies from God toward humans.

One common, contemporary way of dealing with the relationship of these three images is to claim that they are really three ways of talking about the same thing, namely how the death of Jesus saves. The names display their differing emphases, it is claimed, but nonetheless they are three versions of the same theme. Thus, to have a complete statement of atonement, the argument goes, these three should be held together and a complete or full picture of atonement emerges when the three views are combined.

But now, think of the image of the triangle, with the arrows flying in decidedly different directions. The direction of the arrows displays that the difference between these motifs is more than a variety of ways to make the same emphasis. In these motifs, the death of Jesus actually accomplishes very different things. These different accomplishments of the death cannot be satisfactorily reconciled as mere variations on one theme.

Further, there are historical reasons for rejecting the idea that these are three variations of the same theme. Recall that Anselm specifically rejected the ransom version of Christus Victor. In other words, Anselm was not combining his view with another in order to develop a more complete picture. And that goes double for Abelard. Recall that he also rejected the ransom motif but also rejected the satisfaction motif. Abelard was not simply adding additional elements to previous motifs for a fuller image. If contemporary theologians claim that these three motifs are actually variations on the same theme and can be reconciled or integrated, that claim actually ignores important aspects of the images that supposedly are being accepted, as well as ignoring the intent of Anselm and then Abelard to reject the previous motifs.

Alongside the inherited images, this chapter posed a new atonement motif, nonviolent atonement as a narrative version of Christus Victor. Although it has some parallels with the cosmic battle version of Christus Victor, nonviolent atonement obviously differs in significant ways from any of the inherited atonement motifs. It is the only motif that actually builds on the story of Jesus as given in the New Testament. Problems with the existing motifs provoked the need to develop this new model. These problems are both theological and practical. What are the problems? And what do they imply about the character of God? How does nonviolent atonement respond to the problems with the traditional motifs? Answers follow in the next chapter.

3

Atonement and God

FIVE-YEAR-OLD ZACH ASKED WHETHER parents would put their child to death on a cross. The question revealed good, intuitive insight into the inner workings of the inherited atonement images. It is time to explore what these images say about the character of God and the way they portray how God works in Jesus.

Inherited Atonement Images and God

The Climax

For one issue, note the culmination of each atonement motif. For nonviolent atonement, as for the two early versions of Christus Victor described in the previous chapter, the motifs reach their high point with the resurrection of Jesus, which is God's saving act. That culmination poses a strong contrast to the satisfaction and moral theories, in which the climax and the saving element is the death of Jesus. Consider that difference in light of the story of Jesus that we saw in the Gospels. The narrative reaches its climax, not with Jesus' death but with his resurrection. It seems more than appropriate that an atonement motif reflect the resurrection.

What's Not Here?

In light of the traditional atonement images, reflect on the content of the narrative of Jesus as this story is told in the Gospels. Nowhere in the narrative does it appear that Jesus' death was a ransom that God paid to Satan. Nowhere does it appear that Jesus' death was a payment to God to satisfy God's offended honor. Nowhere in the Gospels does it say that Jesus died in order to pay the penalty of death demanded by God's law. Nowhere in the Gospels does it say that Jesus' death was an offering of God's most precious possession as a way to show God's ultimate love for sinful humanity. These claims are brought to the biblical story and imposed on it from outside the story. It has then been assumed that the biblical language reflects these later claims when in fact the biblical language can have other meanings. (In the last chapter of the book, I will return to the question of the biblical language and other possible meanings.)

Inner Logic of the Killing of Jesus

The idea that Jesus' death is an offering to God's honor, as in the satisfaction motifs, or to God's law, as in the penal substitutionary image, or to humankind, as in the moral theory, poses a problem of logic. As the story was sketched from the Gospels, Jesus was living and acting in a way to witness to the reign of God. That witness—for example, forgiving sins—threatened the religious leaders. So they engaged the Romans to have Jesus killed. Jesus did not commit suicide. His life was taken from him violently by evil men, who had evil intentions. But for Jesus' death to be an offering that was necessary to satisfy the offended honor of God or to satisfy the penalty demanded by divine law or to show God's love to humanity, the evil men who engineered Jesus' death needed to be working with or at least fulfilling the will of God. The inner logic of these atonement motifs thus picture the death of Jesus as *both* contrary to the will of God, but in another way, *also* in accord with the will of God.

Inner Logic of God's Role

And even more shockingly, for Jesus' death to satisfy God's offended honor or to satisfy the penalty of divine law or to show God's love to sinful humanity, God had to be orchestrating the death to fulfill God's purposes. The inherited language is that God sent Jesus to die for the sins of humankind, meaning that God sent Jesus to die to satisfy God's own offended honor or to pay the penalty demanded by God's law or to show God's love for humankind. The internal logic of these atonement motifs involves God in two ways—God is *both* the one who was greatly offended when the Son was killed, but God is *also* the one who engineered the death of Jesus—the one who has Jesus killed—for God's own purposes. Here in shocking display is the image of God that worried five-year-old Zach, who wanted reassurance that parents would not imitate God.

Nonviolent Atonement and God

The problems of theological logic are all absent from nonviolent atonement, which features a nonviolent God. In this motif, the death is not offered to God for a divine purpose nor is it God's offering to humankind. Jesus' death itself is not salvific. Rather, the death and resurrection show the radical difference in means between the forces of evil and the reign of God. The powers of evil resort to violence and killing in an attempt to get their way. In contrast, God's means is to restore life where it has ceased to exist—a nonviolent God.

Atonement Images and Lived Faith

Alongside these differences in theological logic between nonviolent atonement and the classic images are some serious practical problems. These problems arise when Jesus is considered as the norm and orientation for the Christian life. The narrative basis of nonviolent atonement makes use of the life of Jesus, while the inherited theories do not. Since an individual encounters God and participates in the reign of God by living in the story of Jesus, this difference is significant.

Living in the story gives a visible dimension to the victory of the resurrection. When people believe strongly enough that God was in the story of Jesus actually to live in that story, then the future reign of God is indeed breaking into and made present in our world. This living witness makes the reign of God visible as it confronts evil and injustice in the world. That visible, lived testimony is lacking from the classic versions of Christus Victor, as well as in the satisfaction and moral images.

Now consider what living in the narrative of Jesus would mean when that idea is inserted into the inherited atonement images.

The Example of Jesus

Reflect on the model posed by Jesus in the inherited atonement images. For the ransom theory, Jesus is innocent but submits to death as God's part of the bargain with Satan. This is a model of passive submission to undeserved suffering and death. The picture does not change for the satisfaction models. God needs the death of Jesus in order to restore order in the cosmos. Thus Jesus, who has not sinned, submits to undeserved suffering and death because God needs his death to satisfy divine honor. The same applies if Jesus' death is said to satisfy the penalty demanded by divine law—Jesus did not disobey the law, but nonetheless as an innocent man he died to satisfy its divine requirement. This modeling of passive submission also applies to any other redefinition of the impact of Jesus' death, whether restoring obedience or worship or taking on of human sin in order to enable redemption. For the moral theory, again Jesus did nothing to deserve death, but he submits to this undeserved death to show God's love. In each of these instances, Jesus models passive, voluntary submission to undeserved or unmerited suffering because God wills or needs it.

Contrast these images of Jesus who submitted passively to unjust death because God wills it with the activist image of Jesus in nonviolent atonement. Rather than passively submitting to evil, the story of Jesus shows that he actively confronted evil or injustice. Examples of this confrontation or active nonviolence include strategies for refusing an insult, blunting the Roman occupation, and exposing an unjust economic system. (We will return to these strategies in detail in chapter 4.) He healed on the Sabbath in defiance of the purity code, confronted racism with his response to Samaritans, raised the status of women in a male-dominant society, and associated with people considered outcasts. He challenged the sacrificial system in the temple. This witness continued through his arrest and trial, where he made it clear that the kingdom to which he belonged did not engage in violence. He confronted his accusers with the fact that he did not fight and that weapons were unnecessary when arresting him. He submitted to violence rather than engaging in killing. And even that submission was an action, a willingness to remain true to the reign of God. He could have saved his life by giving up his mission, but he chose to remain faithful to the reign of God. As a result of that faithfulness, the powers of evil took his life from him. And God restored it. Although Jesus lost his life, his example is not that of passive submission, but that of active confrontation of evil and a willingness to bear the consequences.

The Image of God

Alongside the image of an innocent Jesus who submits passively to unjust suffering, consider the image of God that accompanies the model of Jesus for each of the traditional atonement motifs. For the ransom motif, God is a God who willingly gives the Son to die for the sake of God's other children. For the satisfaction theory, God arranges for Jesus to be human and divine in order that Jesus can die to supply the death needed to satisfy God's offended honor. Or for penal substitution, God sends Jesus as human and divine in order to die to satisfy the penalty required by God's law. Or for the moral influence motif, God is a God who is willing to have one of God's children killed in order to show ultimate love for the rest of God's children. In other words, according to the inner logic of each of these motifs, God uses or arranges or sanctions the violent death of innocent Jesus for God's own purposes. This is a violent God, a God who employs violence, a God who orchestrated the death of God's own Son. It is not really surprising that feminist theologians have written that these atonement images pose an image of divine child abuse.[1] And most certainly, we confront again the image of God that worried Zach when he asked about the rights of parents.

Compare this image of a God who uses and sanctions violence from the inherited atonement theories with the image of God in nonviolent atonement. In nonviolent atonement God does not use or require the death of Jesus. Rather, God responds to the violence perpetrated on Jesus by resurrecting Jesus from the dead. Here is the image of a nonviolent God. This is the character of the God who is revealed in the narrative of Jesus. Rather than sanctioning or administering death, the God revealed in Jesus restores life, and the promise is that this restoration of life will one day apply to all God's people.

This comparison of atonement images has revealed a clear contrast in ways God is portrayed. For the inherited atonement images, the salvation worked through Jesus depends on violence sanctioned or engineered

---

1. One of the earliest mentions of divine child abuse occurs in Brown and Parker, "For God So Loved the World?" A similar discussion is in Brock, *Journeys by Heart*, 52–57.

by God. Jesus was handed over to be killed as a ransom, or Jesus died in order to satisfy divine honor or divine law or Jesus died in order to show God's love for humankind, or to restore obedience or worship or absorb human sin as the basis of redemption. For each of these inherited atonement images, Jesus' mission was to submit to death. He was sent from God with the mission to undergo that death to fulfill a divine need.

Nonviolent atonement portrays God in a different light. Jesus' mission was to embody the reign of God. This mission was to live rather than to die. Since the reign of God posed an ultimate threat to the rule of evil, Jesus' death may have been inevitable. However, dying was not the purpose of Jesus' mission. Rather, it was the consequence of carrying out his mission faithfully. The role of God was not to sanction Jesus' death for divine purposes, but to overcome death and to restore life. This identifies the reign of God as the ultimate power in the universe. From a human perspective, this is a nonviolent God, who works God's will without resort to coercion and violence.

Living the Images

The discussion of the models of Jesus and of God in these atonement motifs may seem like an abstract discussion, but it has real consequences. Consider a woman who is being abused by her husband, and goes to her pastor for advice. She hears, "You are a Christian, use Jesus as your guide." The model of Jesus who submitted patiently to undeserved suffering because God the Father needed it encourages the abused woman to continue to submit and to find meaning in undeserved abuse in hope that some good might result from her suffering. It is doubly harmful when it is accompanied by a patriarchal theology that places the man as head of the woman in the way that God is said to be the head of Jesus Christ. Also consider a girl who has been abused by her father or another male relative. This theology holds up a model that tells her to honor her father by submitting just as Jesus honored his Father by submitting to unjust suffering needed by God. Because of this problematic modeling, many feminist theologians have rejected the traditional understandings of atonement. These motifs pose a harmful model for women. When I have given lectures on these issues, I have heard many testimonies from women saying, "I was a victim of that abusive theology. Don't ever let anyone tell you to stop talking about the harm it can cause."

This model of Jesus who submitted passively to suffering was harmful for enslaved African Americans. Slaves were taught to submit to masters, to submit to beatings and other unjust and inhumane treatment, just as Jesus had done. The same model of submission would apply to African Americans who continue to experience discrimination because of the color of their skin. The model would encourage them to submit passively to the injustice they still encounter. Many writers of black theology and of womanist theology (African American women theologians) have rejected the classic atonement images and the unhealthy models of Jesus and of God that they present. James H. Cone, a founder of the black theology movement, wrote that satisfaction and moral atonement motifs accommodated slavery and racism by separating reconciliation with God from God's liberating deeds in history. Although Cone rejected any salvific meaning in the suffering of the cross, he later likened the cross to the lynching tree for African Americans, and since resurrection was victory over the cross it is a symbol of resistance for African Americans.[2] For African American women, these atonement images provided the double jeopardy of modeling both women's submission to male abuse and African American submission to white racism. In her critique of inherited atonement imagery, Delores S. Williams, prominent womanist theologian, relates the innocent and undeserved suffering of Jesus to the surrogacy of black women, namely the many abusive and oppressive roles that have been forced upon them. She argues that accepting satisfaction or substitutionary atonement would mean validating this unjust suffering, and render Jesus the "ultimate surrogate figure."[3]

The same can be said of any race or ethnic group that experiences oppression. Some specific examples that come to mind are the many people of Latinx descent who live in the United States, particularly those without legal status; Palestinians, who are treated as second-class citizens, and whose land is being continually encroached upon; and the native peoples of North America, whose land was stolen while those not killed were either crowded onto reservations or forced to assimilate into white culture. For each of these, the models of traditional atonement would encourage passive submission to injustice.

As an alternative to the inherited atonement motifs that offer a violent God and models of submission to unmerited abuse, I offer nonviolent

---

2. See Cone, *God of the Oppressed*, 209–13; Cone, *Cross and the Lynching Tree*.
3. Williams, *Sisters in the Wilderness*, 161–67, esp. 162.

atonement as a way of understanding the saving work of Jesus with a nonviolent God. This motif offers a model of active, nonviolent resistance to abuse and oppression. It is a model that encourages women abused by men to assess their situation and take steps to escape it. African Americans and other victims of racial discrimination can draw on this understanding of the saving work of Jesus to confront the oppression of racism. Jesus' posing of ways to confront the Roman occupiers of Palestine can inspire nonviolent resistance by Palestinians, the indigenous inhabitants of North America and many others who have been deprived of land and home through colonial occupation.

Refurbishing the Classic Images

In order to defend Jesus' death as the saving act, some recent interpreters have replaced the outmoded feudal image[4] of satisfying God's honor or the brutal image of satisfying the death penalty demanded by divine law. They suggest other objectives that Jesus' death accomplished. One such option is that Jesus' death returned true worship to God. Another is that Jesus rendered true obedience to God. Yet another is that via an exchange between God and Christ, God in Christ identifies with humanity to the extent of taking on the shame of human sin and thus making their redemption possible. With some of these new emphases, redemption may be applied through the resurrection. However, these efforts cannot overcome the fact that the new language is just additional ways of maintaining the idea that it is still the death of Jesus that impacts God; and Jesus' death is still the prior condition on which God offers salvation; and God is still the one who needs the death and arranges the death for God's purposes. Renaming the purpose of Jesus' death and disguising God's role in it may soften it a bit but such revisions do not change the fact that the motif still focuses on Jesus' death as needed by and offered to God. From the other side of the salvation equation, salvation is still dependent on a God who requires death and arranges death as the condition of salvation. These efforts, and any additional suggestions of new language for death, cannot avoid the fact that for the death to have saving import, God must be behind it, willing the death in some way. Even when the idea is couched

---

4. Chapter 18 expands on the feudal context.

differently, these efforts still assume a God for whom violence is the basis of salvation.[5]

Application to All People

It may seem as though nonviolent atonement works only for people who experience situations of abuse or oppression, but that impression is incorrect. Nonviolent atonement speaks to everyone. Nonviolent atonement challenges violent men to confront the sin in their own lives and to change it. Racism does not happen by itself. Nonviolent atonement challenges perpetrators of racism to repent of this evil and to join together with those who experience racism to oppose it. The victims and the perpetrators of racism come from different sides of the problem, but they can join together in opposing racism.

Similarly, without actively participating in economic exploitation, middle-class people nonetheless enjoy a comfortable lifestyle in the United States, which is related in part to forcing other countries to have less. This inequity is seen, for example, in the trade imbalance that the United State has run since 1976. In recent years, this country has imports that are over forty billion dollars higher than its exports, which means that the goods and resources produced elsewhere benefit the United States more than the producing countries. Even a middle-class lifestyle, modest by American standards, participates in a system that deprives people in poorer countries of the necessities of life. Nonviolent atonement encourages people to seek out ways to witness against economic exploitation and oppression.

Patriarchy, racism, and an exploitative economic system constitute examples of structural or systemic violence. Violence of one kind or another is endemic to all levels of American society. All Christians who live in the story of the nonviolent Jesus are called to oppose this pervasive violence, whether structural or direct. The narrative of Jesus expands the discussion of how following the God revealed in the story of Jesus engages Christians in opposing this violence.

Nonviolent atonement is an atonement motif that speaks to or for every Christian, calling on each Christian to witness to the presence of the reign of God in a world that has not yet come to identify with the

---

5. For a discussion of representative efforts to defend the inherited atonement images, see Weaver, *Nonviolent Atonement*, 220–79.

reign of God. Living in the story of Jesus presents people with many ways in which individuals, and the larger society, fall short of the reign of God. But with that recognition also comes awareness that the God who raised Jesus also calls people to live today in the story of Jesus. And with their lives, they can testify to systemic injustice and act in ways that demonstrate that their participation in the systemic injustice is involuntary. With the grace of God, they live as a witness to the reign of God and experience salvation as they belong to the reign of God.

As a motif, nonviolent atonement depends on the idea that Jesus confronted injustices of various kinds. When reading the narrative of Jesus on which the motif is based, instances of that confrontation appear in terms of Jesus' first-century context. This narrative displays what the reign of God looked like in a particular place in human history. The calling of Christians today is to use that model as the basis for thinking about how to continue the witness of the reign of God in the world and to make Jesus' story present in our world. And when that witness happens, the future reign of God is already present and being made visible, and Christians today are participating in the resurrection of Jesus and continuing Jesus' mission of making the reign of God present in the world.

Conclusion

This book promised to talk about the God who was revealed in Jesus. An outline of the story of Jesus became the basis for further theological discussion. God's resurrection of Jesus identified the story of Jesus as God's story. Christian faith proclaims it a saving story. Describing the story theologically, it became the atonement motif called nonviolent atonement. This motif said something important about God, namely that God does not save with violence or by sanctioning violence, but by restoring life. This learning from nonviolent atonement poses a clear contrast to the actions of God in the inherited atonement images. From the story of Jesus, it becomes visible that the saving action of God does not come through violence, as in the inherited atonement images, but through resurrection. The God on display in nonviolent atonement is a God who does not work through violence—a nonviolent God.

The contrast of violence and nonviolence in atonement images has practical application. In the inherited atonement images, Jesus passively submitted to the violence on which salvation depended, an unfortunate image for anyone in a subservient position. It makes Jesus a model of passive submission to injustice. In contrast, since nonviolent atonement makes use of the life of Jesus, living within the narrative encourages Christians to confront the injustices of the world around them. People who live out the nonviolent story of Jesus are working with the grain of the universe, which was created by the God revealed in Jesus.

This discussion of atonement images has displayed quite vividly how both theology and ethics are derived from the New Testament's narrative of Jesus. Following chapters explore further some implications of living in the life of Jesus. The next chapter explores the teaching by Jesus that undergirds and is expressed in his nonviolent way of confronting injustice.

4

New Testament Teaching and Nonviolence

Jesus' Teaching

THE LIFE OF JESUS displays the fact that he did not resort to violence, but lived out the reign of God in ways that actively challenged injustice. It is this narrative that most of all makes clear the nonviolent character of his life and his mission. That is, seeing and believing that Jesus rejected violence is not simply dependent on biblical authority or on the authoritative status of one particular passage of the Bible. Accepting the nonviolence of Jesus is rather a matter of reading and engaging the story of Jesus as a whole. The story is then the context in which to understand what Jesus says about the rejection of violence and how to resist evil without resorting to violence. Presenting this teaching fills out the understanding of nonviolence given visibility by the story.

Perhaps Jesus' most well-known teaching on the rejection of violence occurs in the Sermon on the Mount in Matthew 5–7. This text spells out much farther what it means to live out the reign of God. He spoke of blessings for troubled hearts, the poor in spirit, those who mourn, the meek who lack the wherewithal to make a big impact on society, the merciful, and the peacemakers. Much of the Sermon on the Mount deals with loyalty—the difference between loyalty to or serving the reign of God and living according to common expectations. There are statements about being faithful in marriage, avoiding divorce, not putting one's trust in worldly riches, seeking the reign of God, treating others as one would like to be treated, and much more.

One of the most striking sections of the Sermon on the Mount concerns Jesus' statements about not retaliating in kind. Citing statements from the law (Exod 21:24; Lev 24:20; Deut 19:21), he said, "You have heard that it was said, 'An eye for an eye and a tooth for a tooth.' But I say to you, Do not resist an evildoer." Although long interpreted as a command to passivity and nonresistance, this statement actually means "Do not mirror evil" or "Do not respond with similar evil." Thus, Jesus follows immediately with three examples of active responses that do not mirror the offense: "If anyone strikes you on the right cheek, turn the other also; and if anyone wants to sue you and take your coat, give your cloak as well; and if anyone forces you to go one mile, go also the second mile" (Matt 5:38–42). These three injunctions have been interpreted as Jesus' further instruction to remain passive and to do nothing in the face of evil, or to go even farther in the direction commanded by the aggressor. But I accept a different interpretation.[1]

Notice that Matthew talked about being struck on the "right cheek." In that culture, the left hand was the unclean hand and would not be used in public. Thus, the only blow that could touch the right cheek would be a back-handed slap by the aggressor. Such a slap is not designed to injure but to insult. It would come from a higher status person insulting a lower status person—master over slave, husband over wife, parent over child, Roman over Jew—reminding the one slapped of his or her inferior social standing. Retaliation in this instance would provoke and seemingly justify additional violence on the part of the aggressor. But Jesus suggests that when insulted in this way, the person insulted should take charge of the situation by turning the left cheek toward the aggressor. This move would refuse the insult and invite another hit, this time by a closed fist, which would be a mark of equality. If the aggressor does strike the target, the aggressor has lost the encounter by treating the lesser status person as an equal. But doing nothing is also a loss of face for the aggressor, since the person slapped has taken the initiative by an act that refused the insult. In essence, turning the other cheek is an instance of active nonviolence, an assertion of full humanity by a supposedly lesser person, but done in a way that has the potential to change a situation and avoid a violent follow up.

The setting for the statement about giving cloak along with coat—undergarment with outer garment—is the debtors court. Common in

---

1. The interpretation here follows Wink, *Engaging the Powers*, 175–84, and Wink, *Jesus and Nonviolence*.

Jesus' day was the poor tenant farmer who owed debts impossible to pay to a rich and exploitative landowner. The law allowed the debt holder to require something of value as collateral for the loan. For a poor person, the collateral might well be his only possession of value, namely the coat on his back that he slept in. However, the law also had a stipulation that the poor person could claim it again at night for sleeping, with the knowledge that it would be surrendered again the next morning if repayment was not possible (Exod 22:25–27; Deut 24:10–13). Jesus suggests that when the coat is demanded for collateral, the debtor should strip off his underwear as well, hand both to the debt holder, and then leave the court naked to parade that way for the rest of the day. In a society where the shame of nakedness fell on the one who caused it, this act would expose the exploitative nature of the system. Again, it is a nonviolent way to expose a situation that needed changing.

Going the second mile concerned the Roman military occupiers of Palestine. Military regulations permitted a soldier to commandeer a civilian at any time and require him to carry the soldier's sixty- or even eighty-pound pack for one mile. However, to minimize the resentment of the locals for this forced labor on behalf of the hated occupiers, military regulations also limited the distance to one mile for any one requisitioned civilian. The civilian who followed Jesus' suggestion would actually put the soldier in violation of his own regulations. Since violators of regulations risked punishment, one can even image the tables turned entirely, with the soldier begging the civilian to put down the pack before the soldier got in trouble.

These creative ways of responding to aggression and injustice are intrinsic to Jesus' proclamation of the reign of God. They demonstrate that followers of Jesus do not confront evil with more evil, violence with retaliatory violence, but rather seek to change the situation in a way that keeps open the possibility of reconciliation. The story of Jesus contains additional actions that provide further examples of ways to challenge an injustice or change a situation. Jesus healed on the Sabbath when it violated the purity code, which was a protest that returned the day to its intended purpose as a day of healing and restoration. His cleansing of the temple was a confrontation that acted out returning the temple to a place where people could encounter God's forgiveness.

Immediately following the three examples in the Sermon on the Mount of ways to respond to aggression, Jesus said "Love your enemies" (Matt 5:44). Here, "love" is not a term of liking and affection. It is rather another version of the examples of ways to respond without retaliating. Jesus is telling his followers that when confronted with an enemy, they should act in such a way as to change the situation. Do something to move the situation away from a conflict and toward a resolution which preserves the humanity of the aggressor as well as the offender. The three examples just noted are such actions. Jesus' injunction about loving enemies is a reminder that such actions are not to be done out of an attitude of vengeance or hostility, but with a view to moving the encounter to one that has a resolution—hitter may see slapped person as human, debt holder sees poor person as individual in need, soldier learns that not all Jews are hostile. These suggestions for challenging the injustice of a situation are thus in the same category of responses as Jesus' challenges to the purity code by healing on the Sabbath or traveling through Samaria and interacting with a Samaritan woman.

Teaching of Paul

Teachings of Jesus are not the only place the idea appears of not responding to evil with the same kind of evil. Paul follows Jesus' line when he writes, "Do not repay anyone evil for evil . . . If our enemies are hungry, feed them; if they are thirsty, give them to drink; . . . Do not be overcome by evil, but overcome evil with good" (Rom 12:17, 20, 21).

Paul repeats the idea in 1 Thessalonians 5:15: "See that none of you repays evil for evil, but always seek to do good to one another and to all." The author of 1 Peter follows suit: "Do not repay evil for evil or abuse for abuse; but, on the contrary, repay with a blessing" (3:9).

These sayings indicate that throughout the New Testament there is an ongoing appreciation of the idea of not responding to evil and violence with more of the same, and instead to act in a way that changes the situation or defuses the confrontation.

The Logic of Nonviolence and Nonretaliation

Love of enemies, acting to change the situation, not returning evil for evil points to a real consequence that is most often missed. By retaliating in kind, by responding to evil with the same or more evil, one is becoming like the enemy, like what one purports to hate. A small boy gets his big brother to beat up the one harassing him. But in so doing, the big brother is becoming an even greater purveyor of violence, a bigger harasser. Ratchet up the scale of violence to the level of a terrorist attack, a very violent act. And the government that pursues the attackers employs even more violence, which provokes yet bigger efforts at retaliation. Such increases can continue to the level of nuclear weapons. Country A fears the nuclear arsenal of Country B. Country A thus builds more nuclear weapons, and in the process becomes an even bigger employer of weapons. Since both sides make claims to be the righteous side, escalation is always a danger.

Confronting the idea of becoming what one hates throws a different light on Jesus' teachings, and their continuation in writings of Paul and Peter. Love your enemies, do not repay evil for evil, is not a mere heroic ideal that would never work in the "real world." It is rather a frank recognition of how the "real world" actually works—violence begets more violence and conflicts continue, and one side mirrors the violence that it purports to hate in the other. These words of Jesus and Paul and Peter are statements about how to de-escalate conflict and how to lessen violence in the real world.

Of course there is risk involved in returning good for evil and attempting to change the situation. But there is also a guaranteed risk involved in responding to evil or violence with more of the same. Responding to violence with violence is guaranteed to cause harm and eventually death. In addition, success with violence is by no means guaranteed. It is often claimed that violence is the only way, the only language, that the other side understands. But in effect, both sides make that claim. However, only one side can win, but both can lose. Since both sides employ violence, violence is guaranteed to fail 50 percent of the time, and usually more since even a "winning side" experiences losses. When this risk of employing violence is faced honestly, the risk of returning good for evil, that is, of acting in a way that stops the cycle of violence and changes the situation, might well pose less risk and entail less destruction, and may even have a good outcome.

Nonviolence in Theology

We have just finished a look at New Testament teachings that suggest nonviolent ways to confront situations of evil and injustice. Stated generally, these teachings suggest refusing to retaliate against violence or evil in kind, and instead to take an action that changes the situation. Jesus gave three examples of such actions in the Sermon on the Mount, and acted out others. The writings of Paul echoed the idea of not retaliating and instead returning good for evil. This teaching fills out the understanding of the rejection of violent means that is made visible in the life of Jesus.

Profound theological implications appear when we make visible the rejection of violence in Jesus' life and teaching. Christian faith has always proclaimed that God was revealed in Jesus. Since God is revealed in Jesus, it follows that God should be understood in terms of nonviolent images. In the previous chapters, we saw how the inherited atonement images assumed that God commissioned violence to achieve salvation for humankind. Understanding the nonviolence of God calls for a nonviolent atonement image. I posed nonviolent atonement as one such image. Following chapters develop a number of additional dimensions of the idea of a nonviolent God who is revealed in the nonviolent story and teaching of Jesus.

Theology Reduced to Ethics?

On first hearing, it may seem as though the entire discussion of Jesus and the reign of God is being reduced to the discussion of nonviolence. However, in response to this challenge there are two things to keep in mind. For one, as the discussion of the atonement images demonstrated, ethical issues have been absent from standard or inherited theology. A later chapter will make the same point for the discussion of Christology. For the most part, ethics has occurred as a separate discipline in the comprehensive outline of religious and theological subjects. Developing theology from the narrative of Jesus integrates his life into theology. This approach gives ethical issues, and specifically issues of violence and nonviolence, a visibility they have not had previously in theology. When ethical issues have heretofore been absent from the discussion of traditional atonement and of the inherited tradition of Christology, bringing these issues into the conversation can seem like an exaggeration of them on first hearing.

Second, recall the many dimensions of violence that were surveyed in the introduction. Violence covers direct violence carried out with weapons and words, as well as the systemic violence of poverty and racism and sexism and patriarchy and more. These latter kinds of violence might also be identified as concerns of social justice. Looking at the life of Jesus shows that his actions have implications for all of these issues. Thus, to discuss the implications of living in the life of Jesus brings these social issues into the theological conversation. Items from this wide-ranging discussion of implications of the life of Jesus appear in the remaining chapters of this book. To discuss the life of Jesus is to discuss the variety of ways that the reign of God made visible in Jesus confronts the violence—both direct and systemic or structural—of the world around us.

Why It Matters

In the inherited view of God, God uses violence and commands violence. It occurs in a number of ways in the Bible. These include commanding massacres as recounted in the Old Testament, sending or requiring Jesus to die for the sins of humankind, and executing violent judgment at the end of earth's time as reported in some interpretations of the book of Revelation. This book provides responses to all those kinds of divine violence.

However, developing understandings of a God who does not use violence is more than an abstract theological discussion. It has implications for the way Christians live and how they see and understand the world. Living in the reign of God, living to make present the life of Jesus, poses a profound challenge to the violent world in which we live.

There is a profound belief in the United States that freedom depends on war. This belief is anchored in the way the story of the foundation of the nation is told, beginning with the Revolutionary War of 1776. This belief in the linking of freedom and war is widespread and deep-seated. When I was still teaching, frequently I asked students in my classes what would have happened had there been no war in 1776. Almost invariably a student would answer, "We would still be oppressed by the British," or "We wouldn't have our freedom." With a twinkle in my eye and a hint of sarcasm, I would reply, "Since Canada did not have a war of independence, that means that Canada is an oppressed country." In other words, the example of the United States' neighbor to the north counters the claim that freedom necessarily begins with or depends on war.

Consider the many ways that violence is presumed and accepted in our society, beginning with the supposed link between war and freedom. The link is pervasive in the telling of American history, along with the belief that the United States wins because it has God on its side. Thus, in conventional understanding, a war was necessary to free the colonies from the oppressive British. A war was necessary to free the slaves and preserve the Union. A war was necessary to save democracy from the Kaiser in World War I. World War II was the good war, necessary to save the Jews.[2] There are other ways to interpret these wars, which we do not need to pursue here, since the point now is to see the prevalence of the assumption in our society that freedom depends on violence and war.

A side note concerns the war in Vietnam. One reason that it was such a traumatic event for the United States was precisely because it did not fit the common assumption that the United States secures freedom through war, and that the United States always wins because God is on the side of the United States.

Our national violence is often pictured as a continuation of stories from the Old Testament. The civil religion of the United States portrays the nation in ways that parallel a reading of the history of Israel. Robert Bellah, renowned scholar of civil religion, described these parallels—as Hebrew slaves in Egypt escaped the tyrant Pharaoh through the exodus and journeyed to the promised land, oppressed people escaped Europe to a new world and fought a war to free themselves from a tyrant king. As civil religion compares these two stories, England is parallel to Egypt, North America is the promised land, the war of 1776 becomes an exodus, King George channels Pharaoh, and George Washington fills the role of Moses. These parallels create unofficial but very real religious connotations for the nation, with a war as the pivotal event.[3] The reverence given symbols such as the flag and the national anthem signal this ultimate significance.

For another place to see the connection between God and American wars, one need only reflect on the prevalence of the song "God bless America," and the importance that people place on the phrase "under God" in the pledge of allegiance to the flag.

Beyond these images of violence, war, and God in the national self-understanding, think of the other violent images that abound in our society. "War" is the term used to indicate that in one way or another a

2. For a different interpretation, see Grimsrud, *Good War That Wasn't*.

3. My essay "Responding to September 11" shows the impact of civil religion. The classic description is Bellah, "Civil Religion in America." A text that contributed to my understanding of the proclivity to violence in United States society is McLoughlin, *Revivals, Awakenings, and Reform*.

struggle is serious—as in the war on terror, the war on poverty, the war on cancer, the war on drugs,[4] the war on HIV, the culture wars, or the war on women. Violent language and military terms abound in the sports world. Football players talk about "the guys I go to war with." Sportscasters routinely refer to the "war in the trenches" or the "war on the boards." Baseball players and quarterbacks who possess a strong throwing arm are said to have a "gun" or a "cannon" for an arm. Quarterbacks throw the bomb. A runner attempting to steal is "gunned down" at second base. A team that acquires a new player is said to have "an additional weapon in the coach's arsenal."

Think of the prevalence of violence in entertainment. Action movies abound, where "action" is a euphemism for violence. There is violence disguised as fun in cartoons and violent video games. Couple these forms of "fun" violence with the research, easily available with a quick Google search, that shows that children who spend lots of time with such violent images are more likely to act out violence. The impact of these violent images acts in the same way that advertising works. In advertising, an image is repeated in an attractive fashion with the intent to create a need where none previously existed or to set up a wish that can be fulfilled only by acquiring the product advertised—guys will attract beautiful women if they drink the right brand of beer or use the correct shaving lotion, girls will attract good-looking guys by wearing a certain brand of jeans or a specific shade of lipstick. If these ads did not work, companies would not pay to show them. Just as ads have an impact on the psyche of people who see them, research shows that frequent viewing of violent entertainment also has an impact—children are more likely to act out aggressively, people assume that there is more violence in society than actually exists, and people more readily believe that violence will solve problems, both in our society and around the world.

Finally, on top of all that violence in our society, recall the violence of the Old Testament and its stories of violence commanded by God. If God kills God's enemies, it seems natural that people kill their enemies, particularly when their government proclaims that killing to be necessary and invokes God's blessing on it. People who fight wars in the belief that God is on their side are simply imitating what they believe that God does. Chapters 9 and 11 will extend this particular discussion further.

---

4. Alexander, *New Jim Crow*, argues in graphic detail that the so-called "war on drugs" is actually a war on people of color.

Given the prevalence of violence in United States society, it is important to go beyond the description of a biblical and theological foundations. The following chapter will suggest that alternatives exist, if there is a will to look for them. Along with this discussion of nonviolent alternatives, the chapter will also display how different the character of nonviolence can appear, depending on the framework in which it is viewed.

5

Active Nonviolence

THE DESCRIPTION OF JESUS' life and teaching in previous chapters displays Jesus' rejection of violence and the nonviolent character of his teaching and his ministry. There is thus an ample biblical precedent for the practice of nonviolent activism today. That precedent faces the many dimensions of violence that abound in our contemporary world. When the God of the universe, the creator God, is made visible in the life of Jesus, it becomes clear that Jesus' way of living reflects the grain of the universe created by that God. One can thus expect to see ways in which nonviolence appears and works in the contemporary world, whether or not it is prefaced by claims of Christian faith. This chapter then sketches an understanding of how active nonviolence is relevant for today's issues of peace and justice.

Nonviolent Activism

Witness by Church Function

The church and Christians can witness to injustice in these areas in many ways. Internal practices constitute a part of this witness. The rite of baptism joins people, regardless of social status, race, gender, or the way one loves, into the body of Christ that is the visible witness to the world. Eating the bread and drinking the wine of communion acts out the practice of sharing goods and treasure in a materialistic society with great disparity in the distribution of wealth. Decision-making in which all voices are heard and valued is a model for a watching world.[1] Further, church agencies that render short-term help in times of disaster and long-term development assistance or refugee resettlement serve as models of caring for the vulnerable and those in need. Activities of the church in the local community, such as assisting programs for the homeless or for restorative justice or helping to settle refugees and immigrants, perform services that reflect the values of the reign of God made visible in Jesus.

But situations arise that are not sufficiently addressed by these functions of the church. Regarding economics and political systems alone, all societies have issues to confront with regard to denial of justice for segments of the population. The question concerns how followers of Jesus should live and act so as to make the reign of God visible when faced with injustices. What happens when injustice exists in the status quo? How does the grain of the universe become visible in the face of discrimination of various kinds—against people of color or people without legal papers or refugees or Muslims or people who are LGBTQ—or exploitative working conditions, and much more? How should contemporary Christians continue the mission of Jesus to make the reign of God visible? How should Christians move society in the direction of alignment with the grain of the universe in the face of such entrenched conditions? Consider these suggestions for dealing with problems, concerning both individual and then societal-wide or global examples.

Nonviolence by Individuals

For responses by individuals, consider first traditional nonresistance as practiced by the Amish and some Mennonites, in which Christians refuse to respond to a provocation. They would accept willingly for themselves an assault or an injustice such as racial discrimination or low wages, since all forms of resistance and protest or strikes or union activity are considered to involve some level of violence. Passive nonresistance is an identifiable option that certainly fits within the framework of Jesus' teachings on loving enemies. But in many cases perhaps a more active response is warranted and applicable in an average household. For example, parenting can incorporate these active, peace-making principles. When a child is acting aggressive, perhaps a parent will, instead of a smart slap, give the child a short "time out" to reflect on his or her behavior. For a more

1. Mast, *Go to Church*.

serious offense, instead of a sound spanking, the parent may suspend playdates with friends for a few days. Active nonviolence can also be used in instances of violence in one's household, such as has been documented where intruders were confronted with kindness and offers of help, and the invasion was subsequently halted.[2]

In today's drumbeat of reports of mass shootings at schools, churches, shopping malls, and other public spaces, we often miss the large number of shootings that were averted by nonviolent intervention, such as by throwing a harmless object like a basketball at the shooter to distract him or by engaging him in conversation. In fact, an FBI report on mass shooting incidents between 2000 and 2013 shows that in the vast majority of instances where civilians successfully disrupted a mass shooting, the civilian was unarmed.[3] Another approach is to study a martial art that teaches how to physically restrain an intruder without causing great bodily harm or death.[4] Notice that these examples form a continuum from least to most assertive while always refraining from physical harm and lethal violence.

Nonviolence in Society

The United States appears to be in a state of perpetual war. Consider these responses to military or police violence. As a witness against war, some have written polite letters to the White House to suggest peaceful ways to deal with international conflict. Others have published sarcastic letters in their local newspaper or have written letters to elected representatives with heated denunciations of warlike activity by the government. Some people have participated in public protests and demonstrations when organizers acquired a permit for such activity or as long as a permit on public property was not required. Others have protested without permits and have risked arrest through such activities as lunch counter sit-ins and library read-ins and lie-ins in congressional offices or die-ins in public places to protest the shooting of unarmed black men by police officers. Others have blocked highway traffic or helped to occupy tribal sites to protect the lands of First Nations peoples from unwanted development.

---

2. For examples, see Willimon, "Bless You, Mrs. Degrafinried," and "Florida Women Disarm Intruder."
3. Federal Bureau of Investigation, "Study of Active Shooter Incidents."
4. Thomas, "Martial Arts."

News media have reported on many such activities. In such highly visible actions, some have left when threatened with arrest, while others have submitted to arrest as a further witness against the injustice under protest. Still others have engaged in specifically illegal activity by cutting fences to enter or otherwise trespassing on military property to attempt to prevent the movement of military equipment or have even pounded on warheads to act out turning swords into plowshares. Again, notice that these examples are ranged from least to most assertive or confrontational but do not employ violence.

We can envision another list of activities that call attention to injustice inflicted disproportionately on people of color such as lead-laced drinking water or poor-quality schools or police harassment. These activities might range from polite letters to hiring lawyers for legal suits to public marches to occupying mayoral or congressional offices to blocking traffic on major highways.

Such lists of activities both legal and illegal is by no means exhaustive. The limits on imagining such activities are confined only by the creativity of participants.[5] It is possible to argue that each of these suggestions—and many more that could be added—are active ways to make visible in our world the nonviolent reign of God.

The Continua[6]

An important dimension of these examples is that they are arranged as a continuum of nonviolent activism, listed from least to most assertive or confrontational. No activity results in harm,[7] lethal danger, or death to those confronted, although certainly there is a risk of harm to those who engage in such nonviolent confrontation. Eventually those who carry out the most assertive actions have submitted to fines and even imprisonment rather than to perpetrate physical harm or vengeance on people. These are continua of increasingly assertive nonviolent resistance, but resistance that does not injure or maim or kill people.

---

5. Sharp, *Methods of Nonviolent Action*; Sharp, *Waging Nonviolent Struggle*; Ackerman and DuVall, *Force More Powerful*.

6. The discussion of the continua draws on material in chapter 6 of Weaver and Mast, *Nonviolent Word*.

7. See below for discussion of loss of business revenue due to strike or boycott.

However, a common assumption often accompanies a list of such activities. The assumption is that the continuum contains additional steps. For example, as the next step beyond learning martial arts, an individual might buy a gun and take training in its use for self-defense. A person concerned for violence in society might become a police officer with the intent to use a weapon infrequently. At a still wider level of concern for society, a person might join the National Guard, which deals with border security or domestic actions such as assisting with hurricane recovery. Another step on the continuum might be joining the military in a noncombatant capacity; then joining the military and accepting a combat role. Finally, at the extreme, one might join the military and prepare to use nuclear weapons.

Notice that for such additions to the continuum, the underlying assumption changes. It has become a continuum that describes the employment of increasing levels of violence. When this set of options employing violence is assumed to be a natural continuation of the previous continuum of nonviolent actions, the character of the entire continuum changes. The very defining characteristic of the first half of the continuum shifts. It no longer contains examples of nonviolent resistance. Instead, all items listed are now assumed to exercise levels of violence, beginning with the discipline of a child. It has become a continuum that measures the use of violence, from minimal to great. When confronted with this continuum, the question for people who reject violence then becomes one of deciding how much violence they will tolerate, how much compromise with violence they will make in order to offer some challenge to injustice.[8] Some defenders of redemptive violence make this application specifically. They argue that since we are already using violence in child discipline or in protests, we should recognize the positive contributions of some forms of violence, including on occasion military violence.[9]

---

8. For this reason, the Amish and some conservative or traditional Mennonite churches that profess a commitment to complete nonresistance would not participate in public marches and protests and other movements for justice because they are considered exercises that employ violence—even as they might acknowledge the injustice involved. For an example of the assumption that civil rights marches and protests exercised a level of violence, but calling for compromising with this violence in order to do some good, see Burkholder, "Limits of Perfection."

9. For this argument in debate with my view, see Boersma, *Violence, Hospitality and the Cross*, 43–51; Boersma, "Violence, the Cross;" and Boersma, "Response to J. Denny Weaver."

In response, I suggest instead that there are in fact two kinds of continua, those that assume the rejection of lethal harm and violence in the pursuit of justice and peace, and others that accept the use of violence, including lethal violence, for the sake of justice and peace. The first reflects efforts to make the reign of God visible in the face of injustice, while the second reflects "Pilate's kingdom" or the empire; that is, that rebellious part of reality that does not yet recognize the reign of God. The point that can mislead is that these two kinds of continua have one point in common—they begin at the point of nonresistance. From that singular, shared point, however, they diverge in increasingly disparate directions.

Parallels to Jesus

The contemporary church acts in ways that resonate with Jesus' life, teachings, and healing. These activities include sharing communion, baptizing, inclusive decision-making, and reflecting his acceptance by eating with those the religious establishment labeled "sinners." A polite letter or pointed meme on a social media platform might correspond to one of Jesus' comments such as "Render to Caesar what is Caesar's and to God what is God's." A sarcastic or forceful letter/meme might resonate with Jesus calling the Pharisees "snakes" or "blind guides" or "beautiful white tombs filled with rotting flesh." Traveling through Samaria and interacting with a woman might be like a lunch counter sit-in during the Civil Rights Movement, while trespassing on a military base or illegally offering water and shelter to migrants crossing the border recalls healing on the Sabbath or the temple protest. In our time, beyond lunch counter sit-ins and library read-ns and bus boycotts, I can imagine Jesus approaching militarized police with bunches of flowers to stem police brutality or calmly helping to occupy an office or business or public service to stop its discriminatory activity. He might lead his followers to break immigration laws in order to offer shelter, food, and water to migrants fleeing across the border for their lives.

This chapter noted examples of witness to the grain of the universe that develop from the normal activity of the Christian church. It also described various examples of public, nonviolent protest, placed on a continuum of nonviolent resistance. Both witness and public protest find precedents in the story of Jesus. The point is that nonviolent action is not an aberration. Such action grows out of or is a continuation of the idea that Christians and the church pose a visible witness to the reign of God and visible in the grain of the universe with eyes of faith.

It is appropriate for contemporary Christians to continue to exercise such nonviolent actions in our modern social context. The calling of Christians is not to copy these biblical suggestions exactly, but rather to use them as a spur to think of actions that make sense in our contemporary setting. The possibilities are limited only by one's imagination.

As a counter to the abundant instances of violence that surround us, this book shows that God is not the purveyor of violence that is often assumed. The God revealed in Jesus is a loving God, a nonviolent God. This book offers readers a choice of the God they will serve and worship—the violent God, or the nonviolent God revealed in Jesus. It is my hope that the image of a nonviolent God will encourage people to act peacefully.

Examples

With this encouragement to confront injustice nonviolently, it is important to provide some specific examples of effective nonviolent actions. Returning good for evil or seeking to change a situation can happen at many levels. After the terrorist attacks of September 11, 2001, there was overwhelming support for a violent response from the United States. I wrote an article that posed a different kind of response, one that would have changed the situation. At that time, Afghanistan still had three million refugees from the recent war against the Russian occupation. I suggested that rather than invading Afghanistan to remove the Taliban, the United States would gain a lot more friends and do more to head off future terrorist attacks if it sent money to hire local people to build homes for refugees. The cost in both dollars and lives would have been exponentially less than what military action has cost since 2001.[10] A similar suggestion appeared in early 2009. As the administration in Washington prepared to send more troops to Afghanistan, George McGovern, ex-United States senator and presidential candidate, published an editorial in the *Washington Post*. He wrote that funding school lunches in Afghanistan would do more to fight terrorism than more soldiers.[11]

Given the money and lives spent in military actions in Afghanistan and Iraq since 2001, with no satisfactory outcome in sight as this

---

10. Weaver, "Responding to September 11."
11. McGovern, "Calling a Time Out."

is written, I still believe that actions such as building houses for refugees and funding school lunches would have been more productive responses than invasions to the attacks of September 11. Retaliation merely keeps a conflict going.

Public protest and demonstration were utilized regularly during the civil rights struggle in the United States in the 1960s, often led by African-American churches. One organized demonstration was a protracted boycott of public busses in Birmingham, Alabama. African Americans refused to ride the public buses until they were granted the right to sit wherever they pleased in the bus. Walking, even long distances, called attention to the injustice of segregated seating on buses. Another protest tactic was when African Americans sat in the whites-only seats at lunch counters, and asked for service. In essence, these "sit-ins" created the image of what racial justice looked like in that public setting. When the African Americans were refused service, and they were either ignored or the counter was abruptly closed, the establishment lost money. Since those sitting at the counter had money and were willing to pay, the refusal of service cost the diner money and further exposed the injustice of segregation. In essence the demonstrators were acting out how a lunch counter should be serviced. Many other successful examples of nonviolent activity are described in the book *A Force More Powerful*.[12]

Two other large-scale, modern examples worthy of particular mention are the Revolution of the Candles that began in Leipzig, Germany, and the Singing Revolution in Estonia. What began as weekly prayer meetings in the Nikolai church in Leipzig, grew into mass marches of hundreds of thousands of people that led eventually to the fall of the Berlin Wall in 1989.[13] That this movement began in church underscores the church's role in witnessing to nonviolent struggle. The Singing Revolution that began in Estonia in 1987 was a series of mass demonstrations at music festivals that featured spontaneous singing, accompanied by Estonian rock musicians, of national songs and hymns forbidden during the years of the Soviet occupation. Eventually 300,000 Estonians, a quarter of Estonia's population, gathered to sing in Tallinn. There were various acts of defiance, including masses of people who served as human shields to protect radio and TV stations from Soviet tanks. In 1991 these actions

---

12. Ackerman and DuVall, *Force More Powerful*.
13. Swoboda, *Revolution of the Candles*.

led to Estonia achieving independence from the Soviet Union without bloodshed.[14]

The Christian Century once carried a story about an elderly African American woman, Mrs. Degrafinried, who confronted an armed prison-escapee that had forced his way into her house. She just told him that she was a Christian lady who did not use violence, and that he should put his gun down. He did. She prayed with him and fixed him breakfast. When the police cars came, Mrs. Degrafinried and her husband yelled out to the police to put their guns away because the prisoner would come peacefully. He did. Later that afternoon, two other prison escapees entered a backyard where a couple was barbecuing. The husband went into the house to get his gun. The prisoners shot and killed him, and kidnapped his wife, who was later released.[15] Although not all stories end this way, here is a graphic example of the difference between meeting violence with violence and acting to change the situation. The assumption is that there are only two answers, but Mrs. Degrafinried demonstrated a third answer.

Nonviolent, creative actions may be less dramatic than those above. In the patriotic ethos after the attacks of September 11, 2001, peace-oriented people close to me encountered some challenges. A teacher taught at a school where the principal required every room to have a patriotic display. Rather than a flag with a military display, my friend put up a bulletin board of red, white, and blue hands working for peace around the world. In the office where my wife worked, all the other desks displayed an American flag for a patriotic display. Rather than lifting up the United States in a special way, my wife chose to display a United Nations flag to symbolize solidarity with all the peoples of the world. Such creative gestures also convey a commitment to the nonviolence of Jesus and a search for ways to change a hostile situation.

One does not have to be a Christian to accept the truth of nonviolence. Gandhi was a notable example. A less well-known example is Badshah Khan, a Muslim from the Pashtun area of Afghanistan. Khan was descended from Muslims with a long tradition of retaliating against

---

14. See "Singing Revolution."

15. Willimon, "Bless You, Mrs. Degrafinried." This story can serve as an answer to the well-known question, "What would you do if a gunman came after your wife/mother/daughter with a gun?" For a thorough analysis of all the possible answers to this question, including Mrs. Degrafinried's kind of response, see Yoder et al., *What Would You Do?*.

offenses. His people had engaged in generations of killings to avenge killings. But Khan came to the conclusion that vengeance only continued a cycle of violence. He swore to reject violence. Khan lived with Gandhi as an equal partner in the struggle to end colonial rule in India, and organized a nonviolent activist force of 100,000 Muslim men who marched with Gandhi.[16]

Nonviolent activity does not always lead to a victory. Stated differently, success may be defined as simply surviving. An example is the small Palestinian village of At-Tuwani, whose inhabitants have centuries-old titles to the land. It is located in the south Hebron hills of the West Bank that has been occupied by the Israelis since the Six-Day War in 1967. The several hundred Palestinian inhabitants are shepherds and farmers. The first Israeli settlement appeared in 1982, with others following. In spite of virtually continual harassment—violent attacks on shepherds and school children, destruction of olive trees, encroachment on their land, and more—the Palestinians have maintained a steady practice of nonviolent resistance as they attempt to maintain a routine life. Their resistance has gained international attention. Since 2004, Christian Peacemaker Teams, a nonviolent resistance group sponsored by Mennonites and Quakers, and Operation Dove, an Italian human rights group, have supplied a permanent international presence in support of the residents of At-Tuwani. In the face of the harassment, the residents maintain a program of active nonviolent resistance and school their young people in it. Children of the village often carry cameras to document incidents and provide information to the wider world. With this nonviolent resistance of nearly four decades, the residents of At-Tuwani embody the frequently seen and referenced Palestinian slogan, "To resist is to exist."[17]

Some Alternatives

There are things to learn from what might have been done to avoid war. A few examples illustrate. Europeans could have settled in North America without extermination of the native population, as illustrated by William Penn's efforts in Pennsylvania. Much is made of the necessity of a war to free the colonies from England. However, research reveals

---

16. For Badshah Khan's story, see Easwaran, *Nonviolent Soldier of Islam*, and Pal, *"Islam" Means Peace*, 97–123.

17. See "At-Tuwani" and "About CPT at-Tuwani."

that only a third of the colonists favored independence, a third actually supported England, with a third neutral; and there were suggestions on how to handle colonial representation in the English parliament. A war was not intrinsically necessary as the only way to secure representation. For World War II, much is made of the need to stop Hitler and to save the Jews. However, the seeds of that war were planted already in the aftermath of World War I, with the harsh conditions imposed on the defeated Germans. It was bitterness at this imposed suffering that became the seedbed in which Hitler's evil designs could fester and then prosper. With magnanimous gestures by the victors after World War I, World War II might not have happened. Such historical observations are possible for virtually any war. I suggest that these examples of what did not happen bring a different kind of witness to the grain of the universe.

Another example of steps not taken has its significance magnified by some mathematical exercises. The case concerns the settlement of the American West in the aftermath of slavery. At the end of the Civil War, there were an estimated four million freed slaves who were released onto the land at manumission with no resources for survival. For a brief moment, there was a suggestion that freed slaves receive forty acres and a mule. That proposal died quickly, deemed impractical and impossible.

But even apart from divvying up land from the plantations on which slaves had labored, there was land that could have been given to freed slaves. It is estimated that some 180 million acres were given to a few wealthy (white) men from 1850 to 1871 for the purpose of building railroads. These men enriched themselves greatly in the process.

If the four million slaves are arbitrarily grouped in families of four to receive the forty acres, that would be one million families and forty million acres. Land being given away was clearly available for freed slaves, if there had been a will to care for slaves. With some applied math, one could calculate the contribution to the national economy over several decades if these families had been allowed to start their free lives with enough resources to become self-supporting, contributing, tax-paying members of society. United States society would be immeasurably better today if the freed slaves had been allowed to have resources and accepted as contributing members. Finally, in anticipation of the discussion of restorative justice in the following chapter, speculate on what might constitute restorative measures for the native peoples from whom the 180 million acres of donated land were stolen, and for African Americans, who received nothing after 250 years of enslavement.

The Pacifist Dilemma

A common question concerning the exercise of violence is "What would you do if a crazed gunman came after your mother/wife/daughter?" The assumption behind the question, sometimes called the "pacifist's dilemma," is either that one can intervene successfully to kill the attacker and thus save mother/wife/daughter or one does nothing and attacker kills mother/wife/daughter. The question purports to be the conclusive proof that killing is necessary. In fact it is improbable that an individual will be able to recover a weapon and use it successfully against an attacker who already has the advantage. John Howard Yoder's book, *What Would You Do?*, analyzes many of the assumptions behind the question as well as showing that there are actually five other possible outcomes as well—victim or defender could accept martyrdom, the attempt to kill the attacker could fail, plus two nonviolent ways to resolve the situation. The story of Mrs. Degrafinried just noted illustrates one of those solutions. There are never only two options.

That analysis applies as well to a modern version of the question, namely "What would you do for a mass shooter in a school?" Again, there is an assumption that an armed civilian will be able to intervene successfully. In fact, the data does not bear out that assumption. A study of mass shootings between 1982 and 2012 reveals not a single case of a killing stopped by a civilian using a gun, while several attempts to intervene resulted in additional bloodshed. Rather than greater safety resulting from putting guns in the hands of more people, it is actually the case that there is a relationship between proliferation of guns and a rise in mass shootings.[18]

Conclusion

From the perspective of the Christian story, nonviolence is not an abstract principle that exists apart from Jesus and is then read into his story. Rather, we read the story and observe that rejection of violence is an intrinsic element of that story. Since God is revealed in Jesus, it is apparent that nonviolence characterizes God and the way things should function in the world that God created. Thus, rejection of violence characterizes

---

18. For this data and the assumptions behind claims that proliferation of guns promotes safety, see Follman, "More Guns."

the best way to live in God's universe. It has been said that working with the nonviolence of Jesus is to work with the grain of the universe. This chapter has displayed a number of ways in which that grain becomes visible—from the idea that finding ways to change a violent situation to halt a cycle of violence to instances where empirical data developed apart from theology validates the theological conclusions. People who are not Christians have the capacity to perceive the grain of the universe. Thus, Gandhi and Badshah Khan could perceive that violent retaliation only perpetuates violence and then adopt nonviolent methods. Meanwhile, for Christians, nonviolence nonetheless takes its ultimate validation and significance from the fact that God is revealed in the nonviolent story of Jesus.

The discussion of forgiveness and restorative justice in the next chapter is another example in which evidence developed apart from theology validates what we learn from the story of Jesus.

6

Atonement, Forgiveness, and Restorative Justice

IN OCTOBER 2006, THE United States and much of the world was shocked when a shooter opened fire in the Old Order Amish school of West Nickel Mines in Lancaster, Pennsylvania, and killed five children and wounded five others. Then the nation looked on in amazement as the Amish announced that they had forgiven the shooter and reached out with material assistance to his wife.[1] This story constitutes a graphic example of the kind of forgiveness that I believe receives theological justification from the nonviolent atonement image portrayed in chapter 2.

Understanding forgiveness has important implications for the way we think about God as well as for our relationships with others. Thus it concerns both God's forgiveness of human sin and human forgiveness of sins—whether our forgiving others or our forgiving ourselves. Forgiveness then becomes one element of restorative justice.

Forgiveness in Psychology

Quite apart from theological considerations, psychologists talk about forgiveness. In fact, according to recent research in psychology, practicing forgiveness is a healthy activity. The common expression is "forgive and forget," but that is not what forgiveness means in psychology.[2]

---

1. The story of the shooting at the West Nickel Mines school, along with a general introduction to the Old Order Amish, appears in Kraybill et al., *Amish Grace*.

2. The description of the practice of forgiveness in this chapter follows Enright, *Forgiveness Is a Choice*.

As understood in psychology, forgiveness means to let go of the anger that a person feels toward the individual or group or institution that has committed the wrong. A person who carries that anger is allowing the wrong to control the emotions. For example, someone may say, "Because this individual wronged me, I will never be able to _____." The claim is that because of a wrong received, a person can never again be happy or visit a certain place or engage in a specific activity or any number of other things. Advice columns in daily newspapers, for example, frequently feature letters from people who have refused to speak to a parent or sibling or one-time friend because of some offense, real or imagined. This angry person is carrying a psychological burden that impacts that way he or she lives. And in this case, the psychologist says, the person wronged is giving the perpetrator control over emotions or actions. Forgiveness means to let go of the anger so that it no longer controls emotions or actions. This process of letting go allows the individual to be free of the burden of anger being carried. The result is improved psychological health of the one who forgives.

A typical program of forgiveness in psychology begins by acknowledging that the person has indeed been wronged. And it involves recognizing the burden that comes with carrying the anger, along with a desire to be free of this burden. The process of forgiveness then requires offering a small, unmerited gift to the perpetrator. This gift may be as small as saying, "I forgive," but it is the beginning of the process of letting go of the anger toward the perpetrator. If the perpetrator acknowledges his or her harm committed, reconciliation may sometimes occur between victim and perpetrator. If the perpetrator does not acknowledge the wrong committed and reconciliation does not occur, the one offering forgiveness is nonetheless keeping that possibility open. But even if there is no reconciliation, the goal of forgiveness is for the person harmed to become free of the burden of anger that binds and controls.

This kind of forgiveness certainly does not mean "forgetting." In fact, the statement "I forgive" is a clear recognition that a wrong was committed. It means that in spite of that wrong, the individual will work at letting go of anger toward the perpetrator. Offering forgiveness does not mean that a perpetrator is absolved of accountability for the wrong committed. On the contrary, true forgiveness means recognizing who is responsible. With forgiveness, restoration is required whenever possible; but forgiveness can occur even if the perpetrator refuses to accept responsibility. For reprehensible deeds, the person who receives forgiveness may need to be confined. The point is that forgiveness is not about how serious the wrong was or whether the perpetrator confesses and offers restitution. Forgiveness concerns the one who practices forgiveness. And it is practiced for the health of this individual whether or not the perpetrator expresses remorse and offers restitution.

To be emphasized is that this practice of forgiveness is not easy. It can be very difficult. For serious offenses, the one wronged may need to repeat the process many times, each time with a bit more success. In essence, this kind of forgiveness is a way of life, a way to live without retaliating and without holding grudges about what has happened. Psychologists describe this ability to practice forgiveness, that is, to live without built-up anger, as one of the keys to happiness.

Forgiveness and Love of Enemies

In chapter 4 we observed that Jesus said, "Love your enemies." This love is not the romantic love of affection. Rather, we saw that it meant not to retaliate in kind, not to respond to evil or violence with the same kind of evil or violence. It means to respond to evil or confrontation by changing the situation. In the Sermon on the Mount, Jesus gave three examples—turn the other cheek, give underwear with outerwear, and go the second mile. Such responses diffuse a situation and have the potential to change a tense relationship. Sayings from Paul and Peter express the same idea, namely rather than responding to evil with evil, one should respond to evil with good.

I suggest that the practice of forgiveness as described here constitutes another way to express love of enemies by acting to change the situation. Offering the unmerited gift to the offender is an act of returning good for evil. The act of letting go of anger—that is, of forgiving—certainly benefits the one who forgives, but by offering the unmerited gift to the offender, the possibility is open of a restored relationship. I suggest that the practice of forgiveness is another dimension of Jesus' statement "Love your enemies" and of Paul and Peter's injunctions to "return good for evil."

And forgiveness has yet another link to the previous chapter. We saw that working with the nonviolent Jesus was to be in line with the "grain of the universe." Retaliating against violence and evil with more of the same continues a cycle of violence, while loving enemies and returning good for evil—that is, working with the grain of the universe, changes the situation and reduces violence. In this chapter we have talked about the practice of forgiveness as another example of expressing love of enemy and changing the situation. And with forgiveness, there is research evidence from psychology to show that practicing forgiveness really does improve the health of the one who practices it. Parallel to the way that Gandhi and Badshah Khan could sense the grain of the universe apart from Christian faith, in the current discussion, research in psychology done without reference to Christian ethics has demonstrated the truthfulness of the practice of forgiveness.

What psychologists have discovered through their research corresponds to what Christians can find in the teaching of Jesus. Forgiveness is another example of the grain of the universe, another example that the nonviolence of the Christian story is not an abstract principle that exists apart from Jesus and is then read back into the story. Rather, we read the story and come to the understanding that rejection of violence is intrinsic to that story. Since God is revealed in Jesus, it is apparent that nonviolence characterizes God and the reign of God and God's means of acting in the world. When we know that Jesus' rejection of violence reflects the God who created the universe, we can then observe that the truth of the rejection of violence is visible in the world. Thus, rejecting violence, loving enemies, returning good for evil, practicing forgiveness, are the best ways to live in God's universe. Research in psychology can demonstrate the benefit of practicing forgiveness, but the ultimate validation of forgiveness comes from the narrative of Jesus in whom God is revealed.

Forgiveness in Atonement Images

In the inherited understandings of atonement, in particular for the satisfaction and penal substitution motifs, God can forgive sinners only because Jesus has first paid the price for sins. For the satisfaction motif, it will be recalled, sinners have offended God's honor and distorted the order of the universe. God cannot forgive until satisfaction is made for that sin. But since Jesus made satisfaction on our behalf, God can indeed forgive those who repent and turn to God. Similarly, for penal substitution, God cannot forgive until the penalty demanded by God's law has been paid. Since Jesus was punished in our place, the penalty demanded by the law was satisfied, and God can then forgive sinners who avail themselves of Jesus' sacrifice. God cannot forgive those who do not accept Jesus' sacrifice on their behalf. Stated differently, God holds onto God's anger and withholds forgiveness until compensation has been paid to God and sinners have appropriated it for themselves.

Now apply the learning from the discussion of forgiveness in psychology to this description of forgiveness in the inherited atonement images. In satisfaction and substitutionary atonement images, God uses or sanctions violence, and God holds on to anger until God's justice has been satisfied. God arranged for Jesus to die in order to fulfill a divine need, whether understood as satisfaction of divine honor or to pay the penalty demanded by God's law. In other words, for these atonement images, God's forgiveness depends on God's prior sanctioning of violence against Jesus. These atonement images link forgiveness to divine violence. Stated another way, while human forgiveness as depicted in psychology works on letting go of anger, God holds on to anger, exacting punishment or satisfaction on Jesus before forgiveness can occur. In these images of forgiveness, God acts differently from humans. Humans offer the unmerited gift of forgiveness to the perpetrator, while God demands punishment as the basis of forgiveness.

Compare the violence-based divine forgiveness of the satisfaction motifs with God's forgiveness as depicted in nonviolent atonement. All human beings are involved in the forces of evil in the world. These are powers with which the Romans and religious leaders cooperated in killing Jesus. It is thus possible to say that all human beings have been involved with the powers that killed Jesus. But when these powers killed Jesus, God responded by raising Jesus from the dead. Resurrection then poses an invitation to join in and live in the story of Jesus and participate in the reign of God, including a future resurrection. In the language used for psychology, God has let go of anger against those who cooperated with the evil powers that killed Jesus and has offered the gift of fellowship with God. This offer is an unmerited free gift, given to sinful humanity by a gracious God. God lets go of anger against sinful humans and forgives. This is divine forgiveness without exacting punishment.

This divine forgiveness in nonviolent atonement reflects the same impulse that human forgiveness does as described by psychologists. God offers unmerited forgiveness to sinners, which can be understood as parallel to the impulse of forgiveness offered by human beings as described in psychology. These complementary conclusions constitute another instance of the grain of the universe becoming visible when viewed through eyes of faith. The result is another dimension of a nonviolent God, namely that divine forgiveness also features a God who acts without violence.

Forgiveness and Restorative Justice

Offering forgiveness does not in and of itself amount to justice or achieve justice. However, there is an approach to justice in which forgiveness has a role. This system is restorative justice, which poses a contrast to retributive justice, the usual practice of the justice system in the United States as well as most countries of the world.

Retributive justice focuses on determining the innocence or guilt of the offender. A guilty verdict then requires determining the appropriate punishment, that is retribution for the offense or crimes committed. The assumption is that crimes are committed against the state (the structures that represents "the people") and justice is done when proper punishment has been meted out. Victims are essentially bystanders of the process, except perhaps when called upon to describe their sense of injury that will impact the form or amount of punishment.

In contrast, restorative justice involves the victim in the process in a central way. As the title indicates, the goal of this approach to justice is to restore relationships to the extent circumstances permit. Through sanctions, counseling, or other means, the offender is eventually brought to recognize the harm committed and to accept responsibility for it. With that recognition, the offender then takes action to repair or restore the harm done, with the victim as the object of these reparations.

Restoration can happen without forgiveness on the part of the victim. These acts of reparation can vary greatly, depending on the original offense, and in the case of some serious offenses, offenders must still be confined for their good or for the safety of the community. From the side of the victim, if or when the victim expresses forgiveness, beyond restoration there can be reconciliation of victim and offender. Achieving this reconciliation, if at all, may be a long and difficult process to achieve. Restorative justice is not a way for offenders to "get off easy." It may be difficult to achieve, and reconciliation may be a long and difficult process for the victim.

School systems have begun to use restorative practices as a better way to keep young people in school. Communities have begun instituting restorative practices, particularly for young people, as a way to keep them out of the criminal justice system. Significant research shows that offenders who submit to a restorative justice program have less likelihood of repeat offenses than do those who go through the standard penal or retributive justice system. In this case, I suggest that restorative justice, and then reconciliation which includes the practice of forgiveness, reflect the grain of the universe.

Conclusion

The Parable of the Prodigal Son (Luke 15:11–32) brings together this discussion of atonement images, forgiveness, and restorative justice. It is a story that portrays forgiveness as letting go of justifiable anger, along with a move toward restoration and then reconciliation. In the parable, the younger son asked for his inheritance, which was already an insult to the father and to family honor. The son then took his money, left home, and went to a far country where he wasted his money in wild living. Famine came and, having no money, the son hired himself out to feed pigs. In this desolate state, he reflected on the security of home. He resolved to return home and to offer to work for his father as a hired hand. As he approached, his father saw him while he was still some distance away. The father ran and threw his arms around the returning prodigal, welcomed him back to the family, and proclaimed a great feast in celebration. Meanwhile, the older brother was angry. His prodigal brother was getting a free pass along with a celebration, while he had never had a celebration.

The figures of father and prodigal reflect the impulses of nonviolent atonement. The father is an image of God, who has been sinned against by humankind; the prodigal who offended the father and the family is like sinful humans who sinned against God by participating in the death of Jesus. But as God restored Jesus to life and offers grace to sinners without exacting a penalty or compensation, the father welcomes the son without penalty and proclaims a great celebration of his return to the family. But from the reaction of the older brother, it appears that he believes the returning prodigal should have to do some kind of penance, such as work as a servant until wasted money has been repaid. The older brother's reaction aligns itself with the satisfaction images of atonement. This discussion of forgiveness adds to the understanding that the God revealed in and made present by Jesus is a nonviolent God.

And once again the image of a nonviolent God appears, this time in the parable of the prodigal son.

There is yet one more point to make about forgiveness and the God who forgives without punishment. God offers forgiveness without exacting a penalty, but that forgiveness is not free. The parable illustrates this point as well. The father's arms were always open with the offer of forgiveness, just as God's offer of forgiveness is always open. However, the prodigal had to act in order to receive that forgiveness. The prodigal had to recognize his offensive state, and be willing to make a change. That change was his decision to return home and confess his wrongdoing to his father. His offer to work as a hired hand can be interpreted as an offer of restoration, even if the father refused the offer. Forgiveness frees the offended person from anger (in this case the father), but the perpetrator does not receive that forgiveness without making a change. My last word on forgiveness is to emphasize that forgiveness as letting go of anger is not a free pass to the perpetrator. For reconciliation to occur, the response to forgiveness is confession and restitution by the perpetrator, and that may be a long and difficult process. With just a bit of imagination, this welcoming of the prodigal and his acknowledgement of wrongdoing and willingness to work as a servant serves as an image of restorative justice and reconciliation.

7

Jesus and Economics

What Does the Bible Say?

WE HAVE OBSERVED HOW the story of Jesus and his teaching presents a nonviolent way to live in the world. We also observed how examination of that life evolved into a discussion of atonement theology, and then a discussion of nonviolent living, and understanding of forgiveness. However, incidents from the life and teaching of Jesus concern more than direct violence, atonement theology, and forgiveness. In this chapter, we will consider what Jesus did and said concerning economic issues.

Jesus' Teaching

Jesus had several things to say about money. When he launched his public ministry in the synagogue in Nazareth, for example, his reading from Isaiah included bringing "good news to the poor." Quoting from Isaiah shows Jesus' familiarity with the writings that Christians identify as the Old Testament. Writings by the prophets contain many condemnations of greed and exploitation. Amos condemned those who became rich by exploiting the poor. "They sell the righteous for silver, and the needy for a pair of sandals" (2:6), take grain from the poor through levies, bribe judges (5:11–12), and generally build a rich lifestyle on the backs of poor people (6:1–7). Jeremiah condemned those who build an exorbitant lifestyle through exploitation of the poor and vulnerable.

> For scoundrels are found among my people;
> they take over the good of others. . . .
> Like a cage full of birds,
> their houses are full of treachery;
> therefore they have become great and rich,
> they have grown fat and sleek. (5:26, 27–28)

Jesus' proclamation of "good news for the poor" certainly fits with such prophetic words. It also reflects his saying from the Sermon on the Mount about giving the undergarment along with the outer coat. That act would expose an exploitative debt holder, one who would "trample on the needy, and bring to ruin the poor of the land" (Amos 8:4), that is, build a rich lifestyle on the basis of exploitative labor practices.

It also needs to be stressed that Jesus (and the prophets) do not condemn wealth or the acquisition of wealth in and of themselves. What is condemned is acquiring riches by exploitative or dishonest means, and hoarding wealth for its own sake. Instead, Jesus taught that those who have wealth should be generous with it, which appears in his statement of how to host a meal.

> When you give a luncheon or a dinner, do not invite your friends or your brothers or your relatives or rich neighbors, in case they may invite you in return, and you would be repaid. But when you give a banquet, invite the poor, the crippled, the lame, and the blind. And you will be blessed, because they cannot repay you, for you will be repaid at the resurrection of the righteous. (Luke 14:12–14)

A dimension of generosity with wealth depends on recognizing where ultimate worth resides. Jesus challenged his followers to avoid simply accumulating earthly wealth as an end in itself. "Do not store up for yourselves treasures on earth, where moth and rust consume and where thieves break in and steal; but store up for yourselves treasures in heaven, where neither moth nor rust consumes and where thieves do not break in and steal. For where your treasure is, there your heart will be also" (Matt 6:19–21). In other words, one should not be identified by or bound by earthly possessions.

> Consider the ravens: they neither sow nor reap, they have neither storehouse nor barn, and yet God feeds them. Of how much more value are you than the birds! . . . Consider the lilies, how they grow: they neither toil nor spin; yet I tell you, even Solomon in all his glory was not clothed like one of these. But if

> God so clothes the grass of the field, which is alive today and tomorrow is thrown into the oven, how much more will he clothe you—you of little faith! And do not keep striving for what you are to eat and what you are to drink, and do not keep worrying. For it is the nations of the world that strive after all these things, and your Father knows that you need them. Instead, strive for his kingdom, and these things will be given to you as well. (Luke 12:24, 27–31)

Living generously, living without worrying about food, clothing, and possessions sounds irresponsible in the context of our twenty-first-century world. The words about living without worry should probably be understood in the context of the common purse of Jesus and his disciples. John 12:6 mentions the common purse. When Jesus was visiting in the home of Mary and Martha, Mary anointed his feet with expensive perfume. Judas protested loudly that the perfume should have been sold and the money used to care for poor people. However, Judas' words were insincere. "He kept the common purse, and used to steal what was put into it" (John 12:6).

Having a common purse meant that Jesus and the disciples pooled their money and shared expenses equally. Sharing equally would mean living without each disciple having a personal account but it also meant that no individual was ever left stranded. That idea may have been in Jesus' mind when he spoke with the rich young man who asked what he needed to do to have eternal life. In addition to obeying all the commandments, Jesus told the young man, "Sell your possessions, and give the money to the poor, and you will have treasure in heaven; then come, follow me" (Matt 19:21). Given the idea of a common purse, this was not a suggestion that the young man become destitute. It was rather an invitation to join the followers of Jesus who supported each other and lived loosely connected to earthly wealth and possession.

Jesus' suggestion for living generously with wealth challenges the common assumption that to live happily or successfully means to accumulate wealth, and that one of the goals of life is to accumulate wealth and become as rich as possible. As one seemingly harmless reference to this assumption, notice the language frequently used by a TV news anchor who comments on a prize won in a local drawing. The announcement is something like, "A local woman is one hundred dollars richer today." The key word here is "richer." The assumption behind the news anchor's statement is that everyone is striving to get richer, to accumulate wealth.

Here is the assumption of accumulation, the perpetual desire for more, the idea that more is always better. But following Jesus' suggestion about living generously and being willing to share, the operative word can or should switch from "more" to "enough." The words of Jesus challenge us to realize when we have enough money to live in our context. Any additional wealth can then be shared with those in need. The challenge for people living in the story of Jesus is to revise attitudes from accumulation of more wealth to be satisfied with enough wealth.

The Example of Zacchaeus

The account of Jesus' interaction with Zacchaeus illustrates the condemnation of ill-gotten wealth and poses an example of restoration (Luke 19:1–10). As Jesus passed through Jericho, Zacchaeus wanted to see him. Since he was short, Zacchaeus climbed a tree to see Jesus from a perch above the crowd. The text identifies Zacchaeus as "a chief tax collector, and rich." This job description meant that he worked for the hated Roman occupiers. It also permitted graft, allowing Zacchaeus to skim money from tax payments into his own accounts. Even though he was an Israelite, the local population would have despised him.

Zacchaeus's attitude toward wealth changed through his encounter with Jesus. As a result of it, he announced that he would give half his wealth to the poor. And since he promised to restore money gained through fraud, most certainly he had engaged in dishonest transactions. Although we cannot know precisely what transpired when they met, the confrontation with Jesus resulted in a complete remaking of Zacchaeus's life. In terms of repaying money with interest, he was practicing what today would be called "restorative justice." As the name implies, restorative justice seeks to restore harm caused by wrong doing. Restorative justice stands in contrast to retributive or punitive justice, the orientation of the justice system in the United States and many other countries. In this orientation, "doing justice" means to punish the wrongdoer. In contrast to seeking restoration of harm done, retributive justice is satisfied when a wrongdoer is punished. In retributive justice, justice would have been done when Zacchaeus was punished. But by restoring ill-gotten money with interest, Zacchaeus was practicing restorative justice. When he saw Zacchaeus's restoration of money gained dishonestly, Jesus declared,

"Today salvation has come to this house, since he [Zacchaeus] is also a son of Abraham."

Large-Scale Applications

This discussion of economics and comments on wealth by Jesus and by Amos and Jeremiah reveal that care for the lowly, the poor, those without economic clout is important in the reign of God. The God revealed in Jesus cares for the needy, for those who struggle to care for themselves.

Structural Violence

Discussion of these concerns about wealth and exploitation and poverty bring us to the structural violence of economic policy in the world today. The gap between the most wealthy people—the often-referenced 1 percent—and lower-income people continues to grow as tax policies and the economic structure favors the wealthy. The wealthy, often with money made from large corporations, contribute huge sums to lobbyists and to political candidates in order to procure ever-more-favorable laws concerning businesses and taxes. These practices and the laws that result exert structural violence on lower-income people. Opposition to raising the minimum wage, with claims that business would lose money by paying higher wages, falls into the same category. In addition, government acts that cut healthcare spending for lower-income people increase structural violence against poor people.

Even when the economy flourishes, as marked by the major stock-market indicators, lower-income people still struggle. Money in the hands of the wealthy and in large corporations is not creating jobs, and wealth is not trickling down to low-income people. An intricate web of structures is exerting the systemic violence of poverty on many people in the United States. As I write, recent statistics easily available with a Google search show that the 1 percent control nearly 35 percent of the wealth of the United States while the lowest 90 percent control a total of 27 percent of the country's wealth. This disparity is the greatest since the Great Depression of the 1930s, and the gap is increasing. It seems clear that tax and economic structures are favoring the few at the expense of the many. This is structural violence.

The violence of economic structures and policy exists at multiple levels. A particular example concerns tax money allocated by local governments to build stadiums for professional teams. A recent case comes from the city of Detroit, which faces serious financial challenges. In 2014, severe measures were taken to avoid bankruptcy, including the reduction of pension payments previously promised to city workers. Meanwhile, the city will pay $283 million toward a new stadium for the city's privately-owned hockey team, the Detroit Redwings. The claim made for this stadium, and for similar stories in other cities, is that money spent on stadiums will stimulate economic development and benefit all residents of the city. But numerous studies show that such expenditures *almost never* produce the promised development. Also ignored in this support for stadiums at the expense of pension payments (and healthcare expenditures and support for education, and more) is that money placed in the hands of pensioners or teachers and other public employees would also stimulate development and most of the money would be spent locally.

Systemic violence exists in the international arena as well. The free-trade agreements vigorously advocated by the United States benefit multinational corporations. The claim is that free-trade agreements benefit everyone by allowing goods to move freely between countries. Nonetheless, in practice such agreements harm people at the lower end of the economic ladder. For example, the North American Free Trade Agreement (NAFTA) between the United States and Mexico allowed corn from the United States to be sold in Mexico. This agreement benefited large growers in the United States. However, small farmers in Mexico could not compete with the large and highly mechanized American growers. When cheaper corn from the north flooded into Mexico, many Mexican farmers went out of business. They are now crowded into already-crowded Mexico City, hoping to find scarce work as day laborers.[1]

Whether intended or not, tax structures, economic policies, and trade agreements are working together to keep poor people poor, making it difficult for them to escape poverty. Lessons from Jesus' story offer challenges to these practices and policies, both nationally and internationally. Jesus' comments on money do not suggest a specific economic system. However, his words do supply criteria that enable us to evaluate the justness and fairness of any economic system. A system that reflects principles of the reign of God cares for all people, and desires for all

---

1. For an analysis of the impact of NAFTA on corn producers in Mexico see Harder, "Violence of Global Marketization."

people to have enough resources to live. Those who have great wealth are called upon to be generous with their wealth, and to live in ways that benefit society as a whole.

It would appear that current tax and economic policies and international trade agreements fall short when compared with Jesus' concern. Recall what he said about the vanity of riches, and his concern for poor people, his words about caring for refugees (strangers), healing the sick, clothing the naked, and feeding the hungry. There is a disjuncture when one confesses an ultimate commitment to Jesus but uses every possible means to amass extravagant wealth while opposing government programs and tax policies that benefit the poor and unemployed. In this instance, there is a higher commitment to the "god" wealth than to the Jesus who said that those would inherit the kingdom of God who feed the hungry, give thirsty people a drink, welcome strangers, clothe the naked, take care of sick people, and visit prisoners (Matt 25:35–36).

Exploitative Bananas

I once had an opportunity to observe for myself another version of such economic exploitation. I was part of a delegation from my church that went to Honduras in order to establish a sister church relationship with a congregation in that country. One of our activities was to visit a banana plantation. We saw bananas being harvested. Laborers in the field hung the newly picked hands of bananas on moving wires that carried them to vats where other workers dunked them in disinfectant to kill any insects still hitchhiking on the bananas. From the vat they were put in boxes and loaded on a truck that took the bananas to a port where they were loaded on a ship for transportation to the United States. The bananas never touched the ground in Honduras. Upon arrival in the United States, they would be distributed for sale in local grocery stores. I recognized the brand, and I have purchased them myself.

Of interest in this story is that the plantation owner had recently managed to suppress a movement to unionize the plantation workers, who sought better wages and working conditions. The only benefit to Honduras of these bananas that never touched the ground were the low wages paid to plantation employees. Meanwhile, a North American owner enriched himself greatly. He owned a major league baseball team, and just before our trip the team had signed a star player to a contract for more than one hundred million dollars. Bananas grown in Honduras did almost nothing to provide nourishment for Hondurans. These bananas enriched directly a very few people in the United States, while enabling many people in the United States to benefit by eating a healthy diet that included bananas. When we eat bananas—and I eat a banana almost every day—we are participating in this unjust system. The same kind of story could be told for pineapples and coffee and many other foods as well as for most of the clothes we buy. Consuming even modest amounts of goods in the United States involves all of us in a system that exploits large numbers of the world's population.

Such a story, accompanied by the earlier discussion of tax and economic policies, may tempt us figuratively to throw up our hands in despair. Since we have to have food to eat and clothes to wear, it may seem that we can do nothing about the exploitative system in which we are enmeshed. But I can suggest several overlapping actions that any individual can do. Look for ways to make public protests that raise awareness of these exploitative practices. Such public statements call attention to injustice, while also giving us a chance to say that although we participate in this unjust system, our participation is involuntary and against our will. Visiting the banana plantation with my church group and then talking about the experience at home and now writing about it in this book constitute one such example of a public protest. But one need not go abroad to find opportunities for protest. For example, at the big public market in my city, often groups are present who call attention to this exploitation. One can sign their petitions or join a group and become involved with their activities. Wherever possible, we should buy local. Spending money at home stimulates the local economy, and buying local avoids the immense time, energy, and money spent transporting food and goods produced elsewhere. We can attempt to influence public policy. Contact government officials and legislators to ask for changes in government policies that abet the exploitative practices. As I write, there is a national movement, involving public protests, to exert pressure on governments to raise the minimum wage. I participated in one of their protests, which stopped traffic briefly in my city to call attention to the low minimum wage. Engage in protests and actions against corporations that engage in these practices. If enough people raised their voices, practices could change. For example, protests by students have convinced several major universities to stop buying university logo apparel from a major manufacturer with unfair labor practices in a foreign sweatshop.

All these actions and more, limited only by one's imagination, constitute active nonviolence that confronts structural violence.

This chapter began with a discussion of Jesus' comments on wealth and economics. The second half of the chapter extended the analysis to the level of economic policies and structures both national and international. At that level, it becomes evident that structures and policies can cause harm to people, particularly poor people. Structures allow wealth to accumulate at the top of the economic ladder at the expense of those lower down. Such harm falls in the category of structural violence, and the discussion of economics, particularly the function of structures and wider policies, becomes a violence issue.

God and the reign of God are made visible in the life of Jesus. Thus, the words and actions of Jesus expose the systemic violence of modern economic structures and point the way for those who live in the reign of God to pose alternatives. Understanding of economic issues is a dimension of understanding that the God revealed in Jesus is a nonviolent God.

8

Racism, Ethnicity, and Gender

ALONGSIDE THE STRUCTURAL VIOLENCE of poverty are structures that cause harm to ethnic minorities and to women. Because some stories of Jesus have implications for both of these kinds of violence, they are treated together in this chapter.

Racism and Gender

Samaritans

The Gospel of John 4:1–39 tells of a time Jesus travelled from Judea in the south to Galilee in the north of Palestine. This journey meant that he passed through Samaria. Actually being in Samaria was itself a remarkable event. According to the strict purity code, the Samaritans were of mixed ethnic heritage, which made them "unclean." Those who followed the strict law would not defile themselves by traveling in Samaria or interacting with Samaritans. Thus, Jesus' presence in Samaria was already a breach of the code. Then to compound this breach, when he stopped at the village of Sychar he asked a village woman for a drink of water. According to the purity code, a menstruating woman was considered unclean. Since one could not tell whether a woman was menstruating, men who observed the purity code would not touch a woman or a vessel that she had touched. When the disciples saw Jesus' interaction with this woman, they were greatly surprised. Not only was Jesus interacting with a Samaritan, it was a woman, and he accepted a drink from her jar. While there are many levels of meaning that can be developed from this story, the point I want to draw out here is that Jesus took specific steps to cross and challenge hurtful boundaries of race or ethnicity and gender.

Jesus' Parable of the Good Samaritan (Luke 10:29–37) also contains a challenge to racism. The term "good Samaritan" has passed into our everyday language as merely a way to designate a good or helpful person. But in this parable, the Samaritan was of the despised race. It was the supposed upstanding folks of society, the Levite and the priest, who were likely fearful of violating the purity code, and who passed by the wounded traveller. The lawyer who questioned Jesus must have received something of a shock, when he had to declare the Samaritan, the member of the supposed inferior and despised race, as the good neighbor. A parallel today might have a United States congressperson and a prominent preacher in the roles of Levite and priest, with a homeless woman or an immigrant without legal papers playing the Samaritan.

A Gentile Woman

In the context of boundary crossing, a story of particular interest concerns Jesus' interaction with a gentile woman (Matt 15:21–28; Mark 7:24–30). She is frequently identified by Mark's designation of her as a gentile, a Syrophoenician woman. As a gentile she would have been one of the wealthy minority of foreigners living in territory occupied by the Romans. Jesus had gone north of Galilee into the area of Tyre and Sidon in Phoenecia, where he hoped to stay incognito. However, the woman learned where he was staying. She came and pleaded for him to help her daughter, who was possessed by a demon. Jesus' initial response was to declare, "I was sent only to the lost sheep of the house of Israel." In other words, Jesus' understanding of his mission did not include gentiles such as this Syrophoenician woman, and he was dismissing her plea. But she got down on her knees and begged. Jesus replied sharply: "It is not fair to take the children's bread and throw it to the dogs." Since dogs were generally scavengers and considered unclean, Jesus was here rejecting the woman's entreaty with what was arguably an insult. The woman was not deterred. She countered, "Yes, Lord, yet even the dogs eat the crumbs that fall from the masters' table." Her retort clearly made an impression on Jesus. He changed his mind, and on the basis of her great faith, he promised that her daughter would be healed. This story is the only account in the Gospels where an interlocutor got the better of Jesus—and it was a woman and a gentile. After the woman dared to cross the boundary separating her from a Jesus, Jesus also confronted and crossed the boundary between gentiles and Jews, as well as the boundary between women and men.

In the stories that deal with Samaritans—the parable of the Good Samaritan and Jesus' interaction with the Samaritan women—Jesus was raising the status of a despised ethnic group. For the Samaritan woman, he was not only raising the status of a Samaritan, but also raising the status of a woman above her location in the social hierarchy. The intervention by the gentile woman, which at first gave Jesus pause, exposes another dimension of raising the status of women. She was a gentile and thus outside the narrow scope of his mission, and yet Jesus listened and heeded her plea.

These interactions by Jesus across ethnic or racial and gender boundaries put on display that these distinctions do not divide people in the reign of God. All are welcome and included. The God revealed in Jesus loves and welcomes all on an equal footing.

Contemporary Applications

Discrimination against Women

These stories from Jesus' life of crossing barriers between Jews and Samaritans and between men and women have clear application in contemporary United States society. Systems or structures persist, often informal and unspoken, that cause harm to women. Women still face barriers to full participation in society. Informal structures may keep women out of some jobs or limit their advancement in others. Statistical studies show that women do not yet receive equal pay for equal work. Discrimination can occur as men, who do not intend to discriminate, continue to hire people like themselves (that is, men) because they fit better into the established culture. Such structures are harmful to women and constitute examples of systemic violence. Harm can occur at many levels, as when little girls pick up the idea in school that girls are not as good as boys at math and science. There is no question that spousal battering constitutes violence against women. But recent cases of spousal battering and sexual assault that made national news appeared to show that judicial and disciplinary processes tend to protect popular, high-profile men rather than the women that they abused. Thus, in any number of ways, there are still systems and structures, some legal and some informal, that cause harm to women. Following the way of Jesus means challenge these barriers.

Racism

Harmful divides continue across racial boundaries. In no way was the problem of racism solved by the outlawing of slavery and the victory of the North in the Civil War. Neither was equality achieved by the welcome gains made by the Civil Rights movement. We find an achievement gap in schools between white students and African American students, unemployment is higher among African Americans, more African Americans than whites live in poverty, and the number of African Americans in the professions is not yet great. The systemic violence of racism is a present reality.

Recent publications describe the institutionalized racism in the criminal justice system. Michelle Alexander's *The New Jim Crow* described the way the so-called "war on drugs" has been aimed primarily against people of color, although statistics show that the percent of people using of illegal drugs is the same in white as in black communities.[1] The result of the war on drugs is mass incarceration of African Americans. With a felony on their records, these people have difficulty finding jobs and housing for the rest of their lives, which results in the creation of a permanent underclass. *Pulled Over* by Charles R. Epp, Steven Maynard-Moody, and Donald Haider-Markel describes the "investigatory stops" that cause African Americans to distrust the police.[2] Investigatory stops are those that use a minor violation, such as failure to signal a lane change, to stop a driver when the real purpose of the stop is to search the car for drugs and weapons. In a pattern well-documented by the authors across the country, these stops are aimed primarily at people of color, although the vast majority are innocent. The result has created great suspicion of police among African Americans, while white people who are not subject to such stops continue to trust the police.

Womanist theologians—that is, African American women theologians—have written that black women have experienced discrimination both as women and as people of color. The particular discrimination they experienced as women occurred in the African American church, which

---

1. Alexander, *New Jim Crow*.
2. Epp et al., *Pulled Over*.

has been predominantly patriarchal and run by men. During the Civil Rights movement, women did much of the behind-the-scenes work, while men were out in front and received much of the credit. African American women have experienced the discrimination faced by all women, but also experienced discrimination because of their race and lower socioeconomic status. These three—race, gender, and poverty—form the threefold focus of womanist theology.

In her book, *Sisters in the Wilderness*, prominent womanist theologian Delores Williams discussed these three forms of suffering and discrimination in terms of black women as surrogates. In the time of enslavement, black women nursed and cared for white babies as surrogates for white women. The white masters used black women as sexual surrogates, while white women were considered pure and delicate. Enslaved black women did field work that was actually the work of men. After emancipation, black men were harassed and lynched with the intent of keeping them subservient. Black women often did the work of these humiliated men. To support their families, black women left their own children at home in order to work as maids in white families and to care for children of white women. In all these ways and more, Williams said, black women were surrogates for both black and white men and for white women. Williams wrote to encourage black women to reject the surrogacy roles and to affirm their own personhood and agency. As was mentioned in the earlier discussion of inherited atonement images, Williams wrote that accepting Jesus' death as a suffering death needed by God was a theological validation of all this unjust surrogacy foisted on black women.[3] The fact that Jesus made assertive moves to acknowledge Samaritans and women and raise their status points to the importance of the womanist understanding, and the need to take positive steps to oppose racism.

White Privilege

Literature easily available describes the assumptions of "white privilege" that continue unabated. White privilege is the sense that persons of the majority ethic group can expect to see people like themselves who understand their culture and speak their kind of English wherever they go—in stores, banks, doctors' offices, movie theaters, an insurance agent's

---

3. Williams, *Sisters in the Wilderness*, 162–67.

office, speaking with their children's teachers, and much more. And as they circulate among people like themselves, those in the majority can and do assume that their skin color will not raise suspicion or be held against them. Since white people can circulate freely, white privilege may blind white people to the problems faced by minority people in the same society. Persons in this majority ethnic group can live without knowing about the cultural practices of African Americans and other minorities, although the members of the minority must learn "white" culture in order to move about easily in society. White privilege exerts an assumed superiority and silent power that gives white people a head start and reminds minorities continually of their minority status, leads members of minorities to feel out of place or unwanted, and functions as an informal but very real form of discrimination. It thus constitutes a silent but real instance of systemic violence.[4]

Leonard Pitts, whose syndicated column appears in my local newspaper, used two incidents that made national news to paint a graphic picture of white privilege. In one scene, a sixty-three-year-old white man stood in a city street with a rifle. When police arrived, he refused to cooperate and acted in a rude and insulting manner toward the officers. The officers spent forty minutes talking him down. He was not arrested and the next day they returned his rifle. In the second scene, a twelve-year-old African American boy was playing with a realistic-looking toy gun. Officers were called. Without attempting to talk him down, the boy was shot dead two seconds after an officer exited his car. According to the columnist, these two incidents illustrate the difference made by assumptions behind white privilege and the benefit of the doubt that goes it with.[5]

Given the existence of "white privilege," most white people experience it silently (and benefit from it) in spite of their intention to avoid the evil of racism. The opposition to racism visible in the story of Jesus and given theological viability in nonviolent atonement calls every Christian, and most certainly those in the dominant ethnic group, specifically to be aware of racism and to engage actively to oppose it.[6]

An example of opposition to discrimination early in the 1940s was the founding of Koinonia Farm by two white couples, Clarence and

4. On white privilege, see Wise, *Dear White America* and Harvey, *Dear White Christians*.

5. I read the syndicated column as Pitts, "Helping Fox's Bill O'Reilly."

6. For an insightful analysis of the many facets of racism and white privilege in the United States, see Hart, *Trouble I've Seen*.

Florence Jordan and Martin and Mabel England. Other black and white families then joined. In an era when racial segregation was legal, this farm posed an example of integration and equality of black and white people. Clarence Jordan called it a "demonstration plot" for the kingdom of God. It persevered even in the face of hostility and violent opposition, including bombing. Although the legal situation has changed for the better, those in the majority still need to look for specific ways to counter the subtle discrimination of white privilege that still exists.

White people or those who identify with the majority culture cannot give away white privilege. However, with awareness of it, those who benefit can start to view society fairly. They should use their status to change the racist system, to look for ways to challenge injustice and to include rather than exclude African Americans and other minorities.

Another category of people who face discrimination are those who live in the United States without immigration papers. These people exist without legal rights and are subject to exploitation because of their lack of official standing. In biblical language, these are the "strangers within your gates" to whom God's people are called to minister.

These multiple instances of discrimination display the need for people who live in the reign of God to continue to challenge systemic racism. Jesus' challenge to racial and ethnic boundaries of his day points to the need to challenge systemic race prejudice today.

People who are gays and lesbians still lack full acceptance in the society of the United States, as is true of many countries of the world. Workplace discrimination still exists, hate crimes still occur, full legal rights for gay and lesbian couples are still in question, and more. In light of Jesus' advocacy for people who experience discrimination, I believe that Christians are called to accept gay and lesbian people as full participating members of church and society. The God of restoration and healing, who is present in Jesus, and fully revealed in the resurrection, is the God of people who are gay and lesbian just as much as of straight people. I cannot imagine that Jesus, who went out of his way to be accepting of Samaritans and women and lepers and others of his day, would reject gay and lesbian people today.

Chapters 6, 7, and 8 have discussed several areas in which the life of Jesus make visible the grain of the universe, the character of the reign of God on earth. It is clear that the reign of God rejects the use of violence, practices forgiveness, pursues economic policies that protect poor people, and values men and women equally and people of all races equally.

Christians who live within the story of Jesus thus display the character of the reign of God on earth. Christians who challenge racial injustice and discrimination against people who are LGBTQ are indeed an advance sample—a demonstration plot—of the future reign of God breaking into the world now. The next chapter changes focus from the character of the reign of God on earth to a discussion of a few things we can say about the character of God as revealed in the story of Jesus.

9

The Omnipotence of God

MUCH IS MADE OF the fact that God is omnipotent. I agree. But the real question concerns how to understand the omnipotence of God.

Quite often the omnipotence of God is connected to great violence and destruction. The assumption is that an omnipotent God controls everything that happens, which means that God must be in charge of evil and destruction as well as great blessings. Such destruction and violence attributed to God has also been identified as both blessing and punishment.

However, the theology of this book works with the belief that God is revealed in the life and work of Jesus. Since Jesus rejected violence, the God revealed in Jesus' story should be understood in nonviolent terms. Posing nonviolent atonement is one aspect of showing that God is nonviolent. We now address another challenge, the common assumption that God employs great violence and destruction for a variety of purposes.

Divine Violence

Violence with God's Support and Blessing

In inherited theology, God is linked to violence in a number of ways. For one, there are claims that God has blessed the exercise of violence. In other words, God has been credited with and thanked for helping Christians to kill their enemies. Examples here provide a brief sample from across the centuries.

It is well known that crusades by Christians against Muslims occurred in medieval Europe. Those crusades were proclaimed by the church. The object of the crusades was to march to Palestine and to take back Jerusalem from the Muslims. Killing Muslims and Jews was certainly considered acceptable in pursuing this goal.

In seventeenth-century England, both Catholics and Protestants carried out massacres against the other side. For example, in 1649 Puritan armies commanded by Oliver Cromwell massacred three thousand Catholics, both soldiers and civilians, in the Irish town of Drogheda. Of such work, Cromwell, the Puritan leader would write, "The Lord is pleased still to vouchsafe us his presence and to prosper his work in our hands," and to claim the "righteous judgment of God upon these barbarous wretches."[1]

If we have read our American history honestly, we know that there were many massacres of the native people who lived here before Europeans arrived. The language of one account is particularly noteworthy. The Puritan settlers in Connecticut came from England with the idea that war was a way to destroy evil and fulfill God's purposes. In 1636, they burned a native village to the ground. Four hundred Pequot natives, including women and children, died in the flames. William Bradford, governor of the colony credited God with success and thought it an occasion for thanksgiving. He wrote: "It was a fearful sight to see [the Pequot natives] frying in the fire.... But the victory seemed a sweet sacrifice, and they [the Puritans] gave prayers thereof to God, who had wrought so wonderfully for them."[2]

Without going into detail, it is safe to say that thanks has been given to God for assisting in the defeat of or the killing of enemies in all American wars since then.

Violence as Divine Punishment

In another kind of violence attributed to God, violence or destruction is called God's punishment on sin or on a wicked society. For example, when Hurricane Sandy devastated parts of New Jersey and New York in October 2012, there were claims that it was God's punishment on the states of Delaware and New Jersey because they legalized marriage of people who

---

1. Quoted in Cahill, *Love Your Enemies*, 143.
2. Quoted in Brock and Parker, *Saving Paradise*, 352.

are gays and lesbians. Hurricane Katrina devastated New Orleans in late August 2005. Newspaper articles reported a variety of reasons claimed by preachers for which God was supposedly using the hurricane to punish either New Orleans or the United States. Reasons given for punishment included shedding innocent blood through abortion, the presence of gay bars and LGBTQ people on Bourbon Street and in the French Quarter, endangering Israel by withdrawing Jewish settlers from the Gaza Strip, and "being in Iraq under false pretenses." The African American mayor of New Orleans also said that Katrina was a message from God to the black community for "not taking care of ourselves," and for the "black-on-black crime" of young black men killing each other.

Such statements about divine vengeance often appear after major disasters. These comments then provoke angry reactions from sections of the public. This anger is not because people think that God would not purposely do such violence or cause such suffering. Rather, people respond angrily because they think God's violence and killing would not be directed at the United States or at their particular segment of the United States.

Claims that God is punishing the United States may seem a bit strange. But there are precedents. In his second inaugural address, Abraham Lincoln said, in effect, that the great destruction and bloodshed of the Civil War was God's punishment for the sin of slavery.

> If we shall suppose that American Slavery is one of those offenses which, in the providence of God, must needs come, but which, having continued through His appointed time, He now wills to remove, and that He gives to both North and South this terrible war as the woe due to those by whom the offense came, shall we discern therein any departure from those divine attributes which the believers in a living God always ascribe to Him? Fondly do we hope—fervently do we pray—that this mighty scourge of war may speedily pass away. Yet, if God wills that it continue, until all the wealth piled by the bondsman's two hundred and fifty years of unrequited toil shall be sunk, and until every drop of blood drawn with the lash, shall be paid by another drawn with the sword, as was said three thousand years ago, still it must be said, "the judgments of the Lord are true and righteous altogether."[3]

---

3. Cherry, *God's New Israel*, 202.

But the precedent for claiming divine punishment on the United States began long before Abraham Lincoln. It goes all the way back to the founding Puritans, the Puritans who thought that the smell of burning natives was a sweet aroma and sacrifice to God. They had come in 1620 to found a society they believed was based on a covenant with God. Laws would be based on the Bible, and only converted church members could hold public office. In their understanding of the covenant, if they prospered it was due to God's blessing, and when problems occurred, it would mean that God was displeased.[4] Things went well for a few years, but the religious fervor could not be sustained and a steady religious decline developed within two decades. A bit later they experienced a series of disasters—several shipwrecks, outbreaks of disease, a series of raids by natives in 1675–76, and huge fires in Boston in 1676 and 1679.

The Puritans believed that this series of disasters meant that God was punishing them for failing to carry out their side of the covenant. Something had to be done. Therefore, church authorities convened a big church synod that began on September 10, 1679. The synod met for ten days while the church leadership talked about why God would be punishing them. In the report of their findings, they presented a list of thirteen areas of sin and religious decay for which God was punishing them. These sins included declining church attendance, swearing and taking God's name in vain, doing secular activities on Sunday, a decline in the family and family values, excess drinking, immodest dress by women, mixed dancing, and more.[5]

Thus people who claim that God is punishing the United States for sin today are standing in a 350-year-long tradition that begin with the assumption that disasters were God's punishment on New England's colonial society. Disagreements concern not whether God is capable of such violence and destruction but whether it is some segment of the United States that is being targeted.

Alongside credit to God for killing in war, and claims that destruction constitutes divine punishment, there is yet one more kind of divine violence to consider.

---

4. For Puritan covenants, see Walker, *Creeds and Platforms*, and Cherry, *God's New Israel*, 37–41.

5. Smith et al., *American Christianity*, 204–16.

Divine Violence as Comfort

I have a friend whose brother was killed in a traffic accident. In following years well-intentioned people told my friend that God would have "'good' reasons" for ordaining his brother's death. My wife's aunt died very quickly from cancer that was beyond treatment before any symptoms appeared. Her husband reported to me that many people told him, "God had a plan for [your wife]." These two examples represent many such comments; they are quite common. These words are offered with the best of intentions. The one who offers the comment intends to bring comfort or meaning to the individual who has lost a loved one.

In one version, these comments that are intended to bring comfort go back to John Calvin, the leading reformer in Geneva, and one of the most important figures of the part of the sixteenth-century Protestant Reformation from which the Puritans came. His major work was a big systematic theology called *The Institutes of the Christian Religion*. In the *Institutes*, Calvin wrote that if a traveler gets separated from his companions and is killed by robbers, or if a tree falls or a building falls and kills a man, these deaths are due to "God's secret plan." If there is a severe draught, Calvin said, not one drop of rain falls without God's permission.[6]

There are good intentions behind the words about "God's plan." When things seem senseless or out of control and people do not understand why something happens, it may seem comforting to believe that God has a "plan." If there is a divine plan, then things cannot be completely meaningless.

But think about it. These supposedly comforting words about God's secret plan have two important aspects in common with the God who blesses the killing of enemies and the God who causes great destruction with hurricanes. Each of these assumes that God kills or that God sanctions killing. And because it is assumed that God guides the violence, the implicit assumption is of an omnipotent God who controls all things. The biggest difference between God's sanction of people killed in wars, and God's killing in disasters, and divinely willed death by traffic accidents and cancer is the number of deaths in each instance for which God is responsible.

Undeniably, there can be a sense of comfort that results from the idea that God is somehow in control of violence and destruction, even if

---

6. Calvin, *Calvin: Institutes*, 197–210.

we do not understand why. However, since humans cannot control God or change God's plan, the idea of a divine plan can easily lead to feelings of helplessness.

Of course, other people make the same beginning assumption about God's control, but come to a different conclusion. When they see a world full of violence and chaos, they conclude that a good and loving God must not be in control. Such conclusions are common among folks who become atheists—if a good and loving God actually existed, they believe, this God would not be allowing such suffering, death, and destruction.

The question arises, how do we know about God? Or, stated another way, is the God who causes such destruction and death the God who is revealed in the story of Jesus?

Speculative Knowledge of God

One way to know about God is to speculate on the basis of certain claims that seem obvious. For example, God is said to be omnipotent, which means all-powerful. Since we know that God is bigger and more powerful than we are, it seems obvious that an infinite God would be omnipotent. When we are compared with God, we are really puny. From my boyhood, I remember the preacher talking about how an all-powerful God could lift an infinitely heavy weight. On a good day, with perhaps some help, I might be able to put seventy-five pounds over my head. Some professional football players can lift 450 or 500 pounds. But even that 500 pounds is really puny when compared with the infinitely heavy weight lifted by a presumed all-powerful God.

Or consider the violent God, the God who uses and sanctions violence to punish a disobedient people or a wicked nation. The need for punishment is presumed obvious. Whatever the human violence or wickedness, the violence or punishing capacity of God is presumed to be greater. Punishment supposedly happens with greater violence exercised by God. Here is a parallel to the small boy bullied on the school play ground who calls on his big brother to beat up the bully. Violence is met with greater violence. And God then exercises the greatest violence of all, now and in final judgment.

Or, think about how much of our immediate environment and world we can actually control. We control very little. It seems that an all-powerful God therefore must be in control of everything—including wars, disasters, aunts dying of cancer, and brothers killed in car accidents.

Consider the results of these speculative conclusions about God. The God who can lift the ultimate weight in comparison to the very small human weightlifter is a God envisioned in the image of human kind. The God who mirrors human violence with great violence of punishment again is a God envisioned in the image of humankind. Finally, the God who controls all in comparison to the human being who controls very little is, once again, an image of God made in the image of humankind. Each of these speculative answers ends up with an image of God that is an extension of a human image.

But, if God is revealed in Jesus, then such speculation about the meaning of omnipotence is not the place to begin to understand God. Christian faith does not suggest, "Assume God is all-powerful and then observe all the disasters happening and attribute everything to [or blame everything on] God." Or, "Assume God is all-powerful and then define it in terms of a bigger and stronger version of what people can do." Rather, Christian faith suggests another place to look to know about God. The understanding of God's omnipotence should be developed in terms of what is revealed about God in the story of Jesus.

Learning God from Jesus

Omnipotence Means "Able to Restore Life"

We read the story of Jesus in the Gospels. From that story we know that Jesus did not kill anyone, but that he did confront injustices. Jesus raised the status of women and he challenged racism against Samaritans. He taught about sharing and living generously with wealth. He forgave people, and challenged them thereafter to lead changed lives. If we accept that God is revealed in this story, then it seems clear that the God of that story is a God who is on the side of rejecting violence, and a God who is on the side of confronting racism and for inclusion of people who are gay and lesbians, and for sharing and living generously with wealth. The God of that story is the God who affirms life over against the forces of racism, exploitation, and exclusion. And most important of all, this affirmation of life appears in the resurrection of Jesus, the restoration of life where it had ceased to exist. If we truly believe that God is visible in the story of Jesus, it is there that we learn the character of God.

Our understanding of God's omnipotence should be derived from this narrative. The Romans and religious leaders killed Jesus in order to remove him as a troublemaker. It was a typical human response. In their attempt to solve problems, human beings often turn to violence, to killing and destruction. With modern weapons, the destructive capacity is enormous. But human beings cannot restore life. In contrast, the God revealed in the story of Jesus supports life, supports bringing justice to the downtrodden. Ultimately God restored the life of Jesus when it had ceased to exist. A characteristic of the omnipotence of God, I suggest, is that God can restore life where it has been annihilated. The idea of a God who can restore life is not God created in the image of humankind. This understanding of omnipotence is derived from the resurrection of Jesus, and it is the promise for all those who participate in the reign of God today.

The Source of Destruction

But, if omnipotence means the capacity to restore life, and God is not directing the destruction and violence in the world, who is responsible? The short answer is that *people* are and this means that *we* are. Sometimes that responsibility is direct, as when people make the choice to use weapons or when a person decides to get drunk and then drive a car. However, quite often that responsibility is indirect but nonetheless real. If God is not the power behind the evil in the world, that leaves people as the source of the evil in the world. That may sound harsh, but just consider a bit.

We, that is all people, are enmeshed in a web of bad decisions and evil that extends far back in time. Eventually it becomes visible in disasters like Katrina. What does this web look like? It has many components. Here is a brief sample, only slightly schematized to illustrate the point.

The production of the oil that powers our cars pollutes the natural environment—the BP disaster in the Gulf of Mexico in 2010, a bigger one in Nigeria that did not make news in North America, and many others—and then burning that oil driving our cars contributes to the pollution that causes global warming. And global warming appears to be contributing to the increasing severity of storms. Often ignored in the reporting on the impact of the storms and flooding is the extent to which decisions by human beings contributed to the devastation caused by these storms.

In the case of Katrina, more than two centuries of decisions about dikes and dams and draining of marshlands, actions taken for the benefit of large farming interests, industrialization, and urbanization, halted the silt build-up from the river and drained wetlands. As a result, much of the barrier that would have absorbed the force of the storm was long gone. Such decisions, coupled with reluctance to spend money on dikes for the protection of poor residential areas, added greatly to the damage caused by Katrina. This data helps reveal the human, not divine, element behind the destruction caused by these storms. And in spite of our intent to live justly, in spite of our good intentions, every time we get in our cars we are participating in this web of evil and injustice.

I felt my involvement in this oppressive web very personally when I was walking the streets of Haiti some years ago with Christian Peacemaker Teams, or on the streets of the Congo with Mennonite Central Committee in 2009. In Haiti our purpose was to use nonviolent activism to give visibility to the oppression of dissidents being carried out by the government of the time. In the Congo I was presenting lectures on nonviolent atonement theology. Both trips had a component of nonviolence; both trips were for recognizably good purposes. But with twenty dollars in my pocket for souvenirs, I was more wealthy than most of the people around us, and that did not count the resources way beyond their reach that had enabled us to be in Haiti and the Congo for those good reasons. The point here is that in spite of the fact that I was a justice-seeking Mennonite who lived a modest lifestyle, I still sensed acutely that I was immersed in and benefiting from being part of the wealthiest nation in the world, the nation that assumes without question its right to consume 30 to 40 percent of the world's resources, including oil, although the United States has only 6 percent of the world's population.

Overcoming Despair

This sense of belonging to this web of injustice can be overwhelming. Examples here have barely scratched the surface of it. There is a temptation to throw up our hands in despair and to stop talking about it because anything we do seems to make so little impact on the whole.

Oscar Romero, Archbishop of San Salvador in El Salvador, was assassinated on March 24, 1980, long before his efforts to assist the poor of El Salvador were finished. A poem frequently associated with Romero but written in honor of deceased priests deals with the fact that one life seems to have such a small impact.

A Future Not Our Own

> It helps now and then to step back and take a long view.
> The Kingdom is not only beyond our efforts, it is even beyond our vision.
> We accomplish in our lifetime only a tiny fraction of the magnificent enterprise that is God's work. Nothing we do is complete, which is a way of
> saying that the kingdom always lies beyond us.
> No statement says all that could be said.
> No prayer fully expresses our faith.
> No confession brings perfection.
> No pastoral visit brings wholeness.
> No program accomplishes the Church's mission.
> No set of goals and objectives include everything.
> This is what we are about.
> We plant the seeds that one day will grow.
> We water seeds already planted, knowing that they hold future promise.
> We lay foundations that will need further development.
> We provide yeast that produces far beyond our capabilities.
> We cannot do everything, and there is a sense of liberation in realizing that.
> This enables us to do something, and to do it very well.
> It may be incomplete, but it is a beginning, a step along the way, an opportunity for the Lord's grace to enter and do the rest.
> We may never see the end results, but that is the difference between the master
> builder and the worker.
> We are workers, not master builders, ministers, not messiahs.
> We are prophets of a future not our own.[7]

As the poem suggests, seeing that the web is a product of decisions by human beings is actually a place to begin seeing hope. The web of evil

---

7. Although commonly known as the Archbishop Romero Prayer, this poem was written by Bishop Ken Untener to be read by Cardinal John Dearden in November 1979 for a celebration of deceased priests. The text is from the website of the United States Conference of Catholic Bishops, reprinted with permission of Little Books of the Diocese of Saginaw, Michigan, which supplied the preferred title.

is a product of human decisions. That means that it can be opposed. If the bad things that happen and the way things are come from God's "secret plan," then it is essentially fruitless to oppose evil and injustice. But seeing that the web of evil is the product of human decisions makes clear that it can be opposed and other decisions are possible. That thought should provide some hope and comfort. We cannot change everything, but we can work at changing the conditions we do touch. We can do something and "do it very well." How Christians live right now *does* matter.

Being able to oppose human decisions means something else as well. It means that we can give testimony that our involvement in the web of evil is involuntary. By the way we live, we show that we really believe that God's mercy floods the world, that the reign of God is victorious in the resurrection of Jesus. Living within the life of Jesus gives visibility to what God has done in the world with the resurrection. Here is where we see God in the arena of these evils. God is not absent from disasters. God is visible in the efforts of people who display God's mercy in the midst of suffering and disaster. God is visible in the efforts of those who oppose violence and work for justice in the midst of violence and oppression. By working for justice and opposing oppression, Christians are putting on display now the beginning of God's future resurrection and restoration of all things.

God's Ultimate Control . . .

Seeing that this web of evil is the product of centuries of human choices contains another ray of hope as well. God is not in charge of day-to-day evil as part of a "secret plan," but God *is* ultimately in control. The emphasis here is on *ultimate* control. God's ultimate control is visible in the resurrection of Jesus, which is what Easter is really about. We should celebrate Easter as the most important Christian holy day—the day that acknowledges where the real power in the universe resides, and testifies to what the future holds.

The theological meaning of resurrection is that God has ultimate control. The God who can overcome death—the final enemy—the God who can restore life where it has ceased to exist—that God has ultimate control of the cosmos. That control was manifested with the resurrection of Jesus, which demonstrates that the reign of God has overcome the last enemy, namely death. The outcome of the universe is determined—there will be a restoration of life and creation, even if it is impossible for us to know when that might be and what it might look like. The one thing we can say is that the outcome is assured by the resurrection of Jesus.

... and Human Freedom

We are living in the interim between the resurrection of Jesus and that final outcome. In this interim, God does not control every event. God does not exercise control in the minutia of human existence. In this interim, God's respect for human freedom is absolute. In fact, that freedom is necessary if people's relationship to God and their living within the reign of God is to be meaningful. The reign of God is honored when people chose to be part of it. A coerced belonging would not honor God. The freedom in the interim is what makes living in the reign of God meaningful, and is a display of God's love for humankind.

Perhaps a sports analogy can illustrate the understanding of the idea of freedom in the interim with the outcome already determined. Some years ago I was watching a National Football League playoff game between the Pittsburgh Steelers and Houston Oilers (now Tennessee Titans). Conditions were miserable, a freezing rain. As the end of the first half approached, Houston trailed 14–3, but had the ball. A touchdown would make the score 14–10 at the half, and either team still would have a chance to win. But then Houston fumbled the slick ball. Pittsburgh got a quick touchdown and the score was 21–3. On the following kick-off Houston fumbled again, followed by another quick touchdown. The score now 28–3. And following that score, Houston fumbled the kickoff yet one more time, which led to a quick field goal as the half ended. Capitalizing on the errors, Pittsburgh had scored seventeen points in forty-eight seconds. Instead of the possible score of 14–10 with either team a potential winner, the score stood 31–3 at the half. The TV commentators immediately said that in the conditions of freezing rain, it would be impossible for Houston to come back. In effect, although there was still a half to play, for practical purposes the outcome was already determined. And the commentators were right. Pittsburgh did in fact win, 34–5.

For purposes of the analogy, the seventeen points in forty-eight seconds are like the resurrection of Jesus. These seventeen points in forty-eight seconds determined the outcome of the game, Jesus' resurrection made clear the outcome of the universe. Now, do not take the analogy too seriously! I am not suggesting that the outcome of a football game is as important as the resurrection. The game just supplies an example of how an outcome can be determined before the event is finished. The second half of the game is like our time of living in the interim between the resurrection and God's culmination of the universe. In the interim of the second half before the game ends, the players had complete freedom to play, to make good plays and bad plays, to become injured or commit errors and draw penalties, but the outcome of the game had been determined. In our interim between the resurrection of Jesus and God's culmination we have complete freedom to live, to work with the reign of God or to oppose God, to suffer, and more, but the direction and culmination of God's universe has been determined. When we live in the story of Jesus, we are living and working with the grain of the universe, living and working with the outcome that has already been determined. And it also means that the evil in the world is not caused by God. Evil is rather the product of human decisions apart from God and consists of actions against the grain of the universe.

Omnipotence Means God's Will Prevails

The fact that God has ultimate control but respects human freedom in the interim brings us to what, I suggest, is a second component of the omnipotence of God. In the face of human sin and disobedience, the will of God will ultimately prevail. Omnipotence means that divine will prevails even in the face of human resistance. This divine will is made visible in a very incomplete and imperfect way when Christians attempt to live within the story of Jesus and align themselves with the will of God, with the grain of the universe. The resurrection of Jesus puts on display that the God who can overcome death has ultimate control of the cosmos. And when we act nonviolently, when we pursue nonviolent conflict transformation, when we work for justice in the midst of oppression, we are working with "the grain of the universe," and God's will is "done on earth as it is in heaven."

Earlier we observed a God who is nonviolent within a nonviolent atonement image. Further, we have observed how the reign of God made visible in the life of Jesus opposes the structural violence of economic exploitation, racism, and sexism. Now we have just seen that the God revealed in the nonviolent story of Jesus is not engineering violence and causing destruction in the world around us. These discussions all point to the idea that the God revealed in and present in Jesus is a nonviolent God. But there is more.

What does the idea of a nonviolent God who does not use natural destruction to punish mean for our understanding of God's creation that is often pictured as "red in tooth and claw"? The following chapter responds to this question.

10

The Nonviolence of God's Creation

I ONCE SAT IN my sun room with a cup of coffee, enjoying a sunny morning. A drama in progress on the lawn outside caught my eye. It was a life-and-death struggle between a large earthworm and a robin that was attempting to pull it out of the ground. Half seriously, for a moment I considered running out to rescue the worm. Then I realized that if I intervened, either the robin or her babies would go hungry. I continued sipping my coffee, and the robin won.

This struggle of worm and robin is a glimpse of one link in the food chain. The next link in this particular chain might be the bird's predator. Although cats are often domesticated, by nature they are hunters and meat eaters. From the same sunroom window, I watched a neighborhood cat take a sparrow from my bird feeder. From the cat's vantage point at the corner of my garage, the sparrow's tail was visible below the feeding tray while the feeder hid the cat from the sparrow. The cat stalked stealthily across the yard and leaped to seize a bird that could not see the cat approach. I was in awe of the cunning of that cat. But cats can also be victims. Our local newspaper sometimes carries stories about coyotes coming into town and carrying off pet cats and small dogs. There are many such food chains. By a variety of paths, with small ones eaten by bigger ones, and weaker ones eaten by more powerful ones, we can move on up the food chain until we reach human beings. People also kill fish and animals for food.

The images of the food chain seem bloody and violent. Add in pictures or TV footage of male animals fighting for the privilege of breeding with a female, whether buffalo or bighorn sheep or bears or chimpanzees or gorillas, and many more. These images together bring us easily to the well-known description of nature as "red in tooth and claw."

But is "red in tooth and claw" the whole story or the complete story of the natural world? Does theology have anything to say about the natural world? More specifically, does our image of God have anything to do with the way we view nature? Still more specifically, if the God who is revealed in Jesus is also the Creator, would a nonviolent God create a natural order with violence as its organizing principle? Stated another way, when the nonviolent God who is revealed in Jesus is the Creator, should we expect to see evidence of the nonviolence of God in God's work of creation? Assume the answer is "yes." For a bit, let's examine the natural order from a perspective that expects to find evidence of the nonviolence of God in creation.

Jesus and the Natural Order

Jesus was a human being. As a human he experienced all the feelings and emotions of other people. He got hungry and thirsty, and enjoyed dining with people. He grew tired and slept. He felt sadness when his friend Lazarus died. Jesus felt pain, and most significantly, he died. When we say that God was in the story of Jesus, it means that the reign of God includes and rules over the physical world that Jesus lived in and that we live in. It means that God loves the world enough to be in Jesus in this world on this earth. It means that the world God created was good.

Jesus himself was in tune with nature. In his teaching, he took examples from nature. Since God cares even for common birds like sparrows and ravens, and for the lilies and grass that soon wither, God's care for people must be great (Luke 12:6, 22–28). Jesus knew about agriculture. He referred to the cultivation of fruit and fig trees to produce fruit (Luke 6:43–44; 13:6–9), and was familiar with sowing grain (Matt 13:3–9, 24–30). Jesus' words do not reflect nature "red in tooth and claw."

The many accounts of healings and exorcisms by Jesus go beyond familiarity with nature to show that nature exists within the purview of the reign of God. The power of the reign of God over nature is given even more visibility in Jesus' raising people from the dead—a widow's son (Luke 7:11–15), Jairus's daughter (Luke 8:40–42, 49–55), and Lazarus (John 11:38–44). But the most important indication of all concerning the power of the reign of God over the natural order is God's resurrection of

Jesus. The end of life in the natural world is death. Death means the cessation of existence in the physical world. Jesus' resurrection displays the capacity of the reign of God to overcome even this final ending, namely the cessation of existence. The God of Jesus is the God who restores life rather than taking life.

Creation

The accounts of creation in Genesis 1 and 2 provide two points that are important for shaping our attitude toward the created order. For one, using different images of God as Creator, the accounts in Genesis say that whatever exists was created by God. Therefore, the creation cannot be divine, and it should not be worshipped. I quickly add that saying that it was created by God is a theological observation, not a scientific assertion. It is true for any view of the science of origins that a reader may hold.

A related point is the fact that we are part of the order created by God. Whether the image of creation by spoken word in Genesis 1 or the human-like image of God as sculptor in Genesis 2, human beings are pictured coming into existence in the same way that other living beings come into existence. Thus, whatever view one may hold of the science of human origins, it is clear that human beings belong to and are part of the created order. Out of respect for the earth that originated with God and our place within it, people should live in harmony with it rather than assuming that it can and should be dominated and used up. We should find ways to share the land fairly, and to respect the various environments that have provided shelter for different kinds of species.

The respect for the various environments of earth has been frequently eroded by the misapplication of the term "dominion" in Genesis 1:28. It has been long read as a license to dominate, control, exploit, and use up the earth's resources. Instead, we should understand the term as a part of what it means for human beings to be made in the image of God (1:27). As beings in the image of God, people are entrusted to become God's representative on earth. Dominion means that we have a mission to carry out God's intent to care for and nurture the earth. Since the God revealed in Jesus is nonviolent, we should exercise the power of dominion in the way that God exercises power, which means without coercion, exploitation, and abuse. Dominion means to care for the earth and its inhabitants as farmers or shepherds care for their animals, to care for the earth in a way that works for the well-being of all creatures.

Walter Brueggemann has written about the "wisdom" that recognizes the careful use of resources and is attentive to the interconnections that keep the world healthy. Where these interconnections are honored, there the whole world prospers, and all creatures come to joy and abundance. Without this wisdom, "trouble, conflict, and destructiveness are sure."[1] At this point, it should be more than obvious that past efforts to appeal to nature to justify the domination of women by men or white people's rule of people of color is a fundamental contradiction to wisdom that cares for the earth in a way that seeks the enhancement, nurture, joy, and abundance of all.

Red in Tooth and Claw?

But where does this view of a nonviolent God with nurturing care for the earth leave us with reference to the image of "nature red in tooth and claw"?

Several kinds of observations concerning the natural order indicate that it is not as violent as is commonly assumed. My colleague, biology professor Todd Rainey, described data on primate behavior from a nonviolent perspective. He observed that while apes and monkeys have conflicts, they also have means of settling those conflicts without resorting to bloodshed. What appear to be violent arguments and confrontations are ways that animals who lack verbal ability learn about each other, communicate boundaries for territory and mates, determine distribution of food, and deal with newcomers to the group. Few conflicts result in serious injury, and many primates have practices of conflict resolution and reconciliation. The human species is the only one that routinely fights to the death and kills its own kind in large numbers. Rainey wrote that "many human observers have read their own violent assumptions into their observations of animal behavior." This observation about the conduct of monkeys and apes, he concluded, should challenge humans to reconsider the common "assumptions about both the inevitability and the effectiveness of violence."[2]

---

1. Brueggemann, *Theology of the Old Testament*, 531–32.
2. Rainey, "Nature's Tooth-and-Claw."

In his recent book, *The Age of Empathy*, renowned primatologist Frans de Waal agrees that observers have projected their own biases about violence and competition onto nature.[3] He supplies many examples that counter the image of "nature red in tooth and claw." Although Waal himself does not make the application specifically to nonviolence, many of his illustrations fit in that context. Primates have processes by which food is shared. Most of the apes want to be the first to put their hands on food, and ownership is respected, but eventually food is shared and even the low-ranking individuals eat. Although it is noisy and there is jostling for position, in the end it is a rather peaceful meal scene.

Waal notes that monkeys and apes have disputes among themselves and that chimpanzees do occasionally wage war on other bands and can be vicious. However, as Rainey said, for the most part these primates do not fight to the death. They perform acts of reconciliation through such activities as grooming or bringing food to share. Various species of primates practice cooperative, group-oriented behavior, or engage in practices that show concern for other members of the group. When one in a pair of capuchin monkeys was offered a choice between a reward for itself alone or another that included the partner, the monkeys overwhelmingly preferred the award in which both shared. Clearly they care for each other. Primates develop alliances for protection, and have mechanisms for resolving quarrels. Among Chinese golden monkeys, for example, the dominant male steps between quarreling females and calms them by turning to each in turn for stroking or friendly expressions. Both male and female chimpanzees work for harmonious community relations, with females removing rocks or branches from the hands of angry males. Females also reconcile males after a fight. While dominant leaders attain status from their roles in the group, the group as a whole benefits from having fewer quarrels, and the leader benefits from a more harmonious society. These societies would not thrive with leaders who acted only in their own interests.

The observations from Rainey and Waal align with the idea that the nature created by God revealed in the nonviolent story of Jesus is not fundamentally "red in tooth and claw" as commonly assumed. Caring for the earth as representatives of the nonviolent God means to work with and nurture a natural order that is much less violent and more cooperative than is commonly assumed.

---

3. Waal, *Age of Empathy*.

This description from Rainey and Waal of a more cooperative view of the nature order is the context in which I put the observations about the food chain. Animals do kill for food. However, it is not wanton killing for the sake of killing. Contrast it with the killing of birds and animals by humans, sometimes deliberately and often through habitat destruction, that has led to the extinction of many species. Further, when animals kill for food, they often take the weaker animals, which contributes to the overall health of the food chain as the stronger specimens survive to reproduce. And in any case, a certain amount of culling of the herd is necessary to prevent populations from exceeding what the land can support. Thus, I believe that it is possible to understand the killing by animals in the food chain as compatible with a more peaceful nature than is popularly assumed, and a nature that is compatible with a nonviolent God.

On occasion, assumptions about the violent character of nature have actually caused harm. My colleague Angela Horn Montel, an immunologist, pointed to the violent metaphors in immunology, the science that develops medicine to resist diseases. In the effort to overcome disease-causing germs, scientists frequently say things like "deliver a lethal blow" to germs, or develop an "arsenal of weapons" with cells that "attempt to bludgeon the enemy." There are "battles against foreign invaders," with a germ as "a patient assassin." Such language not only reflects the easy acceptance of violence among the general public. It also has had some unintended and undesirable consequences. For example, this language has contributed to the idea that germs must be wiped out, which has resulted in the production of antibacterial soaps and many other products with antibacterial agents. Such products have sometimes destroyed the protective layer of helpful organisms on our bodies, which makes people more rather than less vulnerable to disease. Studies show increased numbers of cases of asthma, hay fever, and other diseases associated with germ-free environments as compared to children raised in more polluted countries, on family farms, and who attend day care centers.[4]

In several places I have read that cancer patients do better when they have a positive attitude about confronting their disease. When cancer is called a "killer" or there is talk of the "war against cancer," those images lead some people to give up because the struggle seems hopeless. However, with modern medicine, much cancer is now survivable. Describing

---

4. Montel, "Violent Images in Cell Biology"

the struggle against cancer with less lethal names would actually allow more people to have hope and increase their chances of survival.

Furthermore, some devastation for which a supposedly violent God is blamed should more properly be attributed to human activity. Recall the quotes from chapter 8, in which religious spokesmen blamed God for Hurricane Katrina, which devastated the city of New Orleans as well as portions of the Gulf Coast, killed nearly 1900 people, and left hundreds of thousands without access to homes and jobs. But the human contribution to Katrina's destruction on the Gulf Coast mentioned in that chapter applies here as well. More than two centuries of decisions about dikes and dams and draining of marshlands along the Mississippi River, actions taken for the benefit of large farming interests, industrialization, and urbanization, halted the silt build-up from the river and drained wetlands. As a result, much of the barrier that would have absorbed the force of the storm was long gone. Such decisions, coupled with a lack of willingness to spend money on dikes for protection of poor residential areas, added greatly to the damage. New, exclusive residential developments in southern California are subject to mudslides. It is well-known that cutting of mountainside trees to make way for houses removes the vegetation that holds the land in place. Rain then softens the earth, which has the potential to slide down the mountain. When the real contribution of human decisions is factored into these instances of devastation, it appears that nature as well as the God of nature are not as destructive as commonly perceived. Destruction is multiplied when and where people have sought to dominate nature and have not made sufficient efforts to live within it.

The Cosmos

Nancey Murphy is a theologian who writes about the philosophy of science. She makes observations about the natural world that support belief in the nonviolence of God. One comment describes the hierarchy in which the sciences are arranged, and the way that they related to each other. At the lowest level, physics studies atoms and the behavior of particles at the most basic or elemental level of reality. At the next level, chemistry deals with the preparation and properties of compounds made of atoms, followed by biology, which studies whole organisms, including human beings. Murphy describes a branching of the hierarchy at the level of humans. Since human behavior cannot be reduced to biological functioning, psychology deals with the behavior of individuals and sociology with groups. On the other branch of the hierarchy, in the natural sciences, cosmology studies the physical universe. Each of these sciences or ways of studying the world deals well with questions within its level in the hierarchy. However, at the borders between these levels, questions appear that can only be answered at the next level below or above in the hierarchy. For example, chemistry explains that hydrogen and oxygen can combine in the right quantities to produce water, but it is biology, the next level in the hierarchy, that explores the role of water in an organism. Biology might explain how water functions in the human body, but it is psychology that would explain when people want to drink water or prefer a different beverage.

Murphy suggests that theology belongs at the top of this pyramid of ways of knowing or learning about the world. At its level, theology asks and answers questions just as happens in the preceding levels in the hierarchy, but theology does not answer questions that properly belong to ways of knowing in the lower levels. However, it can pose answers to ultimate questions about the nature of reality that appear at the borders of the other ways of knowing. For example, the science of cosmology can explore the immense, almost incomprehensible size of the expanding cosmos. Cosmologists believe that the expansion started with a gigantic explosion billions of years ago. In popular language, this is called the "big bang theory." There appears to be no definitive answer to where the big bang came from or why it happened. Theology can posit one kind of answer—namely that the so-called big bang originated with God, the eternal being. This answer is a hypothesis. Many cosmologists respond differently. They explain the "big bang" without God—suggesting perhaps that the cosmos is involved in some kind of never-ending expansion and contraction—which means that matter is eternal. But this answer is also a hypothesis. In this light, to posit eternal God as first cause with matter being created is just as logical as denying God and seeing matter as eternal. Theology's answer does not prove the existence of God, nor definitively explain the origin of the cosmos. But for those who are willing to listen, Christian theology does make a meaningful observation about the physical world.[5]

It is possible to understand that this God of the "big bang" is the nonviolent God who is revealed in Jesus. Nancey Murphy is concerned

---

5. For Nancey Murphy's philosophy of science, see Murphy, *Reconciling Theology and Science* and Murphy and Ellis, *On the Moral Nature*.

to provide an understanding of God that is in accordance with the revelation of God in the nonviolence of Jesus, but that also envisions God's providential control of all reality while preserving human freedom and the freedom of creation. If creation and human beings are genuinely to have freedom, then God must not use coercion and must be nonviolent. Murphy's argument assumes and works with modern scientific observations, but encompasses them within the reign of God. In atoms, the location and movement of any one particle is random and unpredictable, while the behavior of matter as a whole is predictable. Murphy uses this randomness within predictability as an analogy for the picture of God as the Creator who allows the freedom of creation. The characteristics of the expanding universe after the so-called big bang have allowed life to develop on our planet. Minute variations in these entities would have rendered life on earth impossible as we know it. Theology at the top level of the pyramid of ways of knowing offers God as an explanation from a Christian perspective of the source of the universe, and within this universe humans could evolve in the image of the Creator God.

The God of this process is the God who limited God's own power in order to allow the freedom of creation to develop, and to allow human beings the freedom to cause harm to the earth and to themselves. The noncoercive, nonviolent character of God is thus intrinsic to the process that created human beings. It is also the case that God has to "suffer" the consequences, sometimes deadly consequences, of the freedom given to creation and to human beings. Those consequences include the just-noted devastation of hurricanes and landslides, which is exacerbated by human choices.

The ultimate demonstration of God's acceptance of suffering is allowing Jesus, the Messiah, to suffer and die. To imitate Jesus and to have the "image of God" is to imitate the "moral character of God," which means to refuse to participate in coercion. This imitation of Jesus and the moral character of God can and does mean suffering. But God is not the cause of the suffering. Rather, God is on the side of those who suffer in a life of sacrifice. However, the power of God is also demonstrated in that death does not have the last word. The resurrection of Jesus is the guarantee that the reign of God will ultimately prevail. God's plans for creation do not end with the world as we know it. These plans will be fulfilled in a transformation for which the resurrection of Jesus is the first stage.

This discussion does have implications for how we live within the narrative of Jesus. This theology would challenge us to live in harmony with the created order rather than seeking to dominant and exploit it. It is possible to see that living within the nonviolent reign of God makes sense. It means that living out of the story of Jesus is to live in line with the character of God, and that nonviolent character is shown to be visible in the created world itself. It has been called working with the grain of the universe, a grain established when the Creator is the God revealed in Jesus.

The resurrection hallows this view of God in creation. God's resurrection of Jesus puts on display the capacity of the reign of God to overcome the freedom of creation to annihilate life. The resurrection of Jesus is the beginning of the restoration of humanity and of creation. Thus, resurrection goes beyond an invitation to enter into the nonviolent life of Jesus. It is also an invitation to live in harmony with the grain of the universe, to participate now in God's restoration of the created order in the eschaton.

Our efforts now to care for the earth are in line with God's future. Caring for and nurturing the earth is to work with God's future, which is breaking into the world now. It is the beginning of God's restoration of creation.

Doesn't the idea that God is nonviolent run counter to a lot of the material in the Bible? In light of the claim that God is a God who rejects violence, what do we do with the many stories of divine violence in the Old Testament, and in parts of the New Testament. The next chapters of this book respond to these questions.

11

God of the Biblical Narrative: Violent?

WHEN THE ARGUMENT IS presented for a nonviolent God, one of the most obvious and most frequent problems raised concerns the Old Testament. The violence in the Old Testament and the violence attributed to God described in the Old Testament are well-known. How does this biblical presentation of divine violence relate to the claim that the God revealed in Jesus is a nonviolent God? How is this violence reconciled with the claim that the God revealed in Jesus is a God who does not resort to violence? These are indeed serious questions that must be addressed. To make sure that we fully understand the problem, this chapter presents a sample of instances of violence enacted or blessed by God selected from throughout the Old Testament.[1]

A Violent God

The Great Flood

A familiar instance of violence by God is the story from Genesis 6–8 of a worldwide flood. The great wickedness of people on the earth made God exceedingly angry. God vowed to destroy every living thing with one exception, namely Noah and his family, whom God discovered were

---

1. This chapter and chapters 12 and 13 to follow deal with violence and nonviolence in Israel's history, as reported in both Old and New Testaments. For a thorough overview of the history of Israel, see Bright, *History of Israel*. For an introduction to the Old Testament, see Bowley, *Introduction to Hebrew Bible*. On the New Testament, see Van Voorst, *Reading the New Testament Today*.

righteous. At God's command, Noah built an ark. In one version of the story, he took a pair of all birds, animals, and creeping things into the ark, and in another, seven pairs of animals considered clean and one pair of the remainder. After Noah and his family and these animals were in the ark, rain came and covered the entire earth, even the mountains. Every living thing on earth was killed. Only the living things in the ark survived. This story of the flood, which appears very early in the Bible, features virtually unfathomable violence by God—destruction of almost all living beings on earth, both human and animal.

The Exodus

When the children of Israel, who were slaves in Egypt, escaped in the exodus, God used water to kill the pursuing Egyptian army. The army of Pharaoh, which was mounted in chariots, chased the fleeing Israelites to the shore of the Sea of Reeds. But Moses stretched out his hand, and "the Lord drove the sea back by a strong east wind all night" (Exod 14:21). The seabed dried out from the wind. While the wind held back the water on each side, the Israelites walked through on the dry land. When the Egyptian army pursued, God "clogged their chariot wheels, so that they turned with difficulty" (14:25). Then God told Moses, "Stretch out your hand over the sea, so that the water may come back upon the Egyptians, upon their chariots and chariot drivers" (14:26). The sea covered the Egyptian army, and not one of them survived. Again, God was directly responsible for killing a great number of people.

Law Codes

In the book of Deuteronomy, many violations are punishable with the death penalty. False prophets who speak against God or lead away from God are to be put to death (13:1–5). Any individual who tempts another to worship "other gods," that is, gods other than the God of Israel, is to be stoned to death. This death penalty applies even to family members, such as a brother or a son or daughter or a man's wife (13:6–11; also 17:2–7). The process is spelled out for condemning and then stoning to death a rebellious son (21:18–21). A young bride who is discovered not to be a virgin should be stoned to death. Similarly, when a man has sex with another man's wife, the couple should be stoned (22:13–22).

Conquest of Canaan

Many other times, God commanded people to carry out great violence. At God's command, the Israelite's conquest of the land of Canaan as it is reported in Joshua 1–12 is very bloody and violent. In this conquest, the taking of Jericho is frequently acted out in children's Sunday school classes. Children march around a pretend city, in imitation of the armed force that marched around Jericho carrying the ark and blowing trumpets—one circuit of the city for six days, and seven circuits on the seventh day. Children often delight in singing the well-known children's song, "Joshua Fought the Battle of Jericho." They enjoy acting out the seventh-day sequence—marching, blowing the trumpets, shouting, perhaps falling down with the walls, and celebrating the capture of the city by the Israelites. But children seldom if ever act out the real culmination of the story. The Israelites stormed into the city and massacred every living person, and every living thing of value, "men and women, young and old, oxen, sheep, and donkeys" (Josh 6:21).

Another account of a massacre concerned the capture of the city of Ai. In their first assault, the Israelites were defeated in the attack on the city. Joshua conducted an investigation to determine the cause of the defeat. It turned out that the defeat was God's punishment because of the sin of Achan. He had kept some of the booty from Jericho and hid it in his tent. Because of that sin, God caused the defeat. During Joshua's investigation, Achan confessed. As punishment, Achan and his entire family, his "sons and daughters," along with all his "oxen, donkeys, and sheep" (Josh 7:24) and his other possessions were taken outside the camp. The entire family was stoned to death, and the bodies and their possessions burned. With Achan's thievery punished, the Israelites returned to Ai. They set up an ambush, which drew Ai's defenders out of the city. These were killed, and then the Israelites entered Ai, burned it and killed all the remaining inhabitants. Thus with God's approval, on that day all the men and women of Ai, twelve thousand people, were slaughtered.

Rule by Judges

Some killings are reported with graphic details. Judges 4 recounts the story of prophetess and judge Deborah, who sent Barak against an army led by Sisera under King Jabin. Deborah instructed Barak that God would be with him. God threw Sisera's army into panic, and Barak's army massacred all of them. Sisera fled on foot and came to the tent of Jael, whose clan was at peace with King Jabin. Jael called a weary Sisera into her tent, covered him with a rug and gave him milk to drink. When he fell asleep, Jael took a hammer and drove a tent peg through Sisera's temple, nailing his head to the ground. When Barak arrived, Jael showed him her handiwork. The story concludes, "So on that day God subdued King Jabin of Canaan before the Israelites" (Judg 4:23). Thus, God is given credit for a massacre of King Jabin's army, including the nailing of Sisera to the ground.

Kings of Israel

Saul was anointed as the Israelites' first king. But God became angry and withdrew the kingship from Saul when he did not do enough killing. Samuel, a judge of Israel, had passed along the command of God to King Saul, namely that he was to punish the Amalekites for their opposition to the Israelites when they left Egypt. This punishment was to destroy everything, "kill both man and woman, child and infant, ox and sheep, camel and donkey" (1 Sam 15:3). Saul did kill all the people, except for King Agag, and he spared the best of the livestock. And God passed the word to Samuel, "I regret that I made Saul king, for he has turned back from following me, and has not carried out my commands" (1 Sam 15:10). Thus the kingship was stripped from Saul, and given to David. And Samuel himself "hewed Agag in pieces before the Lord in Gilgal" (1 Sam 15:33). Again, here is graphic violence directly sanctioned by God.

The kingship was lifted from Saul and transferred to David. The story of David begins in 1 Samuel 16, which describes his anointing by the prophet Samuel. The reciting of David's exploits, frequently having to do with fighting and wars and intrigue, occupies the remaining nine chapters of 1 Samuel, all of 2 Samuel, and the first two chapters of 1 Kings. (The story of David is also covered in chapters 11 to 29 of 1 Chronicles.) In 2 Samuel 7 is the account of the promise made to David by God that a son of David would build a permanent place of worship and God "will establish the throne of his kingdom forever" (7:13). And thus to David the promise is made, "Your house and your kingdom shall be sure forever before me; your throne shall be established forever" (7:16).

The chapter following this promise to David contains a summary of wars fought by David. He defeated Philistines and Moabites. He took

1,700 horsemen and twenty thousand foot soldiers from King Hadadezer of Zobah, and then David killed twenty-two thousand Arameans who came to help King Hadadezer. And upon return from these battles, he killed eighteen thousand Edomites. This section of text concludes, "And the Lord gave victory to David wherever he went" (2 Sam 8:14).

God also punished David. Late in his rule, David commissioned a census of Israel's population. This census displeased God. As punishment, David was given the choice of three years of famine in Israel, three months of devastation from enemies, or three days of pestilence in Israel. As a result, God sent the plague, and seventy thousand people died. Thus the story of David contains both God's blessing on killing, and death caused by God as punishment.

Prophets and Psalms

The writings of the prophets frequently refer to violence worked or sanctioned by God. The prophet's message often contains warnings of God's punishment on an unjust nation. One example comes from the writings of Isaiah, who was active for some forty years at the end of the eighth century BCE, at the time of the full emergence of Assyria as a problem for Israel. A complete cycle of this divine punishment occurs in Isaiah 10:5–19, as the punisher becomes the punished. In verses 5–11, the prophet gives voice to God, who is sending Assyria, "the rod of my anger . . . against a godless nation." The godless nation is Israel, "the people of my wrath." Assyria is commanded "to take spoil and seize plunder and to tread them down like the mire of the streets." Since God's hand has already touched those whose idols are worse that Israel's, there is no reason to withhold judgment on Jerusalem and Samaria. But in verses 12–19, Assyria in turn also falls under divine judgment because of "the arrogant boasting of the king of Assyria and his haughty pride." He vaunts himself, claiming "by the strength of my hand I have done it," when it was actually God's doing. Then the divine punishment falls on Assyria.

> The Sovereign, the Lord of hosts,
> will send wasting sickness among his stout warriors,
> and under his glory a burning will be kindled,
> like the burning of fire.
> The light of Israel will become a fire,
> and his Holy One a flame;
> and it will burn and devour

his thorns and briers in one day
(Isa 10:16–17).

Almost a century later, in 612 BCE, Nineveh, the capital city of Assyria, fell to invaders. The prophet Nahum gives voice to God, who takes credit for the destruction of the ones who plagued Israel.

> A jealous and avenging God is the Lord,
> the Lord is avenging and wrathful;
> the Lord takes vengeance on his adversaries
> and rages against his enemies.
> (Nah 1:2)

Following vengeance on Nineveh comes vengeance against the king:

> Your name shall be perpetuated no longer;
> from the house of your gods I will cut off
> the carved image and the cast image.
> I will make your grave, for you are worthless.
> (Nah 1:14)

Nahum's second chapter describes this vengeance as soldiers and chariots rampage through the city. "Devastation, desolation, and destructions!" (2:10). And the Lord takes full credit, for "restoring the majesty of Jacob, as well as the majesty of Israel" (2:2) and for the destruction:

> See, I am against you, says the Lord of hosts, and I will burn your
> chariots in smoke, and the sword shall devour your young lions;
> I will cut off your prey from the earth, and the voice of your
> messengers shall be heard no more. (Nah 2:13)

Many psalms, the worship music and the poetry of Israel, also appear to portray this powerful and vengeful God. Psalms praise or bow in awe before the majestic Creator God, the God of Israel. This God controls all things. This control covers the forces of nature, when the Israelites escaped from Egypt in the exodus (e.g., Ps 78:11–16, 43–48). It also covers the fortunes of nations, where God expresses anger and wrath. When the people sin, God's wrath is poured out on Israel.

> Then the anger of the Lord was kindled against his people,
> and he abhorred his heritage;
> he gave them into the hand of the nations,
> so that those who hated them ruled over them
> (Ps 106:40–41).

God's anger and wrath also turned on the enemies of Israel.

> He struck down many nations
> and killed mighty kings—
> Sihon, king of the Amorites,
> and Og, king of Bashan,
> and all the kingdoms of Canaan—
> and gave their land as a heritage,
> a heritage to his people Israel.
> (Ps 135:10–12)

These verses constitute a brief sample from the Psalms of expressions of the glory and majesty of God, the mercy of God in protecting and restoring Israel, and the wrath and anger of God directed against the sin of the people, both Israelite and pagan.

Conclusion

This sample of vignettes from across the Old Testament could be expanded greatly. They all picture a God who uses violence as punishment and judgment. At times God exercised the violence directly, as in the stories of the great flood and the exodus. Other times it is Israel's leader or Israel's army who follow instructions from God to carry out the violence. And on occasion, when Israel needs punishing, it is the enemies of Israel who are directed to carry out God's violent punishment. The divine violence falls on those who disobey and oppose the will of God, whether Israel or Israel's enemies. Being God's chosen people means not only blessing; it also carries responsibility with punishment for failure to obey.

These stories of divine vengeance and punishment seem to have had an impact on United States history. As reported in chapter 9, the early Puritan settlers lived with the idea that disasters in their colony were punishment by God for breaking their covenant with God. In the same light, Abraham Lincoln considered the violence and destruction of the Civil War to be God's judgment for the sin of slavery. And the idea that hurricane Katrina was divine judgment, even if the claim was later modified, certainly falls within the same outlook.

If these stories and other writings of violence and vengeance by the God of Israel were all that we knew, it would be obvious that Israel's God was a violent God. But these images of divine violence are by no means the only image of God present in the Old Testament. The next chapter turns to these much neglected images.

12

God of the Biblical Narrative: Nonviolent?

THE PREVIOUS CHAPTER DISPLAYED a sample of the well-known stories of violence from the Old Testament and of a God who uses and sanctions violence. But those images of God are far from the only thing the Old Testament has to say about God.

The Old Testament has other images of divine working and other kinds of obedience to God as well. Picturing these additional images will bring out the fact that the Old Testament does not present a uniform picture of God. In fact, it actually poses a conversation about the character and identity of God that readers of the Bible today can and must join.

A Nonviolent God

Creation

Consider the two creation narratives in Genesis 1 and 2. In the first of these narratives, God creates with the Word, by speaking. There is the familiar sequence of six creative days: day one, light and darkness; day two, the dome to separate the waters above from waters below; day three, the emergence of dry land with vegetation; day four, the sun, moon, and stars; day five, swimming and flying creatures; day six, wild, tame, and crawling animals, and male and female human beings. The seventh day was a day of rest.

The narrative of Genesis 2 has a different mode of creation and a different order for the appearance of living things. This account pictures God in the image of a sculptor or potter. All creation occurs in one day, with God kneeling on the ground, fashioning living beings out of clay. First comes a human being, who is created on bare ground. Next comes a garden—Eden—with all manner of plants, and in which the human is placed. As helpers and partners for the human, animals are sculpted next, and brought before the human to receive names. But among the animals none was suitable to be a helper and partner for the human. Thus God caused the human to fall into a deep sleep. During this sleep, God took a rib from the human and used it to craft another human. These became male and female humans, and the man recognized the woman as like him and declared her "bone of my bones and flesh of my flesh."

Reading these stories as scientific accounts presents a number of difficulties, beginning with the order of events in Genesis 1. These problems include the cosmology of a flat earth with a dome over it, the existence of alternating light and dark as day and night without benefit of sun and the rotation of the earth. Plants appear on day three and produce seeds and fruit, and are thus engaging in photosynthesis which requires sunlight that does not appear until day four. Compound those difficulties with the fact that the order of events in Genesis 1 differs significantly from that in Genesis 2. In the first story, human beings both male and female are created last, on a teeming earth and as the culmination of creation. In contrast, the second story features the male human created first, followed by plants and animals and finally a female human. Much ink has been spilled trying to reconcile these creation accounts with science. That impossible task should be abandoned, not only because it is impossible, but because these are not scientific stories and are not intended to correspond to the science known in the twenty-first century.

The two creation narratives open many rich and fruitful theological discussions. The theological point of most concern for present purposes, namely the nonviolence of God, appears clearly when these biblical stories are compared with another creation account from approximately the same time period. This account appears in the Enuma Elish, a Babylonian saga that was inscribed on clay tablets at about the same time as biblical Abraham would have lived. The time at which it was committed to writing does not indicate the age of the stories themselves. The two sources—the Genesis narratives and Enuma Elish—present accounts whose origin was much earlier than the time they were transcribed.

The account of creation in Enuma Elish appears in the middle of a long-running saga about the lives and adventures of the gods. In this saga, young gods prodded the female god Tiamat to rebel against the head god, Marduk. Tiamat and Marduk fought. When Timat opened her mouth to engulf Marduk, he blew the wind into her so that she expanded like a huge balloon. He then shot and killed her with an arrow. With Tiamat vanquished, Marduk took his sword and sliced the round body of Timat in two, like a shellfish. He lifted the upper half up and formed the dome of the sky. He then created stations in this great dome of the sky for various deities—the sun for the day time and moon and stars for the night. Next, Marduk conducted an investigation to discover who had put Timat up to the rebellion. Kingu was revealed as the guilty party. As his punishment, Kingu was killed and his blood was used to make humankind, called "a savage," whose purpose was to serve the gods while they took their leisure.

Both similarities and differences of Genesis 1–2 and Enuma Elish are instructive. The two biblical accounts and Enuma Elish share a common worldview, namely a flat earth with a dome over it that contains the heavenly bodies. They have the same misunderstanding of how the cosmos actually works—day and night existing independent of sun, moon, and stars, which are entities placed into light and darkness. Genesis 1 and Enuma Elish have the same order of creation as far as the latter's details go—light and darkness existing before the heavenly bodies, plants growing without benefit of sunlight. I note in passing that the effort to reconcile the Bible's accounts with science also validates the "scientific orientation" of Enuma Elish, which few writers would want to do.

It is the differences between the two Genesis accounts and Enuma Elish that make visible the orientation of the Bible's accounts. In Genesis, human beings are declared "very good," or are "made in the image of God," and are pictured as the culmination of creation or that for which everything else was made. Such descriptions pose a marked contrast to Enuma Elish's designation of humans as "savages."

Further, whether the creative image is that of a spoken word or the hands of a sculptor, the Genesis accounts display divine purpose and order. Compare these statements of design with the spontaneity and randomness of developments emerging out of chaos in Enuma Elish—the heavens and earth are fabricated from the dead body of a rebellious god, and human beings occur as savage servants in the aftermath of identifying the instigator of the rebellion.

Finally, note again how violent the story is in the Enuma Elish—killing a god and dismembering the body, which then becomes building material for the cosmos, and killing another god whose blood becomes the material from which human beings are made. In light of that violence and blood, it should jump out that the God of the Genesis accounts creates *without violence*. The Bible pictures creation as a product of divine intention and entirely without violence. The Bible begins with images of a nonviolent God.

The Great Flood

But this nonviolent God who lovingly created human beings is the same God pictured in Genesis 6–8 who became angry at the wickedness of human beings. In response to that wickedness, as the previous chapter described, this enraged God engineered a worldwide flood to drown all of them, except for Noah and his family, along with almost all other living beings. The story of the flood concludes, however, with God's promise never again to destroy every living creature, and a promise that the seasons will continue, "summer and winter, day and night, shall not cease" (Gen 8:22).

As was true for the Genesis accounts of creation, this story of the great flood cannot be historically or scientifically true. The problems are many—contradictions within the account (one pair versus seven pairs of clean animals, different lengths of time rain fell, and more), the absence of archeological evidence to collaborate such a worldwide event, the location of enough water to cover the entire earth, the impossibility of collecting animals from innumerable habitats from around the world and loading them on a small ark with sufficient food for the duration, Noah's family handling the feeding and cleaning of all those animals, and more. But as was true for the two creation accounts, this narrative is not intended to be explained in accord with twenty-first-century knowledge of science and archeology. It is rather a theological account, with an important affirmation about the character of God.

The promise that the seasons and day and night will continue without end confirms the affirmation about the order and purpose of creation from Genesis 1 and 2. There is continuity of the understanding of God from the creation stories to the flood account, a continuity of a desire for order and purpose.

Another kind of theological continuity also surfaces in the account of the flood. Although the account in Genesis does not use the term "repent," that God promised never again to destroy every living thing implies that God repented of the destruction caused by the flood. Repentance, accompanied by a promise not to do it again, reflects the idea of a God who does not resort to violence (or no longer resorts to violence).

Some readers may be surprised to read that God could "repent," that God could change God's mind. In fact, that God could repent or change God's mind is a departure from the traditional idea of a God who was and is always the same.[1] To defend this idea of an unchanging God, it is claimed, then God must be responsible for all the violence depicted in the Bible, including the vengeance of a flood to destroy all living things and the massacres described in the previous chapter. But as this book puts on display, the Bible has another picture of God as well, a nonviolent picture. A God who can repent is consistent with that God. It is also consistent with the story of Jesus' encounter with the Syrophoenician woman, in which her pleas led Jesus to change his mind (Matt 15:21–28; Mark 7:24–30).

Another theological reason also exists to picture a God who can repent and change God's mind. Some theologians have questioned whether it makes sense to pray to a God who never changes, who is always the same, who has ordained everything that has happened and has already foreordained everything to come. But prayer is possible if God can and does respond, if the divine mind can change. In other words, a God who can change is the God who can respond to prayer. The idea of a God who can respond to prayer takes the hard edge off the idea of a vengeful God who destroyed every living thing. It is the idea of a God that is compatible with the idea of a nonviolent God.

The Patriarchs of Israel

It is the loving God of creation and the God who repented of destroying all living things that called Abraham. God promised to give Abraham land in a new location, and "make of you a great nation," and through this nation "all the families of the earth shall be blessed" (Gen 12:2–3).

Establishing Abraham as the father of a nation with future blessing sets up the storyline for the rest of the Bible. How Abraham and his descendants understood this calling and attempted to carry it out establishes the plot for the ongoing narrative of the Bible. Will the descendants

---

1. For development of the idea that God's mind can change, see Sanders, *God Who Risks*.

live up to their side of the covenant, and how will God respond when they fail? Understandings in Israel differed on how to live in this story that began with Abraham and about the character of the God of the story. In the previous chapter we saw parts of the story that assumed a violent God was directing Israel. Now I am sketching a different understanding of the God of this plot that began with the call of Abraham.

Abraham and his nephew Lot lived near each other in the south central part of Canaan. Each grew wealthy with great herds of livestock. With the large herds, the land could not support both of them, and their herders quarreled. But rather than fighting over the land, Abraham proposed that they separate. He gave Lot the choice of land and they parted amicably.

Isaac, son of Abraham, also possessed large herds and a large household. He lived in the region of Gerar in the south of Canaan in a region ruled by King Abimelech of the Philistines. Abimelech's people became jealous of Isaac's success and stopped up his wells. Rather than fighting, Isaac moved and dug new wells. This same scenario played out two more times, and after the third move and the digging of new wells, Isaac was left in peace.

These two stories of Abraham and Isaac display a series of accounts that depict nonviolent responses to conflict. One can interpret these stories to say that when there is faith in God's promise of land, then God's followers do not need to fight for it.

The Exodus

The previous chapter described the crossing of the Red Sea as an event in which God drowned the entire Egyptian army. However, another interpretation is possible. People are responsible for the problems that they bring on themselves. The mobile Egyptian army, driving heavy chariots, ventured out into sands in which the wheels bogged down while foot traffic could pass easily over the sand. This army should not have been pursuing these escaping slaves and they put themselves in a vulnerable position. Whether tides or winds pushed the water back, when it returned the Egyptians were caught where they should not have been and were drowned. That is, rather than seeing the Egyptian army drowned by God, it is possible to conclude that the army suffered destruction that it brought on itself.

Conquest of Canaan

The first twelve chapters of Joshua present the conquest of Canaan as an accomplished fact, carried out by bloody conquest. The stories of capturing Jericho and Ai represented that kind of conquest story. However, the book of Joshua also lays out a quite different version of the occupation of Canaan by the Israelites. Immediately after the first twelve chapters describe a supposedly complete picture of the conquest, chapter 13:1 says that Joshua was "old and advanced in years," and "very much of the land still remains to be possessed." The remainder of the book and the book of Judges describes a pattern of settlement that differed greatly from the account in the first twelve chapters. In this second version, individual tribes moved in independently of others, and settlement often occurred by osmosis and integration into the existing society. There were, of course, some military operations, but these were only a part of a much more complex story. The other accounts of settlement by moving in and settling and of incomplete settlement indicate that the description of military success attributed to God was actually a stylized recitation rather than a historical account. Thus the book of Joshua clearly holds open the possibility of another, nonviolent understanding of God and the way God's people settled the land and confronted their enemies.

Rule by Judges

An example with minimal violence in the time of Judges comes from a story of Gideon in Judges 7. When a huge army of Midianites threatened the Israelites, Gideon sent out a call and roused an army. However, God sent the message that Gideon had too many men. He allowed all those who were frightened to return home. Twenty-two thousand left and ten thousand remained. God told Gideon that it was still too many—when victory came people would credit the size of the army rather than God. Gideon then brought his army down to the water to drink. Those who put down their weapons and put their faces in the water Gideon sent to one side, and to the other side he directed the three hundred who scooped water and lapped it out of one hand. He kept the three hundred and sent the remainder home.

For equipment when they faced the Midianites, Gideon instructed each of the three hundred men to carry a trumpet and a torch hidden inside a pitcher. In clusters of one hundred, they positioned themselves around the camp of the Midianites. At Gideon's signal, they all broke their pitchers at once and began blowing on their trumpets and shouting, "A sword for the Lord and for Gideon!" Seeing the sudden burst of light and hearing the noise, the startled Midianites panicked. Thinking that they were surrounded by a huge army, they started running and hacking at each other. Gideon's three hundred men chased after them. Two captains were captured and killed, but there was no slaughter.

This story from Gideon is a victory through a ruse and creative imagination. It is an example of nonviolent resistance, carried out via commands from God with virtually no killing by the Israelites. That Gideon later engaged in military activity and violence does not detract from this particular story as an example of active nonviolent resistance.

Kings of Israel

As the previous chapter displayed, God's blessing was claimed on the wars of King David and he received a divine promise that his line would endure forever. Nonetheless, the wars of David did not go completely without censure. David had planned to build a great temple in Jerusalem. However, he reported that God told him, "You shall not build a house for my name, for you are a warrior and have shed blood" (1 Chr 28:3). Solomon, David's son and future king, was the one to build the temple. Early in his reign King Solomon was renowned for his wisdom. He kept a standing army and was a harsh taskmaster but did not make a name for himself as a warrior. Having Solomon build the temple is thus a censure on David's violence, and is an interpretation that fits with the images of a nonviolent God.

Chapter 6 of 2 Kings features a story of the prophet Elisha who repelled an invasion with another ruse and food. With God's help, Elisha had several times warned the Israelite king of ambushes set up by the king of Aram. Finally, totally frustrated with Elisha, the king sent an army to capture him. But when this invasion force arrived at the house of Elisha, their eyes were blinded so that they did not recognize him. Elisha said that he could lead them to the man they sought. He led them into Samaria, where they were surrounded by the army of the Israelite king, who wanted to massacre the invading Arameans. But instead of a massacre, Elisha instructed the king to prepare food for the Arameans. After they had eaten, the story concludes, "And the Arameans no longer came raiding into the land of Israel." This turning away of an enemy with the help of God and a ruse, followed by kindness, most definitely constitutes an example of active nonviolence.

Prophets

Alongside the God who uses the nations for punishment as depicted in Isaiah and Nahum and the Psalms, the Suffering Servant poems from the second section of Isaiah (in particular Isa 42:1–4; 49:1–6; 50:4–9; 52:13—53:12) present a much different image of God, along with the idea of being willing to suffer for the benefit of others. This Suffering Servant is described in frequently quoted words:

> Surely he has borne our infirmities
> and carried our diseases;
> yet we accounted him stricken,
> struck down by God, and afflicted.
> But he was wounded for our transgressions,
> crushed for our iniquities;
> upon him was the punishment that made us whole,
> and by his bruises we are healed.
> All we like sheep have gone astray;
> we have all turned to our own way,
> and the Lord has laid on him
> the iniquity of us all.
> (Isa 53:4–6)

Scholars do not agree on the identity of the Suffering Servant. Suggestions include the Servant as Israel, as an individual, or as a combination of the two. The traditional Christian interpretation is that Jesus fulfilled the Servant's mission as the suffering Messiah. But regardless of the identity one accepts for the Servant, the God of the Servant is a God who works through patient suffering, that is, a nonviolent God. The God of the Servant stands in marked contrast to the violent God who perpetrates and sanctions massacres of thousands.

Nahum was not the only prophet who wrote about Nineveh. Nineveh has a central location in the book of Jonah. However, Jonah's conclusion differs greatly from that of Nahum. In the well-known story, when God called Jonah to preach to pagan Nineveh, the prophet ran away and ended up spending three days in the belly of the large fish. After being returned to land, Jonah agreed to preach, proclaiming "Forty days more, and Nineveh shall be overthrown!" The citizens of Nineveh responded by repenting and donning sackcloth. When their king heard of these events, he also donned sackcloth and ashes, and decreed, "All shall turn from their evil ways and from the violence that is in their hands." The hope was that God's mind would change and God would not destroy the city. God did indeed relent, and the city was saved.

In the story, this display of mercy by God angered Jonah. After a discussion with God, Jonah built a booth outside the city wall to wait in the shade to see what would happen to the city. God sent a bush that grew to shade Jonah, and then a worm that killed the bush. With the bush gone, Jonah declared himself angry enough to die. God's response: "You are concerned about the bush, for which you did not labor and which you did not grow; it came into being in a night and perished in a night. And should I not be concerned about Nineveh, that great city, in which there are more than a hundred and twenty thousand persons who do not know their right hand from their left, and also many animals?" (Jonah 4:10–11).

The book of Jonah can be understood as a parable that interprets Israel's history. Jonah represents unfaithful Israel punished by captivity in Babylon (the great fish or whale) and then returned to Israel (spit up on the shore) for another opportunity. In spite of their repeated disobedience—symbolized by Jonah's flight and then his continuing anger—God remains faithful to Israel as a merciful God, but a God who also shows mercy even to the enemies of Israel, represented by the city of Nineveh. Thus, the parable actually shows that God cares not just for the Israelites but for all people.

Because of the contrast of attitudes toward Nineveh in Nahum and Jonah, some commentators have suggested that the writer of Jonah intended to provide a response to the image of the vengeful God of Nahum. Note how closely Nahum 1:3 and Jonah 4:2 resemble each other. Nahum writes that "the Lord is slow to anger but great in power, and the Lord will by no means clear the guilty." The prayer of Jonah uses the same description of the Lord, but ends differently. Jonah fled to Tarshish, he says, "for I knew that you are a gracious God and merciful, slow to anger, and abounding in steadfast love, and ready to relent from punishing." Such words placed in Jonah's mouth, coupled with the mercy of God displayed in the parable, positions the book of Jonah as a prophetic softening of divine justice in Nahum with a message of divine mercy. Thus the book of Jonah can be listed among the images of a nonviolent God.[2]

The Exile in Babylon

The monarchy in Israel came to an end some six centuries before Jesus, when the king and other leaders and numbers of people were taken to Babylon as captives. Exile forced the Israelites to rethink who they were and what it meant to be the people of God. For more than four centuries they had been ruled by kings from the dynasty started by David. Now in exile, they had no ruler of their own, no political establishment, no monarch. They had no control over politics and no means to control the direction of Babylonian society through government. Such had been the case much earlier in their history, but it was certainly a change from rule by the dynasty of King David.

The prophet Jeremiah, who was living in Jerusalem, now controlled by the invaders, wrote a letter to these exiles in Babylon. His letter gave them some advice, stated as a message from the God of Israel. Evidently, they spent energy lamenting their lost life in Jerusalem. Jeremiah told them to stop pining after that life. They now lived in a new land, he wrote. They should maintain their identity as God's people in this new land, but settle down and decide to make a life in Babylon. "Build houses . . . ; plant gardens and eat what they produce," get married and raise families and then encourage children to produce grandchildren. The exiles should learn trades that benefited the host society, and "seek the welfare of the city where I [the God of Israel] have sent you into exile, and pray to the Lord on its behalf, for in its welfare you will find your welfare" (Jer 29:5–7). In other words, living as God's people Israel did not depend on having their hands on the means of political control, but the people would find meaning through working for the society in which they now lived.

In a long view of the history of the Israelites, not having a centralized authority such as a king was not new. After they entered Canaan, for nearly two centuries there was no centralized authority. In principle they were to trust God, who would raise up a regional leader when needed to deal with a particular problem. These leaders were the judges and

---

2. For the contrast of Nahum and Jonah see Spronk, *Nahum*, 8–10, 16 and Machinist, "Nahum," 665.

GOD OF THE BIBLICAL NARRATIVE: NONVIOLENT? 143

prophets of the stories in the book of Judges. Now, in Jeremiah's eyes, living in Babylon as God's people was actually returning to the original pattern of trust in God, before Israel had a king. In this life in exile, they were to maintain their religious traditions and worship, which would serve as a witness to the way of Yahweh in the midst of a foreign nation. Nothing about living as God's people depended on having a king or control of government or their own army to carry out divinely sanctioned violence. But as God's people, they could learn to speak the language and develop vocational skills that would benefit the society where they now lived.

Stories in the book of Daniel illustrate this witness. The first chapter of Daniel tells the story of Daniel, Hananiah, Mishael, and Azariah. The palace master renamed them Belteshazzar, Shadrach, Meshach, and Abednego. These young Hebrews were among the captives brought in for education that would enable them to enter the king's service. The young men were willing to learn the local language and a useful skill, which lines up with Jeremiah's suggestion that the captives "seek the welfare of the city." However, as they were engaging in this new learning, they maintained their identity as Hebrews, as people of God. To assert their distinct identity, they rejected the royal food and wine and asked for a diet of vegetables and water. In other words, the young exiles maintained their own cultural and religious identity as Hebrews, which identified them as people who worshipped the God of Israel rather than the gods of Babylon, even as they learned skills that would benefit Babylon's society. In contemporary language, we can say that maintaining a distinct identity was a matter of nonviolent cultural resistance. The outcome of the story is that the Hebrews thrived on their own kind of food and thus they were allowed to continue with it as they worked for the king.

The third chapter of Daniel tells another story of Shadrach, Meshach, and Abednego. Upon intercession by Daniel they were appointed to be civil servants with responsibilities for the province of Babylon. After the three refused to worship the gods of King Nebuchadnezzar and the golden statue that he had set up, they were bound and thrown into a furnace. But when the three were not harmed in the fire, the king acknowledged the God of Israel and gave Shadrach, Meshach, and Abednego a promotion. Even at risk of their lives, the three young men maintained their identity and resisted worshipping the king's gods. Again, using contemporary terminology, this story is one of nonviolent, cultural resistance. These stories portray ways that the Hebrews maintained their own religious and cultural identity, which was a witness to the God of Israel, even as they worked for the good of Babylon.

The story of Daniel and the den of lions in the sixth chapter has a similar outcome and meaning. Daniel was one of three presidents placed by King Darius over 120 satraps stationed throughout the kingdom to look after the king's affairs. Daniel's job performance earned him the favor of the king but jealousy from the other civil servants, who plotted against him. They persuaded the king to sign a proclamation that required worship and prayer to the king only for thirty days. The penalty for disobeying the decree was death in a den of lions. With this proclamation, the other civil servants hoped to create a situation that would lead to the elimination of Daniel, who continued to pray three times daily to the God of Israel. However, after being left in the den of lions over night, Daniel said, "My God sent his angel and shut the lions' mouths so that they would not hurt me, because I was found blameless before him; and also before you, O king, I have done no wrong" (Dan 6:22). As a result, the king issued a decree in support of Israel's God, and Daniel continued to prosper under King Darius.

These stories from the book of Daniel illustrate and put a theological blessing on the cultural resistance of the Hebrew captives. They maintained their identity as worshipers of Yahweh in a society where they had no control of political authority but nonetheless worked for the blessing of the culture in which they were captives. Their witness required courage and it could be confrontational. Today we would call it nonviolent social protest or social resistance. The stories are told with a view towards encouraging that nonviolent witness.

Conclusion

This sample of stories and texts about God and obeying God, selected from across the Old Testament, demonstrates that there are many images of God that pose a counterweight to the well-known violent images. Many of the stories cited in this chapter are well-known individually. What may be new is the idea of connecting them in order to show that together they do present a different image of God than the common idea of the God who exercises great violence in judgment and punishment. When this chapter is put alongside the previous one, it is evident that the Old Testament does not present a uniform picture of God. Rather it presents a conversation—even a debate—about the character of God.

If the Old Testament was all that we knew about God, it would not be possible to determine the character of God by putting a finger, whether an actual or figurative finger, on a particular story and then repeating it loudly. For any story or text thus recited, a text could be cited from the other side of the debate.

But we are not left with the equal-sided shouting match pictured in this chapter and the previous one. A resolution to this debate occurs in the following chapter, along with a discussion of the form of this conversation in the New Testament.

13

God of the Biblical Narrative: A Resolution

ALONGSIDE THE OLD TESTAMENT's debate about the character of God, the New Testament has its own version of that conversation. I will resolve the Old Testament debate as a precursor to dealing with the New Testament.

The Old Testament Debate: A Resolution

The two previous chapters presented contrasting images, actually collections of images, of violence and nonviolence from the Old Testament. On the one side, there was violence perpetrated by God, and stories that depicted violence blessed by God or carried out at the command of God. On the other side were images of a nonviolent God or of Israelites who refused violence and who confronted enemies with nonviolent practices. Both lists could be expanded.

In light of this conversation, the obvious question is whether there is a way to get beyond this conversation. Can we actually decide whether God is violent or nonviolent? One thing does seem clear—that question cannot be answered via a shouting match of dueling texts.

There is a way, however, to move beyond citing one story or another and to reach an answer to the question of whether God is nonviolent. Here is one place that it becomes important to recall the statement from chapter 1, in which it was said that Jesus was the Messiah. Jesus was a son of the Israelites. Jesus was a continuation of the story of the Israelites from the Old Testament, and those people who accepted Jesus as the Messiah (who came to be called Christians) are one continuation of the people of

God who trace their origin to Abraham. Both sides of the conversation in the Old Testament claimed to speak for God and to be living as the people of God. But the story of Jesus most obviously aligns itself with one side of the conversation about God.

The story of Jesus, who rejected violence, finds its roots in the images of the nonviolent God and the nonviolent responses to conflict. There were the images of creation without violence, and the willingness of the patriarchs not to fight for land. When the people trusted the Lord, there was salvation from enemies without violence. Jesus' teaching about sharing wealth and living generously with wealth, about dealing with an oppressive economic system by walking naked, or about going the second mile to embarrass a soldier of the Roman occupation all assume that the people of God are able to act without a king or central authority to validate or enforce their actions. In other words, Jesus is carrying forward the situation that had been the case at least since Jeremiah's letter to the exiles in Babylon. Jeremiah told the captives how to live as the people of God when they no longer controlled the government. In fact, they did not need a king to live as the people of God. Stories in the book of Daniel provided some illustrations. And a century and a half later, Jesus was continuing that tradition, teaching how the people of God can and should live when they are not in control of the reins of power, and demonstrating that they certainly did not need a king to live as God's people. Without needing a king or emperor, they can be a living witness to the orientation and values of the reign of God: sharing of wealth, confronting discrimination against ethnic and racial groups, opposing second-class status for women, and demonstrating nonviolent approaches to conflict. And with reference to the question about the character of God, if we believe that God is revealed in Jesus, then the clear conclusion is that God is nonviolent. A nonviolent Jesus reveals a nonviolent God.

The story of Jesus also speaks to some claims to violence in the New Testament.[1]

---

1. On reconciling violence and nonviolence in the biblical writings, I refer to Seibert, *Disturbing Divine Behavior*; Crossan, *God and Empire*; and Nelson-Pallmeyer, *Jesus Against Christianity*.

The New Testament Conversation on Violence and Nonviolence

The New Testament also contains a conversation about divine violence. Alongside the nonviolent story of Jesus, some parables attributed to Jesus display a vengeful God who pronounces violent judgment on offenders.

New Testament: Violence of God

One example of this vengeful God appears in Matthew's parable of the unforgiving slave (Matt 18:23–35). The parable says that the kingdom of heaven is like a king who wished to settle accounts with his slaves. He called in one who owed ten thousand talents—a huge sum of money—and demanded payment. When the slave could not pay, the king ordered the slave and his family and all his possessions sold. When the slave begged for mercy, the king took pity and forgave the debt. As this slave departed from the presence of the king, he came upon a fellow slave who owed him a hundred denarii, a quite small sum of money. The one who had just experienced relief from the huge debt, seized his fellow slave and demanded payment. When it was not forthcoming, he threw the debtor into debtors' prison until he could pay what he owed. This action disturbed the other slaves greatly, who reported the action to the king. The king called in the unforgiving slave, accosting him with the words "You wicked slave!" and charged that he should have shown the same mercy that he had just received. As punishment, the angry king turned him over to be tortured until he could repay his entire debt. In his conclusion, Jesus's words use the king as analogy for God. He says, "So my heavenly Father will also do to every one of you, if you do not forgive your brother or sister from your heart" (Matt 18:35). In terms of the image of God visible in this parable, God is pictured as a God who tortures those who are not sincere in their forgiveness.

A similar image of God appears in the parable of the wicked tenants, which occurs in the Gospels of Matthew (21:33–46), Mark (12:1–12), and Luke (20:9–19). In this well-known parable, a landowner planted a vineyard, assembled the apparatus around it for a wine press, and hired tenants to run the operation while he was in a far country. When he then sent servants to collect on his investment, these servants were beaten, stoned, and finally one was killed. Thinking that the tenants would respect his son, the owner sent his son to collect the fruits of his investment. But the wicked tenants killed the son. With the son eliminated from the picture, they thought that they would be able to claim his inheritance. When Jesus then asked his hearers what the owner would do, the reply came, "He will put those wretches to a miserable death, and lease the vineyard to other tenants who will give him the fruits in their seasons" (Matt 21:41). The three Gospel writers then have Jesus respond by quoting Psalm 118:22: "The stone that the builders rejected has become the cornerstone" (Matt 21:42). The implication of the quote from Psalms is that Jesus approved of his listeners' answer. His follow-up comment in Matthew's version makes the vineyard owner who applies harsh punishment analogous to God: "Therefore I tell you, the kingdom of God will be taken away from you and given to a people that produces the fruits of the kingdom. The one who falls on this stone will be broken to pieces; and it will crush anyone on whom it falls" (Matt 21:43–44). This interpretation of Matthew's version of the parable pictures God as a God of harsh vengeance.

Another parable compared the kingdom of God to a king who gave a marriage feast for his son (Matt 22:1–14). But the invitees thought they had better things to do and even mistreated and killed the servants who carried the invitation. In response the angry king sent his soldiers to destroy the murderers and burn their city. Then he sent his servants out into the streets to "invite everyone you find to the wedding banquet" (Matt 22:9). As a result the wedding hall was filled with guests. But the king became angry when one of those in attendance was not properly attired for a wedding celebration. The king commanded his servants, "Bind him hand and foot, and throw him into the outer darkness, where there will be weeping and gnashing of teeth" (Matt 22:13). Once again, like the king in the parable, God appears as a vengeful God who exercises great violence.

A similar image of God appears in the two versions of the Parable of the Talents (Matt 25:14–30; Luke 19:12–27). In this parable, a wealthy man left on a journey and gave his slaves money to invest for him while he was away. In each version, one slave hid the talent he was given while the others followed orders and gained significant earnings. Luke adds that on this journey, the noblemen was to acquire royal, ruling power. However, his citizens hated him and sent a delegation to protest his appointment. In each version, on the nobleman's return, the slaves were rewarded for the gains made with the talents entrusted to them, and the slave who hid the talent returned it to the owner. In Matthew's version, the angry owner commanded that the talent from the slave who hid it be given to the one who had the most, and ordered that the slave who hid the talent be thrown into "outer darkness." In Luke's version, the talent is also taken from the slave who hid it, but nothing is said about his fate. However, for those who had protested the rule of the new king, he commanded, "Bring them here and slaughter them in my presence." In either version, God appears in these parables as a vengeful and violent God.

New Testament: Nonviolent God

As a prelude to observing parables with a different kind of ending, recall our earlier discussion of the life of Jesus. He forgave sins. With his responses to women and to Samaritans, he crossed barriers and confronted the systemic violence of racism and sexism. In his teaching, he gave examples of returning good for evil and of responses that changed a situation in order to avoid mirroring evil. At his trial, he told Pilate that the kingdom he represented did not engage in violence. In light of the belief that God is revealed in Jesus, we need to keep Jesus' life and teaching in view when discussing the parables that feature a violent and vengeful God.

Alongside these parables are ones with a different image of God. In at least one instance, the contrast of images of God is explicit. We just saw Matthew's version of the parable of the wedding banquet, which described the violent response to those who rejected the invitation or wore inappropriate clothes to the banquet. Luke's version omits the violent response of the king. The king is still angry at those who make light of the invitation. But the anger spurs the king to send his slave to go "into the streets and lanes of the town and bring in the poor, the crippled, the blind, and the lame." And when there was still room remaining, the slave was to go out "and compel people to come in" to produce a full house. The judgment pronounced on those who refused the invitation: "None of those who were invited will taste my dinner" (Luke 14:21, 23–24).

Judgment still appears in Luke's version of the parable. But in this case, it is not a vengeful and violent judgment. Rather, those who reject the invitation bring judgment on themselves by choosing not to attend the banquet. Those who refuse the invitation are excluded from God. But exclusion is not God's doing. It is rather self-exclusion from a God whose invitation remains open.

With the alternative endings of the same parable in view from Matthew and Luke, it is clear that the conversation about the character of God—violent or nonviolent—that was visible in the Old Testament is also visible in the Gospels in the parables of Jesus. Other parables and sayings and some other interpretations of parables also reflect the side of the conversation that has nonviolent images of God.

Judgment by self-exclusion is visible in Jesus' conversation with the man frequently referred to as "the rich young ruler" (Matt 19:16–30; Mark 10:17–31; Luke 18:18–30). The young man asked Jesus how to be saved. Jesus recited the well-known commandments about not committing adultery, not killing, not lying, and not stealing, and then added one more. To the young ruler he said, "Sell your possessions, and give the money to the poor, and you will have treasure in heaven; then come, follow me" (Matt 19:21). The young man went away grieving because he was very rich. Earlier we saw that this was not a suggestion that the young ruler become destitute. Rather, it was an invitation to pool resources with Jesus' disciples who shared their money in a common purse—none was independently wealthy, but all their daily needs were met. As the man departed, Jesus talked to his disciples about the difficulty that the rich have in entering the kingdom of God. There is nothing here of a violent, punishing God. The young man has selected himself out of the bounty of the kingdom of God.

A most important parable that features a nonviolent image of God is the Parable of the Prodigal Son. The father in this parable is anything but the image of a vengeful God who must exact harsh-but-deserved punishment in order to uphold family honor.

A further example of a nonviolent God may be Jesus' reference to "the sign of Jonah." The Pharisees and Sadducees asked Jesus for "a sign from heaven." It is possible that they were expecting Jesus to validate their view that a movement of apocalyptic violence was near. He refused to give a sign, except to refer them to "the sign of Jonah" (Matt 16:4). If the Pharisees and Sadducees were looking for a statement of God's violent assistance against their enemies, they did not get it. Instead, Jesus referred them to the story of Jonah, which features a merciful God rather than a vengeful God.

Some parables that have been assumed to feature a violent God have alternative interpretations. One example is the parable about the wicked tenants who killed the owner's son. We just observed the most common interpretation, in which God is presumed parallel to the vineyard owner who sent a troop of soldiers to kill the rebellious servants who had killed the owner's son, who is equated with the messiah. However, another interpretation is also possible. Those listening to Jesus would have been poor farmers who had firsthand experience with exploitative landowners. These laborers would know that landowners could be brutal and that rebellion was useless—it would only succeed in getting the rebellious laborers killed. Thus, the laborers would hear Jesus' parable as a warning against rebellion. Rebellion against the landowner would only bring down the greater violence of the landowner, thus continuing a spiral of violence. In this interpretation, Jesus would be breaking from the common expectation that the coming Messiah would emerge from or provoke a violent revolution and that God would ensure victory through divinely engineered violence. This interpretation thus involves a rejection of the idea of a violent God who secures justice through violence.

To consider this alternative interpretation of the parable of the unjust tenants and observing the conflicting endings of the parable of the banquet means recognizing that different images of God do in fact appear in the Gospels. As was the case with the Old Testament writers, it means coming to terms with the fact that the Gospel writers did not always understand God in the same way, and they sometimes drew meaning from Jesus' life in different ways.

Conclusion

The solution to this conversation—or disagreement—about the character of God in the New Testament has the same solution as for the Old Testament. *We look to the narrative of Jesus' life.* It is the narrative that shows that Jesus rejected violence and rejected any idea of a violent revolution. As he told Pilate, "My kingdom is not from here." That is, the values of the kingdom Jesus represented differed from Pilate's kingdom. If Jesus' kingdom were from this world, Jesus said, "My followers would be fighting to keep me from being handed over to the Jews" (John 18:36). It is the story of Jesus, the life of Jesus, and his principled rejection of violence that points to the side of the conversation that best reveals the character of God. As was true for the Old Testament, the Gospel writers also differed in their interpretations, which in part reflected the times in which they wrote. And just as was true for the Old Testament, seeing both sides of the conversation in the New Testament about God and violence is important. Only when the alternative sides of the conversation become visible do we see that there truly is a conversation, and more fully comprehend the significance of the fact that Jesus' life indeed followed a path that rejected violence. If God is revealed in the life of Jesus, as Christian faith professes, then the God of Jesus is a God who rejects violence, a nonviolent God.

The use of the Bible in the previous two chapters has perhaps raised questions for readers about the character of the Bible, and exactly how Christians can and should use it. The next chapter responds to such questions.

14

Reading the Bible Again

THROUGHOUT THIS BOOK, I have used the Bible freely in the discussion. This use occurred without providing much explanation on the nature of the Bible or how to understand it. Some readers may have been surprised by the way the Bible was used, or by some claims made about the Bible. Since the Bible has been the professed authority for Christians, it was perhaps surprising that no explanation was given for the authority of the Bible. This chapter now moves to talk about the character of the Bible, and how it serves theology.

"Scripture Alone"

Reformers in the sixteenth century appealed to the Bible as an authority over against the authority of the pope. *Sola scriptura* or "Scripture alone" became one of the rallying cries of the newly emerging Protestant traditions, and reformers of many stripes based reform on appeals to the Scriptures. However, although these appeals contributed greatly to the Protestant Reformation, this approach also contained the seeds of a problem that is still with us, nearly six centuries later.

The reformers thought that when they appealed to the Bible, the question would be settled. They did not recognize that other reformers as well as their opponents were reading and using the Bible as well, but interpreting it differently, which meant that appeals to the Scripture did not resolve their differences. This problem persists to this day. Disagreements based on appeals to the Bible continue. It is a problem that has spread beyond the original reformers who claimed to be following "Scripture alone."

How to use the Bible is a question that in some way touches every Christian today. Since the last half of the twentieth century, the lines of agreement and disagreement on how to read and understand the Bible are creating new alliances that no longer follow longstanding denominational lines. For example, I can report that the theology portrayed in this book has garnered support from a wide array of Christians, beginning with Catholics and extending across the Protestant spectrum and including the Mennonite tradition with which I worship. At the same time, it has also been challenged by voices that represent that same denominational spectrum of voices.

An appeal to the Bible as a direct source of authority assumes that it functions on the order of a divine rule book. The assumption is that its words jump over the twenty or even thirty centuries since it was written to dictate theology and to give instructions in timeless fashion directly to us for today. Those who truly believe the Bible, it is claimed, will accept this theology and follow these examples and commandments. This approach works well when people are comfortable with the rules discovered and the theology supposedly dictated.

But what happens when other examples and commandments are unthinkable or seem completely outmoded today? Earlier we saw examples of creation stories and biblical cosmology that are rendered incorrect and obsolete by modern sciences. If we followed the example of patriarchs Abraham, Isaac, Jacob, and the kings of Israel, men today would have multiple wives. On numerous occasions in the conquest of the promised land, God commanded the Israelites to massacre enemies (Josh 1–12). There are instructions to stone to death a rebellious son (Deut 21:18–21), to execute adulterers (Deut 22:22–24), to stone to death a wife, brother, son, or daughter who tempts one to worship other gods (Deut 13:6–10). We are not to mix types of cloth or plant a second crop in a vineyard (Deut 23:9, 11), and must never eat pork or shellfish (Deut 14:3–21). Women may not wear what was once claimed as men's clothing such as pants (Deut 22:5) or cut their hair, and are required to wear a prayer veil (1 Cor 11). Jewelry of any kind is forbidden (1 Pet 3:4). Men must have beards since trimming the edges is not allowed (Lev 19:27). Divorce is forbidden (Mark 10:6–12). And more. Some church traditions have applied a number of these injunctions, but all have been ignored by many other Christians.

Rule Book or Story?

Ignoring commands of Scripture may cause uneasiness for people who want to take the Bible seriously. How can one take the Bible seriously when significant parts of it are ignored or rejected? This question comes from the assumption that we should read the Bible as a book of transcendent rules and belief statements, existing above history and directly applicable today. However, this assumptions forces us into the mode of deciding which of these rules and examples to ignore. But ignoring some texts is a *de facto* rejection of those parts of the Bible. I suggest another approach. A better understanding of the character of the Bible itself can indicate a more fruitful way to take the whole Bible seriously, but without simply discarding parts of it as irrelevant.

The unity of the Bible is provided by a narrative, the story of God's people that begins with Abraham and runs through the history of Israel and is continued in Jesus and the early church. In seminary I was excited to learn that the Bible was much more than a collection of inspirational writings. It actually had a plotline—would God's people descended from Abraham live up to their calling as God's people, and how would God respond when they fell short? In the Old Testament we read this long-running saga in Genesis, Exodus, Numbers, Joshua, Judges, 1 and 2 Samuel, 1 and 2 Kings, 1 and 2 Chronicles, Ezra, and Nehemiah. Close-up vignettes appear in Ruth, Esther, and parts of Daniel. The books of the prophets present commentary on events all along this history. Psalms presents the worship music of God's people, Proverbs and Ecclesiastes review some of their wisdom, while Song of Solomon presents sensuous love poetry. Leviticus and Deuteronomy contain their early law codes. In the New Testament, the story continues in the four Gospels and Acts. The Epistles provide commentary on the story for the early church. Apocalyptic writings in Daniel and Revelation present a view of events happening in the world from the perspective of the heavenly throne room.[1] This description of the Bible's books could be greatly expanded, but the important point here is to see that it is the narrative of God's people that ties the books of the Bible together and shows how the various books relate to each other. Thus, the *narrative* unifies the collection of writings that we call the Bible.

---

1. For readings on the history of Israel and the literature of the Bible, see titles listed for chapter 10.

Unity in a Narrative

How is it helpful to see the story of God's people as the unifying factor of the Bible? First, this understanding makes this history *our* history. The history of the people of God is the beginning of our history as people of God. We, the church today, are the continuation of the story of God's people. The story that began with Abraham and goes through Jesus and the early church is the beginning of the identity of Christians today as God's people. This reading displays the entire Bible, and not just the New Testament, as the book for Christians.

Second, recognizing this story that runs from Abraham through Jesus and the early church as the unifying element of the Bible should impact our understanding of the character of the Bible. It is not a pristine, perfect book without error. Seeing that a historical narrative constitutes the unifying element of the Bible means that we should expect to see developments over time and changes in the story, as the people of God grew in their understanding of what it meant to be God's people. We should expect to see disagreements among the biblical writings, we should expect to recognize instances where in retrospect people got things wrong, without thereby rejecting the Bible as untrustworthy. In other words, we should get used to the idea that not all writings in the Bible speak with the same voice, and we can see that some ideas in it are wrong or misguided—but all writings are nonetheless important because only by seeing all the writings can we see the direction in which things were developing and changing. The most important point of all is to see the direction of changes as the writers grew in their understanding of God. And since the important culmination of the story is in the narrative of Jesus, his story becomes the key to identifying which of the earlier voices in the story most truly reflect the will of God. In essence, since we know that the story culminates with Jesus, we are interpreting the entire Bible from the perspective of the end.

Third, seeing the unifying factor of the Bible as the story of God's people enables us to see that everything in the Bible reflects the particular context in which they lived. Quite obviously we live in a different social and political context. Previous chapters in this book mentioned a few instances in which our worldview or context differed markedly from the one visible in the Bible. In the creation story in Genesis 1, for example, the ancient cosmology of a flat earth with a dome over it was visible. In following chapters, in the book of Revelation we will see a three-layered worldview of heaven above, earth, and the underworld. Our political environment in twenty-first-century North America differs significantly from that of the church in the midst of the Roman Empire of the first Christian century.

Our task is not to try to copy and transplant directly the ideas and practices from two or three thousand years ago. Rather than assuming that the history speaks directly to us, we should read their story to understand the direction in which things were moving and changing. Then, in our context we will discuss how to be the continuation of that story, how to keep moving the story in the same direction.

Fourth, seeing a narrative as the basis of the unity of the Bible has significant implications for our understanding of theology. Since the Bible's parts were written and edited together over an extended period of time, discrepancies in the narrative are to be expected. Recall the book of Joshua, where the first twelve chapters of the book present a quite different picture of conquest from the remainder of the book. When the books of Kings and Chronicles report on the same events, details differ. The New Testament features four accounts of the story of Jesus, with significant differences in detail and in chronology. Theology about Jesus is derived from this story. However, the narrative itself needs to be articulated and an explanation given for how it is used. Further, contexts change and new learnings are brought to the text, which requires articulating the meaning of the narrative again in the new context. Deriving theology from a narrative thus means that theology is always open-ended, never finished, always in process, always open for revision. But on the other hand, deriving theology from a narrative actually brings theology closer to our experience. Starting with the narrative locates the history of Israel and of Jesus and the early church in the world in which we live, and we can then visualize the fact that the church today really is a continuation of that story. Christians today are the cutting edge of that story moving through history, and we are always in the process of thinking about the origins of the story and then giving theological articulation to what it means to continue that story today.

Some Christian traditions consider creedal formulas developed in the fourth and fifth centuries to be the authoritative norms that determine the truthfulness of theology today. But from the perspective explained here, namely that theology is always in process, using fourth- and fifth-century statements as the authoritative theological norms is to come into an ongoing story in the middle, and then to attempt to stop further developments in the theological story.

The idea of development within the story is not strange to the Bible. In fact, the Bible makes changes within this history quite visible. By the time of the New Testament, for example, there had been a movement away from the polygamy practiced by the patriarchs and the kings of Israel. In another shift, there is a clear move toward less violence, which culminates with Jesus' rejection of violence. There is visible development in theology. Six times in the book of Acts the writer describes the brief narrative of Jesus used by the apostles to identify Jesus in the months immediately after his death and resurrection (Acts 2:14–39; 3:13–26; 4:10–12; 5:30–32; 10:36–43; 13:17–41). Paul repeats that outline (1 Cor 15) and makes explicit what is implicit in this story, namely that the resurrection of Jesus requires belief in a general resurrection of the dead. Some decades later, as the eyewitnesses to Jesus began to die, the narrative outline visible in Acts was expanded by the four Gospel writers. Meanwhile, the church in Acts expanded the circle of God's people to include gentiles, abandoned the requirement of circumcision for such gentiles, and allowed them to eat of foods previously deemed unclean. New Testament interpreters took the story of Jesus into other worldviews and used the images from these diverse frames of reference to say that with his life, death, and resurrection Jesus belonged both to the realm above and identified with the earthly realm below. Examples are the Greek Logos (John 1), principalities and powers (Col 1), the high priest (Hebrews), a new Adam (Phil 2), and the slain Lamb (Rev 4 and 5). In following chapters we will expand on these particular developments related to the meaning of the narrative of Jesus.

The developments and changes visible in the New Testament all involved decisions about how to communicate the gospel of Jesus Christ effectively in new contexts and how to address new issues as the early church expanded beyond Jerusalem. Sometimes a point was brought out which previously was only implicit, as when Paul made clear that belief in the resurrection of Jesus meant there would be a general resurrection of all dead. Other times minds were changed about acceptable conduct, as when the apostles ruled that gentiles could become part of the people of God without being circumcised.

Living with Change

With changes occurring, it should be obvious that different viewpoints appear in the text of the Bible. Thus, contemporary interpreters are not obligated to, and in fact cannot, harmonize or synthesize all biblical statements on a particular question. It is not possible, for example, to harmonize the blessing of marriage to multiple wives with a clear endorsement of monogamous marriage, or decisions for and against circumcision or slavery.

In practice, Christians have long been applying this understanding of the Bible but without fully acknowledging or owning it. Some changes have taken longer to develop than others. It was well into the nineteenth century before many Christians could condemn slavery in the face of the Bible's apparent sanction of slavery. A more recent example concerns the status of women in the church. Since early in the last century, in many denominations there has been significant movement toward acknowledging the equal status of women, and recognizing that women can and should hold any office and perform any function within the church.

A current change in process concerns the status of people who are gay or lesbian within the Christian church. In the story of Jesus, it is apparent that he accepted Samaritans even though they were an ethnic group discriminated against in his time. The stories of Jesus' interaction with women show that he raised their status in a time when women were subordinate to men. Jesus showed great concern for poor people, for lepers, and other people on the margins of his society. In light of such acceptance by Jesus, it is becoming increasingly clear to many Christians that Jesus would certainly not approve of the exclusion of gays and lesbians from full participation in the life of the church, including serving as ordained leaders and receiving the blessing of marriage.[2]

What I am suggesting is for Christians to be more forthright about the way we are actually using the Bible. Even as the assumption still persists that the Bible functions as a rule book, in practice we are already reading it as a history, whose context we assess as we ask how to continue the story today.

It may seem that understanding the Bible in this historical way places an unreal burden on modern readers. After all, aren't Christians

---

2. For a description of how a prominent Evangelical scholar came to accept people who are gay and lesbian as Christians, and his interpretation of the main biblical texts on which exclusion is based, see Gushee, *Changing Our Mind*.

supposed to read the Bible for themselves? But how can a reader who has never studied the ancient world be expected to know the creation story of the Enuma Elish, or know the context of the world in which the biblical patriarchs and ancient Israel came into existence? How could a modern reader know the specific first-century situations addressed by Jesus' suggestions of turning the other cheek, giving cloak with coat, and going the second mile? When the meaning of today's satirical, political cartoons fades in a few short years, how can a modern reader be expected to correlate the seven seals in Revelation 6 with first-century emperors, as is done in a following chapter? The short answer is that a modern reader cannot be expected to know such things. The solution is to ask for help in reading the Bible.

We encounter many areas of knowledge in which our activity depends on assistance from an expert. We ask a computer specialist for assistance with a computer problem or when we have trouble understanding our new software. When we get sick, we ask a medical doctor to diagnose the problem and then tell us how to address it. When we want to remodel the kitchen or install new book shelves, we call an expert craftsman. We seek out a skilled mechanic to take care of our cars. This list of examples could be expanded greatly. In some cases, we may go beyond asking for help and actually apprentice ourselves, formally or informally, to such experts. Some people ask questions or read manuals and learn to work on their own cars. Others might study what it takes to do more advanced home repairs, or learn to handle some computer issues on their own. And this list could be expanded greatly.

Every Christian cannot be expected to have detailed knowledge of the Bible. Just as we ask assistance of experts in many areas of daily life, it should be expected that for understanding the Bible, we would seek assistance from experts who have spent years developing knowledge of that subject. It is also the case that we can learn from these experts and go on to do significant study on our own. The role of these biblical experts is to help us read the Bible, just as experts help us with computers or remodeling our homes or healing our bodies or caring for our cars. In some cases, these biblical experts teach us techniques and resources that will enable us to do additional Bible study on our own. The point here is that in daily life we depend on and learn from experts in many areas, and we can approach learning about the Bible and studying the Bible in the same way.

The Church's Book

The Bible is the church's book because it contains the story of the church's origins. Without it, we would know little about the first millennia of the story that began with Abraham. But the Bible is the church's book for another reason as well. We are called *Christ*ians. The Bible is by far the best source to the life, teaching, death, and resurrection of Jesus. We read the Bible because it contains the story of the one who defines the primary identity of Christians, namely Jesus Christ. The words of the Bible are important, but they are not the primary authority. The ultimate authority for Christians is the narrative of Jesus that is witnessed to by the words of the Bible.

With the story of Jesus in view as the key to understanding the Bible, it needs to be emphasized that this is *not* a "picking and choosing" of preferred texts, nor is it discarding a part of the Bible. Nothing is being omitted from the canon. In fact, we need the complete text, and we should not shy away from talking about all of it and reading all of it in church. Without the complete text of the Old Testament, we would not see the conversation about the character of God, which helps us to understand the significance of the story of Jesus. The contradictions and disagreements and unsavory elements of the story that led to Jesus point to the authenticity of the ancient text. No editor sanitized it. And only with this full, unexpurgated version in view do we see that there is an unfolding and developing understanding that comes to fruition in the nonviolent story of Jesus.

In the first century, Paul was understanding and bringing Jesus into his context. We who stand in the tradition of Jesus and Paul are engaged in the same task, namely reading the history in a way to continue today the task of bringing Jesus into our world as we continue the story of God's people. Performing this task is by no means a replacement of the biblical writings. Rather we are learning from them how changes were made in applying Jesus to their context, which then assists our efforts to bring Jesus into our world.

Revelation, the last book of the Bible, also deals with the way Jesus is understood in the world, both for the time in which it was written and for today. However, this book poses particular problems for interpretation, both in understanding its meaning and in showing that it too pictures a nonviolent God. The next three chapters deal with these problems.

15

Interpreting Revelation

PERHAPS NO PART OF the Bible has been interpreted in as many ways as Revelation, the last book of the Bible. Revelation is also one of the most important biblical texts to consider in the discussion of God, violence, and nonviolence. Many interpretations display a God who exercises great violence, and a Jesus who returns with a great sword of vengeance and judgment. Both these views are diametrically opposed to the understanding of Jesus and of the God revealed in Jesus that has been presented in our previous chapters. So Revelation merits an extended explanation, in this chapter and the following two.

Revelation contains picturesque imagery, some overwhelmingly beautiful, some hideous and grotesque: a beautiful pregnant woman, clothed with the sun and standing on the moon; God's angels fighting the devil's angels in a cosmic battle; an ugly, seven-headed dragon; four ferocious horsemen and seven famous seals; a city with streets paved in gold, each gate made out of a single, huge pearl, and much more. Some of this imagery has humorous dimensions—think of it being produced today as an animated movie with exaggerated features of beauty, and villains so ugly they bring chuckles. Other humorous scenes appear as well. This imagery has been subject to wild speculation and great diversity of suggestions for its meaning. This chapter will cut through this speculation and chaotic answers and provide an easy-to-understand, common-sense approach to understanding the meaning of these symbols in Revelation.

Perhaps the most common assumption—actually misconception—that occurs in interpreting the book of Revelation is that it predicts the future. More precisely, the assumption is that Revelation makes predictions of events that indicate that the return of Jesus is near. The book's images are then assumed to be clues to events happening now in our world, or that soon will happen in our world. And thus the interpreter claims to have discovered the link between the symbolic images and events occurring now or soon to occur in the world around us. Applying some common sense will unravel the seeming mystery of Revelation as well as the fallacy of making such predictions.[3]

A Book of Predictions?

It is obvious that the book of Revelation contains a great deal of symbolic language. Any reader will want to know the meaning of the symbols. Many people have believed that the symbols referred to events coming true in their own time. If images in Revelation do indeed refer to events coming to pass in our time, then Revelation predicts the future, a future very distant from the time in which it was written.

Scholars agree that Revelation was written late in the first Christian century or early in the second century. Here is a different kind of question to ask when thinking about how to interpret Revelation. In what newspaper would we look to find the events represented by the symbols? Would we go to a library and look in a newspaper published in Rome or in Jerusalem in the year 100 CE, or would we read a newspaper published today, such as the *New York Times*, or watch TV news reported by CNN? If Revelation is predicting things that are finally happening in our time, then we would read *The New York Times* or check CNN to find the events symbolized in Revelation.

But here is where common sense comes in. Think about it. Would a book written around the year 100 CE be talking about things we could read about in a newspaper today, nearly two thousand years later? If it were, think what that would mean. The supposed predictions in Revelation are frequently said to refer to the United Nations, whose headquarters is in New York City. But people in 100 CE did not know about the continent that we now call North America, where the United Nations is located. And in 100 CE there was no city of New York and no country of the United States and North America was unknown. Further, the United Nations consists of nations with fixed borders—governments change, but

---

3. Literature that has influenced my analysis of the book of Revelation in chapters 14, 15, and 16 includes Eller, *Most Revealing Book*; Boring, *Revelation*; Reddish, *Revelation*; and Howard-Brook and Gwyther, *Unveiling Empire*.

INTERPRETING REVELATION 165

borders remain, unless they are rearranged by a war. But this idea of the modern nation state is only two to three hundred years old. The idea of an organization composed of entities not yet known and located in a city that did not yet exist that was located on an unknown continent would have made no sense to people in 100 CE. And there is more. Think about our communication systems that now link the entire world electronically—email and Twitter and the Internet and Facebook and computers that organize all this media and store it in "the cloud." Then there is the international banking system and credit cards by which money is transferred around the world without paper currency or metal money ever changing hands. None of these things would make any sense at all to readers late in the first century.

We could go on with such examples from the modern world. These, however, are sufficient to show that common sense calls into question the idea that Revelation was predicting the distant future. An author writes to an audience, and expects the audience to be able to understand. But it would be impossible for readers at the end of the first century to understand these aspects of the modern world. First-century people would have no frame of reference for understanding any of these things, none of which will come into existence for nearly two millennia. If Revelation is predicting such things, it was entirely beyond comprehension for the readers for whom it was written. That it is making predictions violates the idea that a writer would expect readers to understand, and it turns Revelation into a meaningless piece of gibberish for its first readers.

At this point, some commentators have attempted to salvage a predictive approach by claiming that the author thought that he was writing to first-century readers, but that God was really using the author of Revelation to send a message to later readers, namely readers in the early twenty-first century. But reflect a moment on what that suggestion implies about God. It means that God is dishonest. It means that God would trick the writer of Revelation and manipulate him into writing something that he thought would be comprehensible to his readers, but would not be, because God was actually sending a message to readers two millennia in the future. Besides, this suggestion arrives again at the idea that even though Revelation was addressed to readers in the first century, it was using references incomprehensible to them, and was actually intended for an audience two millennia later.

Another aspect of common sense also leads to rejection of the idea that Revelation is a book of predictions. Within a century or two from the time the book was written, writers began using interpretations from Revelation in attempts to predict the time of the return of Jesus. These predictions have come regularly through the centuries, right down to the present time. Hal Lindsey's book *The Late Great Planet Earth*, published in 1970, contained one of the most famous of such recent predictions. In this book, Lindsey said that Jesus would return within forty years of 1948.[4] Another similar prediction that gained national attention around the same time was Edgar C. Whisenant's book *88 Reasons Why the Rapture Will Be in 1988*. A few years ago, Harold Camping gained national notoriety with predictions for the return of Jesus in 2011.

These examples represent only a few recent predictions. Such predictions have been popping up for centuries. There have been hundreds of such predictions. It is important to see this long history. It is a history of failure. Absolutely every one of these predictions through the centuries has been *wrong*.

A football coach who kept running the same play for no gain over and over again, unsuccessfully throughout many games and seasons, would not retain his job for long. Fans would be screaming for a new coach. The same kind of common sense applies to interpreting Revelation. Common sense indicates that this record of 100 percent failure for centuries shouts out that Revelation is not making predictions, and that another approach to Revelation is indicated.

A Common-Sense Approach

Common sense suggests that the 100 percent failure rate of predictions and the impossibility that early-century readers could understand references to twenty-first century institutions and events requires a different approach. This approach is rather obvious. Assume that the first readers could understand the symbolic references, which means that the references come from the time frame of the first readers. And assume that the message is directed first of all to these readers and not to readers two thousand years in the future. The meaning for modern readers will then be derived from the message intended for first-century readers.

Reading Revelation as though it spoke to its first readers ought not surprise. In fact, most literature with imaginary characterizations is read in this way. For example, recall Jonathan Swift's *Gulliver's Travels*, which featured Gulliver's sojourns with tiny people six inches tall and

---

4. Lindsey, *Late Great Planet Earth*, 43.

with giants who are seventy-two feet tall. No one suggests that because these small people and gigantic people have not been found, that means author Swift was predicting that one day they would appear or that he was making predictions about the distant future. Instead, common sense leads readers to relate the figures in the book to people and events in author Swift's time. Commentators recognize this work as satirical commentary on events and people in Swift's own time, and historians identify particular practices and kings to which he was referring.

Another example is Mark Twain's *Connecticut Yankee in King Arthur's Court*. In this novel, Twain transports a Connecticut engineer from his time back to sixth-century England and the court of King Arthur. The engineer introduces gun powder and other modern inventions and tries unsuccessfully to improve that society. No reader suggests that Twain was predicting anything about the distant future. This book is Twain's satirical critique of mythical notions of chivalry and his praise for American ingenuity.

I am not equating these novels with the book of Revelation, which has a much more profound message about the God who is made present in Jesus. However, just as common sense leads readers to find the references in these fanciful works in the frames of reference of authors Swift and Twain, the same approach leads us to look for the meaning of the symbols of Revelation in the time frame of Revelation's author and his first readers. The operative question is, "What could they have understood?" Or "Is a suggested interpretation comprehensible to first-century readers?"

Focusing the interpretation on what the first-century readers could understand does not render the book meaningless for today. Absolutely not. It is rather that we start to understand how the message applies to us by first understanding how it was relevant for its first readers. And from that we begin to understand Revelation's message for Christians today. As we shall see, Revelation has an extremely important message for twenty-first-century readers.

Reading Revelation

The Subject of Revelation

The first verse of Revelation is in fact the title of the book. It contains an important clue for understanding the subject of the entire writing. It reads:

> The revelation of Jesus Christ, which God gave him to show his servants what must soon take place; he made it known by sending his angel to his servant John, who testified to the word of God and to the testimony of Jesus Christ, even to all that he saw. (Rev 1:1)

This long sentence emphasizes that the focus of the book of Revelation is Jesus Christ. It follows a logical circle, beginning with a revelation about Jesus Christ, which came from God for the purpose of being shown to his followers. It was made known by sending an angel to John, the author of Revelation, who gave a testimony to the word of God, which is another way of referring to Jesus Christ, and then finally another reference to Jesus Christ, with which the long, winding sentence started. The book is being presented as a message about Jesus and from God, given via a writing by John.

Most obviously a message about Jesus would be within the frame of reference of the book's first readers. Since the message is about Jesus, we should expect to find a message that corresponds to the story of Jesus who rejected violence that is told in the Gospels. And since the message of Jesus comes from God, readers should expect to see images of the nonviolent God who is revealed in the nonviolent Jesus. This first verse of Revelation thus sets the stage for what readers should expect to find in the remainder of the book.

In the midst of this long, winding sentence is the phrase "what must soon take place." Some commentators accept this verse as the proof that Revelation predicts the future. If the author did intend this writing as a prediction of things soon to take place, that is, in his immediate lifetime, then his prediction was wrong, just as wrong as all following predictions have been. However, there is a better explanation for the phrase, "must soon take place."

Revelation does not predict the future. But as we shall see, the book does say something about the future. It says that the future belongs to the reign of God. The resurrection of Jesus has validated God as the ultimate power of the cosmos. Since the resurrection of Jesus, human history is occurring in the time between the resurrection and what theologians call the return of Jesus. The book of Revelation is talking about the significance of the resurrection of Jesus for understanding human history in this interim between the first and second appearances of Jesus. Resurrection uses fantastic imagery to say that in this interim the reign of God is already victorious over the evil in the world. God's time is infinitely long. Whatever the scope of God's infinite history, relatively speaking, the length of human history in the interim between the two appearances of Jesus is short. In terms of the symbolism of Revelation, the second appearance of Jesus will be "soon." "Soon" is thus a symbolic way to compare the time of human history to the time of God's history.

A sports analogy can help to explain Revelation's way of talking about the future but without making predictions. Recall the football game in which the Pittsburgh Steelers scored seventeen points in forty-eight seconds at the end of the first half, which determined the outcome of the game. Even though there was still a half to play, the play-by-play announcer on TV proclaimed the game decided. Or for another example, think of the Brazil-Germany soccer match in the semi-finals of the 2014 World Cup. Germany scored one goal early in the match and then midway through the first half added four more goals in a space of six minutes, for a 5–0 lead. Since match scores at this level of soccer are routinely 1–0 or 2–1, a score of five goals was unprecedented. TV commentators called it embarrassing and humiliating for Brazil, and assured viewers that it would be impossible for Brazil to come back from such a deficit. The final score was 7–1. In effect, the outcome was decided in those six minutes and the outcome of the game was known already midway through the first half.

Declarations about who will win in such games are not predictions. They are statements of reality, based on recognized facts about the conduct of football games and soccer matches. Time remains on the game clocks, and interesting things as well as injuries can happen in that interim before the game concludes. Nonetheless, for those who have an understanding of how games are played out, the outcomes are already known. The resurrection of Jesus is analogous to these big leads going into the second half of the football game or the remaining three-fourths of the soccer match. For those with faith to perceive it, the resurrection is the evidence that the outcome of history has already been determined. It belongs to the reign of God. Interesting things can occur with Jesus' followers in the interim until history ends. Some Christians will likely suffer, but nonetheless the outcome of history has been determined by the resurrection of Jesus. This is not a prediction of the future. It is a statement based on understanding the meaning of the resurrection of Jesus in the unfolding of God's history.

The First Readers of Revelation

The first readers of Revelation are addressed in chapters 2 and 3. They are people who belonged to the churches in the cities of Ephesus, Smyrna, Pergamum, Thyatira, Sardis, Philadelphia, and Laodicea. These cities were located in Asia Minor, in what was then a province of the Roman Empire. Today the cities, or the remnants of the cities, are located in the country of Turkey. Some of the cities are still populated, perhaps with different names. Others are marked by ruins in or near today's cities.

Pointing to these cities and the churches located in them underscores the fact that Revelation was written to be read by real people living late in the first or early in the second Christian century. These readers were Christians in cities of the Roman empire. The expectation by the author was that these people would understand the writing, and that it would have a message relevant to their situation in the empire. Seeing that Revelation was directed at seven churches in the Asian peninsula is yet one more indication that the book was not written to predict events two millennia in the future.

Conclusion

This chapter put forward what I called a common-sense approach to Revelation. This approach assumes that the author expected his readers to understand and thus the symbols used would refer to events and institutions within the frame of reference of the first readers in the late first century. A first indication of that approach appeared when we noted Revelation's first verse. It says that the book contains a message about Jesus. Thus, readers of Revelation today should expect to find a message that corresponds to the view of Jesus that is found in the Gospels.

We are now ready to apply the common-sense methodology to some important texts in Revelation. Revelation was written at the end of the first Christian century. The next chapter examines images from Revelation that reflect on the experience of the church between the time of Jesus and the date of the writing of Revelation.

16

Looking at the Past in Revelation

REVELATION DOES NOT PREDICT events in the distant future. However, some of its most well-known sets of symbols actually deal with events in the recent history of the time in which the book was written. I begin with perhaps the most well-known of all images in Revelation, the scene set in the heavenly throne room, where the Lamb opens the seven seals and the fierce and renowned four horsemen appear.

The Heavenly Throne Room

The meaning of the seven seals is as widely debated as any text in the entire book. The text of the seals in the sixth chapter belongs to a larger block of material that begins in Revelation 4 and includes the first verses of the eighth chapter. Applying the common sense described in the previous chapter will assist greatly in understanding the text.

Chapters 4 and 5 of Revelation convey a message that we already saw when reading the story of Jesus in the Gospels. In the narrative, God's resurrection of Jesus provided the ultimate testimony that God was in the story of Jesus, that Jesus' story was God's story. Now, in these chapters of Revelation, this same identification of Jesus' story with God's story is conveyed through a set of splendid and colorful images.

Revelation 4 presents the author's image of the heavenly throne room from which the universe is ruled. The ancient Hebrews were reluctant to mention the name of God. The "one seated on the throne" is a euphemism for God, ruler of the universe. The setting of the throne is described in images befitting the ruler of the universe. Red colors of precious stones—"like jasper and carnelian"—identify the one seated on the throne, and the colors of the rainbow surround the throne. Twenty-four elders dressed in white and wearing gold crowns stand around the throne, while flashes of lightning and peals of thunder issue from it. Seven torches burn in front of the throne, which are said to be the seven spirits of God. The number seven has divine significance throughout Revelation. A crystal-like sea of glass stands in front of the throne.

At the four corners of the throne stand an honor guard of "living creatures"—a lion, an ox, one with a human face, and an eagle. But these are strange living creatures—each has six wings, and they are covered with eyes. These four living creatures sing continually to God, "who was and is and is to come." That is, they sing to the God whose time encompasses all time. This scene in the throne room concludes with a musical salute by the four living creatures and the twenty-four elders who sing:

> You are worthy, our Lord and God,
> to receive glory and honor and power,
> for you created all things,
> and by your will they existed and were created
> (Rev 4:11).

Notice this language. It will be repeated a few verses later to include Jesus as well as God, the one seated on the throne.

Chapter 5 opens with a statement that there is a scroll in the right hand of the one seated on the throne, that is, in God's right hand. This scroll has seven seals. The fact that it is sealed identifies it as a scroll containing a secret or hidden message. Presentation of a secret message obviously arouses curiosity. That curiosity is displayed in the reaction of the narrator of the vision. When the voice proclaims that "No one in heaven or on earth or under the earth" is able to open the scroll and reveal the hidden message, the narrator's disappointment is great. He is said to "weep bitterly." Chuckle at this super tantrum of bitter weeping.

In passing, notice the description of an ancient, three-tiered universe—heavens above, the earth, and the underworld. It is far removed from our current understanding of the cosmos, which features an unfathomably large universe, which is still expanding at a speed virtually impossible to imagine. This image of an ancient view of the universe is a further indication of the social location of the first readers, for whom the three-tiered worldview was their reality, their unquestioned given.

But even as the narrator weeps his disappointment, one of the elders calms him with the words, "The lion of the tribe of Judah, the root of David, has conquered," and therefore has won the right to open the seals and thus reveal the message of the scroll. After the seeming tantrum, readers can almost hear the narrator heaving a big sigh of relief, "Whew!"

Then the narrator spies something between the throne and the honor guard of four living creatures and among the twenty-four elders. It is a Lamb that looks like "it had been slaughtered." But there is something unusual, even grotesque, about the Lamb. It has seven eyes and seven horns. And although the voice had said that the Lion of Judah would open the scroll, it is this strange-looking Lamb that trots over and takes the scroll from God's right hand.

As soon as the Lamb touches the scroll, glorious music breaks out. The four living creatures and the twenty-four elders, each holding a harp and golden bowls of incense, fall down before the Lamb. Chuckle again when considering the contortions the elders must perform as they fall down to honor to the Lamb while holding both a harp and a bowl of incense, and then bursting into song. They sing,

> You are worthy to take the scroll
> and to open its seals,
> for you were slaughtered and by your blood you ransomed for God
> saints from every tribe and language and people and nation.

And then the elders and creatures are joined by a huge multitude of angels. The text says myriads of myriads and thousands of thousands. A myriad is ten thousand. Today we would probably say millions and millions of angels. This huge throng sings again that the Lamb is worthy because he was slaughtered. And then this heavenly throng of creatures, elders, and angels is joined by "every creature in heaven and on earth and under the earth and in the sea" in what becomes an unimaginably large choir. This choir sings:

> To the one seated on the throne
> and to the Lamb
> be blessing and honor and glory and might
> forever and ever.

And finally the four living creatures end the song with a loud "Amen" and the elders worship. And then in verse 1 of chapter 6, the Lamb opens the first seal.

This scene of overwhelming scope and fantastic beauty leaves a reader breathless. We need to pause a bit to recover, and to develop a sense of the meaning of this text. First, consider the figure of the Lamb. It is obviously alive but has marks of slaughter. The Lamb is a symbol of Jesus, the sacrificial Lamb. Since this Lamb is alive but displays wounds, it is quite clearly an image of resurrected Jesus. The meaning to be derived from this image thus comes from Jesus after his resurrection.

This Lamb seemed disfigured—seven horns and seven eyes. Now recall the seven torches that are the seven spirits of God from chapter 4. Since seven is a number associated with God, the seven eyes and seven horns identify the Lamb—Jesus—with God. But further identification follows of resurrected Jesus the Lamb with God. In particular, note the last stanza of the song. The one seated on the throne, that is God, and the Lamb—resurrected Jesus—are celebrated equally by the unfathomably large choir as recipients of "blessing and honor and glory and might forever and ever."

Finally, there is yet one more image of equality between Lamb and God. After no one was found who could open the scroll in God's right hand, now the Lamb—the resurrected Jesus who is identified with God—can and does open the scroll. This is one last identification of the Lamb with God. It tells readers, if you want to know about God, look at Jesus, whom God has raised from the dead. And that, readers will recall, was the meaning of Jesus developed in the earlier chapters of the book in hand.

One important discussion remains for Revelation 5. What happened to the Lion of Judah, a title for the Messiah that was expected to come from the Israelite tribe of Judah as a descendant of King David? The elder had promised that the lion would be able to open the seven seals. The appearance of the Lamb and the huge choir leads readers almost to overlook the lion. But the lion is important. The lion is a symbol of power and of conquering. The Lamb opens the seals on the scroll, but the elder said that the lion would perform that function. In effect, the lion is opening the seals. The lion is also a symbol of the resurrected Jesus. The lion image is that of power and conquering, while the image of resurrected Lamb symbolizes the way that conquering occurred. Conquering was through the death and resurrection of Jesus. Symbols of lion and lamb together make that point.

Recall that in interpreting Revelation, the first readers need to be able to understand. With the meaning of the symbols in Revelation 4 and

5 focused thus far on the resurrected Jesus, most obviously first readers could understand the book. And since the focus is on Jesus, that accords with the opening verse of Revelation, which stated that the book concerned a message from God about Jesus the Word. When the Lamb, an image of resurrected Jesus, proceeds to open the seals, it is a clear indication that one learns about God through Jesus. Now, on to the opening of the seven seals, with these principles of interpretation in mind.

The Seven Seals

It will become apparent that the seven seals present a symbolic look back at a historical sequence between Jesus' time and the epoch when Revelation was written. We will follow the opening of the first four seals and then take stock.

The Lamb opened the first seal, one of the four living creatures yelled out "Come," and a figure appeared riding a white horse. The important identifier for this rider is the language of "conquering and to conquer," which indicates a failed effort at conquering. The second seal was opened, another loud "Come," and a rider appeared on a blood-red horse. This rider had a great sword, and he was allowed to take peace from earth. The third seal follows the pattern, a voice yells "come," and a rider emerges. This third rider sat astride a black horse. He carried a set of scales, while a voice in the background gave the price of grain—a day's pay for a quart of wheat or three quarts of barley, while the price of olive oil and wine remained unchanged. Note that this cost of grain makes a loaf of bread very expensive—a whole day's wages for enough grain to make small loaf of fine bread or a slightly larger loaf of more coarse bread. Such price gouging happens in time of scarcity as during a famine. After the fourth call of "come," a sickly green horse appeared with two riders. This double ugly pair are named Death and Hades. They have authority over a quarter of the earth and kill with swords, famine, disease, and wild animals.

Many efforts have been made to link these four riders to epochs of world history. But recall the principle that the first readers need to be able to understand the symbols. If the contents of the seals are linked to world history centuries and even millennia in the future, the meaning of the seals is beyond the comprehension of the original readers in the cities of Asia Minor.

I believe that the seals represent something well within the understanding of the first readers. The seals represent, I suggest, the series of emperors from the time Jesus was crucified to the epoch in which the book was written. In other words, far from being predictions, the parade of seals is actually a symbolic look back at history since the time of Jesus. The content of each seal contains a symbolic reference to something of significance during the reign of that emperor. Following this suggestion, the first seal represents Tiberius, emperor 14–37 CE. The important symbol here is the statement that "he came out conquering and to conquer." This language indicates a failed effort. I think that this failed effort refers to the crucifixion and resurrection of Jesus, which happened during the reign of Tiberius. The effort to remove Jesus by killing him obviously failed when he was resurrected from the dead. The symbols become clearer as the seals advance.

Seal two corresponds to Caligula, emperor 37–41 CE. Caligula commissioned a statue of himself in the form of the god Zeus and authorized an army commanded by Petronius to invade Jerusalem and install the statue on the alter in the temple. The blood-red horse of the second rider and his ability to remove peace from the earth correspond to this threat to Jerusalem. However, the invasion of Jerusalem did not happen. When the army reached north Palestine, people came out from the city and lay on the ground in front of the horses and stalled the advance of the army. They begged for the invasion to halt and Petronius sent a messenger to ask Caligula's permission to halt the army. Caligula ordered the messenger to return, and kill Petronius and then continue the invasion. But Caligula died before this order could be carried out, and the invasion did not happen.

The scales in seal three and the high price of grain refer to famine. Acts 11:28–29 mentions famine that occurred in the region of Antioch (in today's Syria) during the reign of emperor Claudius and the efforts of Christians in Jerusalem to send famine relief. Acts thus provides a cross-reference to the symbols of famine in the third seal and to Claudius, who ruled 41–54 CE. He was the next emperor in line after Caligula.

The fourth emperor in the succession was Nero, who ruled 54–68 CE. Nero's cruelty is legendary. He impaled people on stakes, covered them with tar, and set them on fire along the big road into Rome. He burned the city of Rome and blamed it on Christians. Knowledge of this fire continues today. Some years ago, a commercial played on the radio for chewing gum that claimed long-lasting flavor. Violin music was heard, supposedly produced by Nero who played the violin. Nero was called to deal with the fire, but the music continued unabated. A voice intoned, "He's not talking while the flavor lasts." A second voice replied, "All Rome could burn by then." Nero enjoyed the games in the arena, in which Christians and other undesirables were thrown to the lions. The cruelty of Nero merits representing him with the double ugly riders on the sickly green horse of seal four.

By this time, readers can observe that the symbols fit well with the sequence of emperors. With seal five comes a shift in scene, namely from earth to heaven. The image that now appears is an altar in heaven, with the souls of martyrs trapped under the altar. These martyrs suffered death because of their loyalty to the word of God. The location of this altar must be near the throne because they call out to God, "with a loud voice," that is, a bit angrily, asking how long it will be before God avenges their killers. In this scene, God does not respond directly, but their cries are heard. However, the response seems cavalier, even humorous. In response to the angry pleas, they are given a white robe and told to just cool down and be patient because very soon more martyrs would be killed to join them. This image calls attention to the ongoing possibility of martyrdom from the emperors and empire that opposes Christians.

This scene shifts with seal five corresponding to a break in the sequence of emperors. Following Nero, in 68 and 69 CE three men—Galba, Otho, and Vitellius—claimed the imperial crown. None survived assaults on his authority long enough to consolidate power.

Seal six is renowned for its images of celestial chaos—the sun turning black, the moon becoming blood red, stars scattering like figs falling in a strong wind, even the sky vanishing—and earthly pandemonium—a huge earthquake moved mountains and islands, civil order disappeared as kings, commoners, and slaves all run panicked through the streets looking for places to hide. Those who see Revelation as a book of predictions usually offer this image as a prediction of the chaos at the end of time. But that it is not. In fact, the sixth seal has a mundane reference point, mundane meaning down-to-earth and located in the real world.

Vespasian, who ousted Vitellius, ruled as emperor from 69 to 79 CE. In 70 CE, in response to an uprising against the Roman occupiers, the army of emperor Vespasian, commanded by his son Titus, invaded Jerusalem. This army destroyed the temple and sacked the city. Virtually no stone was left standing on another. Not surprisingly, the destruction devastated the local inhabitants. The world that they knew was destroyed.

It was as though the sky had fallen on them. The scenes of celestial chaos and earthly pandemonium in seal six reflect the feelings and experiences of the Jews in Jerusalem as they faced the destruction produced by the army of Vespasian. Seal six symbolizes the pandemonium that resulted from the destruction of Jerusalem.

At this juncture in reading Revelation, an important point is often missed. Seal seven is not opened until the beginning of Revelation 8. The depiction of celestial and earthly chaos is only the first scene of seal six. The entirety of Revelation 7 also belongs to seal six. The climax of the message of the seals comes in the second scene of seal six.

The second scene of seal six has two vignettes. One is the famed 144,000 who have been marked with the seal of God on their foreheads. This 144,000 is made up of twelve thousand from each of the tribes of Israel. The book of Revelation contains many symbols. Numbers no less than other images are symbols. 144,000 is not meant to be taken as an exact number, one more than 143,999. It is a symbolic number whose meaning the original readers could understand and that we can understand.

The number one thousand was one of the biggest numbers available to the original readers of Revelation. It should be understood in the sense of "very large number," used in the same way that a person in our time who feels very busy might say, "I have a million things to do today." Then, there were twelve tribes of the children of Israel. Twelve becomes a "God number," a number linked to God's people. Jesus expressed continuity with Israel by choosing twelve disciples. Multiply twelve by itself and the answer is 144. Multiply that answer by one thousand and the answer is 144,000. This figure is a highly symbolic number that identifies God's people with the children of Israel. Using the idea of twelve times twelve and then multiplying by "very large number" produces a highly symbolic way to say that the number of God's people is huge.

Seeing this huge number used to identify God's people leads to the second vignette of the second scene of seal six. Here appears another huge multitude, all robed in white and so large that "no one could count." This multitude consists of people from ethnic groups and speaking languages from all around the world. This huge throng is singing, "Salvation belongs to our God who is seated on the throne, and to the Lamb." This song, like the song from the heavenly throne room, expresses the equality of God and Jesus, the resurrected Lamb. Then the reader learns that this white-robed multitude consists of martyrs, those who have come out of "the great ordeal." This could be a reference to martyrdom generally. But it makes sense to see "the great ordeal" as the destruction of Jerusalem and by extension the havoc produced on Christians by emperors such as Nero. This vignette then ends with another song sung by these throngs, as they worship God and the Lamb and are guided by them.

Let's bring these two images together. There are two huge, heavenly throngs. When we understand the symbolic nature of 144,000, it becomes clear that these throngs are actually pictured as identical in size, both too large to measure. Both throngs constitute the people of God. One image emphasizes that God's people are in continuity with the Children of Israel. The other image witnesses to the fact that gentiles, people from all other ethnic groups, are also joined to God's people. These two huge throngs are then given songs that express their loyalty and their worship of God and of the Lamb—resurrected Jesus—in equal measure. And these two vignettes of the throngs celebrating and worshipping God and the Lamb are juxtaposed with the scene that symbolizes the destruction of Jerusalem.

The message to first-century readers is clear. As horrible as the destruction of Jerusalem might be, it pales in significance alongside the victory of the reign of God in the resurrection of Jesus. When one has eyes on the resurrected Jesus, one knows that even death does not separate a believer from the reign of God. Emperors such as Nero and Vespasian can kill the body and destroy the holy city of Jerusalem, but in the grand scheme of things the reign of God triumphs in the resurrection of Jesus.

It is this message about the meaning of the resurrection of Jesus in the face of recent events that the author of Revelation directed to his first readers. It was an important message. Historians tell us that at the end of the first century, when the book was likely written, the Christians in Asia Minor were not experiencing persecution. They were becoming comfortable with the emperor, and were wanting to participate in the yearly festivals that honored and pledged loyalty to the emperors. Since the emperors were beginning to make claims about being gods on earth, and were demanding ultimate loyalty, participating in the loyalty ceremonies would pose a conflict for Christians, who professed ultimate loyalty to Jesus Christ. With this message about the gloriousness of the reign of God and the reminder of past destruction produced by emperors, the author of Revelation is warning his readers not to be deceived by a seemingly benevolent emperor, and to remember that their first loyalty is to God and to the resurrected Jesus. And that message applies to Christians in North America two thousand years later as well. More on that point later.

This message about the triumph of the reign of God through resurrection corresponds to the meaning of resurrection derived from the narrative of Jesus which we saw in chapter 1. And most clearly, the God visible in the image of the seven seals is the God who conquers, not with violence, but by restoring life. The God visible in these texts is the nonviolent God revealed by the narrative of Jesus. And with that observation, it is coming into focus that the message about Jesus in Revelation is another version of the message from the Gospels. With the first verse of Revelation in view, it ought not surprise that Revelation's message parallels that of the narrative contained in the Gospels.

At the beginning of Revelation 8 the Lamb opened the seventh seal, and there was silence for half an hour. Then begins another cycle of sevens. Since the sequence stops here, it indicates the likely epoch when Revelation was written. Titus, Vespasian's son, ruled as emperor for two short years, 79–81 CE. He was followed by Domitian, who ruled from 81–96 CE. Revelation was likely written during the reign of Domitian, at the end of the first Christian century.

War in Heaven

The symbols in Revelation 12 provide a different look at the same historical epoch covered by the seven seals. In this chapter one finds the image of a woman, beautifully clothed with the sun, standing on the moon, and wearing a crown of twelve stars. She is pregnant and in anguish from labor pains. A huge, red dragon stands waiting to snatch the baby. The dragon is grotesque, with seven heads and ten horns and seven diadems or crowns on the seven heads. The dragon prepares to devour the baby, who is destined to rule all the nations. But as the baby is born, the dragon fails to catch the baby, and it is snatched up to heaven and the throne of God, while the woman flees to a place of safety in the wilderness. Her stay is put at 1,260 days, which is three-and-a-half years.

Meanwhile, the dragon pursued the baby to heaven, where war broke out between God's angels led by Michael, God's head angel, against the dragon and his angels. Here the dragon is called the devil and Satan. He is defeated and with his angels is thrown down to earth. At the defeat of the dragon, a voice from heaven proclaims,

> Now have come the salvation and the power
> and the kingdom of our God
> and the authority of his Messiah,
> for the accuser of our comrades has been thrown down,
> who accuses them day and night before our God.

The voice stated that the means of defeating the dragon were "the blood of the Lamb" and the testimony of the martyrs. Finally, the heavenly voice issued a warning to the earth and sea because the "devil has come down to you with great wrath, because he knows that his time is short." The following scene pictures the dragon pursuing the woman, who escapes into the wilderness with the wings of a great eagle. When the dragon pours water from his mouth to drown the woman, the earth helps by absorbing the water. Finally, unable to capture the woman, the dragon goes off to make war on the rest of her children, "those who keep the commands of God and hold the testimony of Jesus."

Again, a common-sense approach displays the meaning of this text as a message that the first readers could understand. In fact, the message of this set of symbols is parallel to the message from the text of the seven seals.

The key questions are the identity of the woman and the baby and the dragon. It seems clear that the baby snatched up to heaven is a symbol of the resurrected Jesus. The woman must then be Mary, the mother of Jesus. But the symbol represents much more as well. She has a crown of twelve stars, the number that recalls the Children of Israel. Thus the woman in this scene also represents the Israelites, the people of God from whom Jesus was descended. The continuing presence of the woman in the scene also identifies her with those who accept Jesus as Messiah. Thus the woman is also a figure of the church, and the pursuit of the woman by the dragon makes her a symbol of the persecuted church.

Just a bit more thinking is required to identify the dragon. First of all, note that the text actually names the dragon as the devil and Satan. But the numbers attached to the dragon are there for a reason. These numbers give the dragon another identity as well. He has seven heads, seven crowns on the heads, and ten horns. Rome is said to be the city built on seven hills, which correspond to the dragon's seven heads. Review the number of emperors from the vignette of the seven seals. There are seven: Tiberius, Caligula, Claudius, Nero, Vespasian, Titus, and Domitian. These seven would correspond to the seven crowns on the dragon's seven heads. Adding the three short-lived emperors—Galba,

Otho, and Vitellius—to the other seven arrives at the number ten, for the ten horns. This interpretation of the numbers arrives at the conclusion, easily comprehensible to the first readers in Asia Minor, that the dragon is a symbol of the Roman empire. The dragon is depicted as ugly, so ugly that readers should be laughing at the image, which is also identified with the devil and Satan.

This scene of woman, baby, and dragon is another representation of the followers of Jesus—the church—as the earthly representative of the reign of God as it confronts the Roman empire, depicted as a representative of Satan. In this confrontation, the reign of God has already triumphed. That the triumph has already occurred is evident in the message of the heavenly voice that follows the defeat of the dragon. Note the emphasis when the heavenly voice booms out, "*Now* have come the salvation and the power . . . of our God, and the authority of his Messiah." With the "now," it is clear that the decisive event in all of history has already occurred. It is the resurrection of Jesus, which has once and for all overcome the worst that the empire, the earthly representatives of Satan, can accomplish, namely to annihilate a person's existence by killing. This "battle" between the forces of Michael and the dragon is not really a battle with military weapons as battles are usually understood. The author used battle imagery to describe the confrontation of church and reign of God verses Satan and rule of evil personified by Rome. The decisive event in this confrontation is the resurrection of Jesus. This is another depiction of the nonviolent God who conquers, not with greater violence, but by restoring life where it had ceased to exist.

The dragon has been defeated. The defeated dragon is nonetheless still dangerous, which is symbolized by the dragon's pursuit of the woman and her children. The escape of the woman into the wilderness and the earth's swallowing of the river symbolize the fact that the dragon is still dangerous, but that the reign of God has ultimate power and in the end, even if Christians are killed, the reign of God has triumphed. The number of years the woman is to spend in the wilderness—three-and-a-half—is another symbol of the defeat of the dragon by the resurrection. Seven is a divine number. Half of seven is three and a half, a way of using time symbols to say that ultimately in God's time, evil is limited and defeated.

This understanding of the scene of woman, baby, and dragon uses a different set of symbols to convey the same message as the text of the seven seals. In each of these sets of images, the church as representative of the reign of God confronts the might of the Roman Empire. Emperors and empire can do damage to the people of God. But when Christians have their eyes on the resurrected Jesus, they know that ultimately the reign of God has conquered and God is the ultimate power in the universe. This message has nothing to do with predictions of events happening two thousand years after Revelation was written. This message has everything to do with warning the first readers in Asia Minor to remember the true character of empire as revealed in recent history.

Meanwhile, images in the next chapter of Revelation lend themselves to applying this message about the character of empire and victory in the resurrection to the church today.

17

Looking Ahead in Revelation?

As already noted, a frequent assumption is that some images of Revelation are predictions of events that signal the return of Jesus and the end of the world. This chapter examines several of these images. We will see that these images may have an application for today or say something about God's future, but in no way are they making predictions about coming events.

The Unholy Threesome

One of the supposed predictions concerns the appearance of the Anti-Christ. This figure is connected to a beast pictured in Revelation 13. A common-sense reading will bring this image into focus in the real world while showing why it is not making a prediction. And again the nonviolent Jesus and nonviolent God will be apparent.

In the last verse of Revelation 12, the dragon, which we now recognize as a symbol of the Roman empire, established itself on the sand of the seashore. Nearby a beast rose out of the sea. The dragon gave this beast its power and his throne and great authority. Like the dragon, this beast also has multiple heads and ten horns with crowns. This beast had characteristics of a leopard with the feet of a bear and the mouth of a lion. One of its heads had what seemed like a fatal wound that had healed. People were in awe of this beast; they worshipped it and considered it unstoppable. This beast was given the authority for forty-two months (three-and-a-half years) to make war on the saints.

Then a second beast rose out of the earth. This beast had two horns like a lamb, but its voice sounded like the dragon. This beast exercised all the authority of the first beast, and led people to worship the first beast. This second beast orders every person, "both small and great, both rich and poor, both free and slave" to have a mark, the famous "mark of the beast." Those without this mark cannot participate in commerce, that is, buy and sell goods. The mark of this beast is a number, namely 666.

As we have seen, the dragon is a parody of the Roman Empire. With the first beast's multiple heads and ten crowns, it closely resembles the dragon. As a counterpart to Revelation's linking of God and the resurrected Jesus, the dragon and first beast together constitute an evil parody of God and Jesus Christ. Christians worship God and the resurrected Jesus. Worshipping the dragon and the beast then parodies the growing cult of emperor worship, and makes clear that Christians are confronted with a clear choice—worship either the emperor or Jesus Christ, but not both.

The head with the healed wound refers to the myth of Nero. According to the legend, Nero was so evil that he would return from the underworld to continue to cause destruction. The likely meaning here is not that Nero has come back, but that the current emperor, in this case Domitian, has the potential to behave like another Nero.

The second beast, with horns like a lamb but speaking with the voice of the dragon, is another parody of Jesus Christ. The role of this beast is to influence people to worship the first beast and the dragon, that is the empire and its emperors. The mark of the beast, which is the key to participation in commerce, may well be possession of the certificate of loyalty to the emperor that citizens could acquire each year at a loyalty ceremony. But in any case, both Christians and others have an identifying mark. But the mark is not something like a brand or tattoo. It is rather that people are marked by their conduct; their actions portray where their loyalties lie. Their loyalty, whether serving Jesus Christ or the emperor, is truly a mark of identity. Those whose lives display loyalty to the emperor are marked by the beast.

These parodies of Jesus Christ have produced the idea of an "Anti-Christ." Those who see Revelation as a series of predictions believe that these parodies of Jesus Christ, and particularly the second beast, with horns like a lamb, are predictions of a particular historical person, an "Anti-Christ," who will arise in the future and cause great destruction. Countless efforts have been made to identify this Anti-Christ, with the answer usually linked to a current, highly visible personality who is a popular target of public hatred. At one time or another, answers have included various popes, kings of England, figures like Adolf Hitler and Osama bin Laden, and most presidents of the United States. But the images of beasts in Revelation 13 are not predictions. They are parodies of Jesus, and simply portray Roman emperors with traits that are the opposite of Jesus Christ. They are warnings not to be lulled into worship of emperor alongside Jesus and the God of Jesus. Early readers would have recognized this approach easily the way modern readers recognize the meanings in editorial cartoons of donkeys and elephants and bears and bulls and likenesses of current politicians. And in the comparison of Jesus and the God of Jesus with emperors and empire, the nonviolent characteristic of Jesus and of God is self-evident.

The figures of dragon and two beasts constitute an additional parody of a related kind. There is the powerful dragon, the first beast who looks like the dragon and has the power of the dragon, and the second beast who leads people to worship the first beast and the dragon. The dragon as Satan, together with the first and second beasts, constitute an ironic, evil threesome over against God, who is revealed and made known by Jesus Christ and the Holy Spirit, who is immediately present and leads believers to worship Jesus Christ and God. In a number of instances in Revelation we have already seen this parallel worship of God and the Lamb.

The second beast's mark is said to consist of a number. The primary principle for deciding who the number refers to is that it has to be an answer that the first readers could have understood. In the ancient world, letters had numerical values. Various schemes have been proposed that would identify the number with an ancient emperor. While scholars cannot be absolutely sure of the original author's answer, it is likely that the number would identify Nero.

The images of dragon and two beasts constitute yet one more warning not to be deceived about the character of the empire and emperors that may appear benevolent for a time. That message applies equally to our contemporary time. It may be a particularly appropriate warning for Christians in the United States, which proclaims itself loudly as a Christian nation and which has the unofficial but very real expectation that the president will be a professed Christian. The president as professed Christian, who prays in the White House before announcing that he has declared war with the blessing of God, seems to be functioning as one who has two horns like the lamb but speaks with the voice of the dragon.

That is, the leader of the United States, with full approval of a majority of the population, claims to be a follower of Jesus Christ, but leads the nation in waging war, which is counter to the example visible in the narrative of Jesus and counter to the character of the God who is revealed in Jesus.

Let me be very clear here. I am not calling any one person the Anti-Christ, and Revelation is not making a predication about a particular historical person who will be revealed as *the* Anti-Christ. What I am suggesting is that we should examine the actions of presidents and other leaders of our self-proclaimed Christian nation in light of the language in Revelation about speaking like Jesus the Lamb but acting counter to his teaching and example.

The Rider on the White Horse

An image frequently appealed to in support of a God who exercises violence is the rider on the white horse in Revelation 19. This rider has a sharp sword coming out of his mouth. With this sword he will "strike down the nations, and he will rule them with a rod of iron; he will tread the wine press of the fury of the wrath of God the Almighty." The name of the rider is inscribed on his robe and on his thigh, "King of kings and Lord of lords." The beast and all the kings of the earth line up to make war on the rider on the white horse. But the beast and his false prophet are captured and thrown into the lake of fire, and all the rest are killed by the sword that comes out of the rider's mouth. It is claimed that the image pictures Jesus, as he returns at the end of the world to administer great, final, violent judgment on evil doers. But I believe the image has a quite different meaning.

The rider is quite obviously an image of Jesus—his name is Word of God. He is also called King of kings and Lord of lords, an identification for the resurrected Jesus that appears in 1 Timothy 6:15 as well as the designation of the Lamb in Revelation 17:14. The rider is also an image of resurrected Jesus, since he is alive but his robe is blood-stained. Since no battle has occurred, it must be his own blood, a symbol of his crucifixion.

Most obviously this depiction of Jesus uses violent imagery. This imagery is frequently invoked to make the argument that in final judgment, God is violent and that Jesus returns as conqueror who will use great violence against his enemies. The imagery of battle does indeed depict a confrontation, but the image of Jesus depicts a nonviolent conquering that is consistent with the nonviolent confrontation observed in earlier texts of Revelation.

Consider the sword. It comes from the rider's mouth, which indicates that the sword symbolizes words. It is an image of the Word of God. Ephesians 6:17 and Hebrews 4:2 are two other texts that depict the word of God as a sword. With the idea in mind that the sword is an image of the word of God, note how the armies of the kings of the earth are dealt with. They are "killed by the sword of the rider on the horse." In other words, they are overcome by the Word of God. There is no actual battle. The so-called battle has already occurred, as evidenced by the blood—his own blood—on his robe. The battle was won by the resurrection of Jesus, and the word of God declares that victory. Although using the language of war, it is actually another image of nonviolent victory through the resurrection.

This graphic, even macabre, imagery of the beast and false prophet being thrown into a lake of fire, and of birds gorging themselves on the flesh of the kings and their horses, arrives at the same message that we have seen earlier. We saw victory symbolized with the great multitudes worshipping and praising God and the Lamb in seal six, and in the victory of the angel Michael and his forces over the dragon and his angels. Now this victory is visibly pictured in terms of the word of God—depicted as a sword—that disarms all the forces of the world. The power of these forces is demonstrated to be limited, little more than decaying flesh, in light of the God who has raised Jesus from the dead. For those with the eyes to see and a mind to understand, the rider on the white horse uses graphic imagery to convey the same image of nonviolent Jesus and the nonviolent God revealed in Jesus that is present in the narrative of Jesus from the Gospels as well as other earlier parts of Revelation.

A Future Millennium?

The description of a thousand-year reign of Christ on earth, the renowned millennium, appears in Revelation 20. It is another image often treated as a prediction of a future event. Much ink has been spilled debating about the character of this millennium and when it will appear. But I suggest a simple, common-sense interpretation of this millennium, based on our previous observations about the book of Revelation.

Recall that one thousand is a symbolic number, understood in the sense of "really large number," as today we might say millions or billions. In Revelation 20, this "really large number" of years covers all the time between the resurrection of Jesus and the final consummation of the reign of God that is associated with the second coming of resurrected Jesus. In previous texts—the seven seals, the woman and the dragon, the rider on the white horse—we have seen that from the perspective of the reign of God, the evil symbolized by the destruction wreaked by the Romans has already been defeated by the resurrection of Jesus. Now, the defeat of Satan by the resurrection is symbolized by the binding of Satan for one thousand years, that is, for a "really long time." In other words, the image says that even though evil is still around—symbolized earlier by the marauding of the already defeated dragon—Christians should rest assured that the resurrection of Jesus signals the ultimate defeat of evil by the reign of God. This image of a millennium is thus an image that uses a time symbol to convey the same message that was pictured earlier with the seven seals, the defeat of the dragon in heavenly battle, and defeat of all the kings of the earth by the sword from the mouth of the rider on the white horse. By having Satan bound for one thousand years—a really long time—the message is that even though history continues and evil still abounds, remember that in God's unfathomably long time this evil has already been overcome by the resurrection of Jesus.

The New Jerusalem

Revelation concludes with the glorious image of a shining city with twelve gates with twelve angels standing guard and the names of twelve tribes on the gates and the names of the twelve apostles of the Lamb on the foundations. The city is a gigantic cube, whose dimensions are twelve thousand stadia on each side. A stadion was approximately 660 feet, which means that each dimension of the cube is about 1,500 miles. Its walls are 144 cubits or about seventy-five yards thick. The city itself is made of pure gold. The walls are constructed of the precious stone jasper, and a different precious gem decorates each of the twelve foundations of the city. Finally, each gate is a single pearl. This city is often assumed to describe a future heaven. But I suggest a different meaning.

As with the other images in Revelation, this description of the city is highly symbolic. Note the twelves in the number of gates and walls and foundations, as well as the number of angels and tribes and apostles. These twelves identify the city with the people of God. Twelve also figures in the size of the city. It is twelve thousand stadia. This dimension is a product of twelve times one thousand. Remember that "thousand" means "very large number." This dimension does not indicate an actual measurement. It is rather a way to identify the city with God's people by using a gigantic, symbolic number. The shape also has symbolic value. Since ancient cities grew up in haphazard fashion, that the city is a cube—all dimensions equal—symbolizes perfection. Consider also the materials from which the city is constructed—walls of a precious stone and foundations decorated with precious stones, and each of the twelve gates consisting of a single pearl. An aside: If one doubts the symbolic character of this description, try figuring out where the clams are that can produce a pearl large enough to be a gate of this huge city!

Finally, note that the city contains no temple, the traditional place to access God. There is no need for a temple because God the Almighty and the Lamb reside in the city. The city has no need of sun or moon for light because the glory of God provides its light and the Lamb functions as its lamp. Again, these are symbolic representations that put God and the Lamb on the same footing as the source of light, and establish the city as their habitation.

Perhaps the most important question concerns the identity of the city, the New Jerusalem. The traditional answer is that this is a vision of heaven, with streets paved with gold. However, I believe that the description of the city actually indicates a quite different answer. Note that after the statements that God and the Lamb constitute the light of the city, it says that "the kings of the earth will bring their glory into it." These are among the kings who were slain by the Word in 19:21, but the ones here understood the Word and were attracted to the light of God and the resurrected Lamb and now enter the city. Seeing the kings within the city emphasizes that the victory of the rider on the white horse was by the Word, a nonviolent victory. Further, the gates of the city are never closed, and people will bring the glory and honor of nations into the city. Yet, even though the gates of the city never close, nothing unclean will enter the city, and those who practice abominations and falsehoods will not enter the city.

The thing to observe is that the city seems to exist in the midst of the world, where wickedness exists alongside goodness. Kings and ordinary people both can bring honor and glory into the city. Meanwhile, evil still exists right outside the gates, but this evil does not enter the city. I suggest that this vision of the New Jerusalem is a highly symbolic description of the church in the present, the people of God who live in the midst of a wicked world. This is a symbolic depiction of how glorious it is to live in the church as the people of God who live in the joy of the resurrected Jesus. The description of gates always open while evil does not enter is not a statement of spatial location; it is not a statement of physically stepping through a gate to enter a city. It is rather a statement about loyalty. Those who are loyal to God and the resurrected Lamb are in the city, and those who follow the abomination of Rome are not in the city.

Throughout Revelation we have seen several symbolic representations of the victory of the reign of God over the evil committed by the Roman empire. The last scene of Revelation makes this statement one more time. In this instance it is a vision of the church as the New Jerusalem. This glorious representation is a reminder to Christians in Asia Minor to remember the true nature of the emperor and empire when compared with the glorious victory of the reign of God that occurred with the resurrection of Jesus. It is an invitation to the first readers to live in the reign of God in the face of any potential dangers posed by the empire.

Conclusion

In this chapter along with the previous one, we observed a number of different symbolic representations of the clash of loyalties between God and the reign of God with Roman Empire and its emperors. In this confrontation, the reign of God emerges victorious in the resurrection of Jesus. With these symbols in mind, we can see that Revelation had a clear message for the first readers in the seven churches in Asia Minor. The author of Revelation was warning them not to forget the character of empire in a time when the emperor was acting in a relatively benign manner toward Christians. The message was to keep the resurrection of Jesus in view, which renders insignificant anything Rome has done or can do in the face of the glorious reign of God.

In reading Revelation, Christians today would do well to heed this warning for themselves. Christians in North America ought not be seduced by the claims of the United States to be a Christian nation and the very real but unofficial requirement that the president be a Christian. In spite of these words—remember the beast who resembled the lamb but spoke like the dragon—the nation with the largest military budget in the world does not speak for the reign of God, and Christians ought not be deceived by the freedom from persecution that they enjoy in North America.

In terms of the focus of this book, namely seeing that the God revealed in Jesus is a nonviolent God, these two chapters have displayed how the author of Revelation used a variety of images to portray the victory of the resurrection of Jesus. And throughout this variety, the focus was on the ultimate victory over evil by the death and resurrection of Jesus. Furthermore, God and the resurrected Jesus, depicted as the living Lamb with marks of slaughter, were displayed as co-equals. The God who is positioned as a co-equal with the resurrected Lamb must be a nonviolent God. The interpretation of the symbols of Revelation has demonstrated just that, namely the nonviolence of God.

Throughout the book in hand, the implication has been that understandings of theology can change over time as contexts change. The final two chapters discuss important changes in Christology and atonement, the primary theological issues developed in this book.

18

Does Theology Change? Christology

The Possibility of Change

GOD IS THE SAME yesterday, today, and forever, or at least that is how the saying goes. But does theology about God change? And is it all right for people to change their minds about theological topics? These may be surprising or even threatening questions. Theology accepted as orthodox theology is summarized in formal statements such as the Nicene Creed, the language of the Trinity, and the formula from the Council of Constantinople, which all came into use in the fourth and fifth Christian centuries. To be judged orthodox means that the doctrines have been declared true and thus all faithful believers will accept them as the source of Christian faith. Dissent from these doctrines then places the believer in error. As I was once challenged at a conference after I had raised a question about requiring the Nicene Creed, "But without the Nicene Creed, how would we know what to believe?"

But other perspectives exist. I once asked a prominent womanist theologian who visited my class at Bluffton University whether we could revise the orthodox creeds. The first sentence of her answer may shock, but it certainly got the attention of my students. "God never wrote any theology," she said. "All theology, including the orthodox creeds, is written by people, and until quite recently it was written by men. Nothing written by people should be considered absolute, and anything written by people can be changed."

I agree with my guest. An assumption throughout this book has been that theology can and does change, or that Christians can change their minds about theological statements.

This chapter focuses on Christology, the words we use to talk about the nature of Jesus Christ. Change can take many forms. For some aspects in the development of Christology, change has meant expanding the understanding of a given theological idea. An example in the New Testament is Paul's use of the story of Jesus to argue for the idea of a general resurrection. Change has also meant developing new terminology to describe Jesus, a change explored in this chapter. Change may mean determining that a revision is necessary, a suggestion that this book makes. Finally, in yet one more instance, change might mean deciding that an idea was wrong and should be abandoned, which we will see with the discussion of atonement in the following chapter.

Discussing the possibility of change and development in theology calls for a word of caution. Change merely for the sake of change is not intrinsically good. In fact, it can be problematic. Change can move in erroneous directions as well as in positive or helpful directions. As far as Christian theology is concerned, since theology is derived from the narrative of Jesus, all theological change should take place with guidance from that narrative.

Christology

Identification by Narrative

Jesus was identified by a narrative throughout the Gospels. That narrative identified him as the one whose mission it was to witness to the reign of God on earth. His life demonstrated that God cares about all people, particularly those on the margins of society. The reign of God is concerned about living generously with wealth and challenges injustice without violence. God's resurrection of Jesus validates his life and teaching as genuinely the life of God.

However, the Gospels are not the first place that Jesus was identified by a narrative. The author of the Gospel of Luke also wrote the New Testament book of Acts. Acts continues the story of Jesus told in Luke, with appearances of the resurrected Jesus to his followers and his ascension toward heaven. The book then follows the actions and ministry of the disciples and the early church in the weeks and months after Jesus was no longer with them.

On six occasions, Acts recounts statements in which the apostles identified Jesus. One was at Pentecost, when "tongues of fire" descended on Jesus' followers, and people from all across the empire heard others speaking their languages. At this cacophony, a crowd gathered and demanded to know what was happening. Peter's explanation was the well-known Pentecost sermon, recorded in Acts 2:14–36. In response to this message, three thousand people repented and were baptized into the believing community. A bit later, Peter and John healed a crippled man. Again, as recorded in Acts 3:12–26, Peter made a major address that explained their authority for healing. Acts then records four other occasions as well, in which the apostles gave an address that explained their authority (4:8–12; 5:29–32; 10:34–43; 13:16–41). Peter was the spokesman for the apostles in the first five, Paul for the sixth.

Comparing these six statements brings out the characteristic that describes all of them. The basic literary form of these statements is "narrative." Each of these sermons tells the story of Jesus. When the apostles were asked in whose name they acted, or under whose authority they acted, they told the story of Jesus. They identified Jesus by his story, by his history.

When one makes a grid to chart the appearance of various elements in these six addresses or sermons, one sees that they all used the same outline. Two items appear in every statement—that Jesus was killed and that God raised him. The first five addresses occur in Jerusalem, and in referring to the death of Jesus, Peter says "you killed him." He was talking to people who were part of the mob at the condemnation of Jesus. The sixth address, by Paul, occurred outside of Jerusalem in Antioch of Pisidia. From this location away from Jerusalem where Jesus was killed, the way of referring to the agents of death has changed. Instead of "you killed him," Paul now says, "they asked Pilate to have him killed" (13:28). Occurring almost as frequently alongside the mentions of death and resurrection were several other aspects of Jesus' story. Speakers mentioned the fullness of time or citations from the Old Testament to indicate that the God of Israel was the God who was in the story of Jesus. There were mentions of mighty works that Jesus performed. There were mentions of the fact that the apostles and others were witnesses to the events being recounted. And there was mentioned that in this story sins were forgiven or salvation was found, and the story provoked hearers to want to become part of the story.

Comparing the six addresses in this way brings out the fact that they all used the same outline. In a few instances, the report in Acts is quite brief, little more than the declarations of Jesus' death and resurrection. Other times the outline is filled out in some detail, perhaps with a long account of the history of Israel, which culminates in the event of Jesus. It is also the case that the apostles did not always need to tell the story in great detail. They were talking to people in the first weeks after Jesus' death and resurrection, and their audience had often seen Jesus and knew the story.

As the apostles told and retold this story in following decades, the eye witnesses began to die and there were fewer and fewer people who knew the story from their personal experience. This situation is what precipitated the writing of what we now know as the four Gospels. The Gospel writers collected stories and memories and wrote out accounts so that the narrative that identified Jesus would be preserved. They filled out the outline that is visible in the six addresses in Acts. This means that for the early church, their way of identifying Jesus was by telling his story. We can call it a narrative-based Christology.

The Beginning of Theology

Although the early Gospel writers identified Jesus with a narrative, ways to talk about Jesus did not stop with the narrative. One example is Paul's discussion of resurrection in 1 Corinthians 15. In this text, Paul's beginning point is familiar. He used the same outline for the story of Jesus that we just observed in the book of Acts. In this case, Paul expanded the list of eyewitnesses and included himself as the last witness. In his introduction, Paul made a point of saying that this beginning point had not originated with him, but rather he was merely passing on what had been told to him and that they had heard it from him and agreed with it. Paul's introductory comment shows that this narrative way of identifying Jesus was the standard pattern practiced by these early Christians.

Paul had a specific reason for referring to the resurrection in the story of Jesus as something that his readers had heard and said that they accepted. Paul tells them that if they believe in the resurrection of Jesus then they must also believe in a future, general resurrection of all the dead. If they deny a general resurrection, that means a denial of Jesus' resurrection as well, which would mean that the proclamation of the good news about Jesus Christ was also denied and in vain.

The point here is that Paul has used the story of Jesus to argue for a belief that is not specifically included in the story. Paul argued that the idea of Jesus' resurrection is linked to the idea of a general resurrection, and that one cannot exist without the other. And since Paul includes himself as a witness to the resurrected Jesus, he tells his readers in Corinth that a general resurrection is also real.

Paul makes an assumption that allows him to link Jesus' resurrection to a general resurrection. He assumes that what happens to Jesus will happen to everyone. Thus human beings can die with Jesus, and human beings can and will be resurrected with Jesus. Sometimes this linking is called the logic of solidarity. This is simply a way of saying that what happens to Jesus also touches human beings. This logic of solidarity and the idea that Jesus' resurrection signals a coming general resurrection are not stated specifically in the narrative of Jesus that we can read in the Gospels, but is rather drawn out of the narrative of Jesus. Seeing that Paul makes an explicit link between Jesus' resurrection and a general resurrection in 1 Corinthians 15 is an example of expanding theology in the New Testament itself.[1]

Another kind of theological development visible in the New Testament occurs with the language and images used to talk about Jesus. Four different images—Word, Creator, high priest, New Adam—in very different ways all assert that Jesus' story is God's story and that through identification with the Jesus who died and was resurrected human beings are reconciled to God. These images resulted when New Testament interpreters carried the story of Jesus into other contexts and worldviews and used the images from those new contexts to talk about the meaning of Jesus. John 1 refers to the Word that was with God from the beginning, but then also became flesh in Jesus. Thus Jesus, who is both Word from the upper realm and flesh in the lower realm, brings together the upper and lower realms of the cosmos. In Colossians 1, Jesus is both involved in creation and is the firstborn of all creation and through him all things are reconciled to God. The book of Hebrews describes Jesus in the image of the high priest who bridges the gap between God and humanity by giving himself. The image of Jesus as a New Adam appears in Philippians

---

1. For this description of the way that theology developed from the narrative, see Yoder, *Preface to Theology*.

2. In contrast to the first Adam, Jesus did not try to grab at equality with God. Instead, he was fully obedient to the will of God and because of that obedience he was raised and exalted and declared Lord of all.

These four images all assume a version of a hierarchical cosmology, with God in a realm above and human beings below. In this worldview, the problem of alienation from God is understood as the separation of sinful humans in the realm below from God in the realm above. Each of these four images then pictures Jesus as identified with both realms, so that the gap is overcome through identification with Jesus' death and resurrection. This hierarchical worldview does not fit our contemporary picture of the cosmos, which is described as incomprehensibly large and expanding at unimaginable speeds in every direction. Nonetheless, these New Testament images portray the universal relevance of the death and resurrection of Jesus within their context.

Another New Testament image of Jesus that fits better within our worldview is the slain and resurrected Lamb in Revelation 5 and 6. As the last chapter displayed, this Lamb is a symbol of the resurrected Jesus, the Jesus whose story was outlined in the sermons of Acts and filled out in the narratives of the Gospels. These narratives locate Jesus on earth and in human history. He is the continuation of the story of Israel from the Old Testament, and the God who raised Jesus is the God of Israel. In Revelation 6, this slain and resurrected Lamb opens the seven seals on the scroll in God's hand. It is a symbolic way to say that resurrected Jesus is the key to knowledge of God. Since it concerns Jesus who is identified by the Gospel narratives, this is also an image that locates Jesus in human history in terms of the Roman Empire, and identifies him as the key to understanding God's future in human history. Identifying Jesus in this way fits with our contemporary life on earth, as a stimulus to live within the story of Jesus and thus to be aligned with where God is directing human history.

When the early church expanded beyond Jerusalem, it had to develop new ways to communicate the gospel of Jesus Christ effectively in new contexts. The different images for identifying Jesus from the New Testament all involved decisions about how to communicate in new contexts. The writers extracted new insight from the story, and created new language to explain the meaning of Jesus. Theology certainly does change. It is important to note that the theological changes are already visible in the New Testament itself.

Classic Christology

Development of additional ideas and new images did not stop with the end of the New Testament. The New Testament left some questions about Jesus unanswered. One question concerned Jesus' relationship to God. Was he God or the same as God or like God? And the more closely one identified Jesus with God, the more another question surfaced—if Jesus was identified with God, how could he be human or identified with human beings? These questions occupied theological discussions of the church for the next three or four centuries.

The first authoritative answer to these open questions was produced by the Council of Nicea in 325 CE in response to an empire-wide theological crisis. Arius, a priest from Alexandria in what is now Egypt, precipitated this dispute. According to the most common way of telling the story, in discussing the relationship of Jesus to God, Arius wanted to preserve the uniqueness of God. Thus, Arius proposed that Jesus was divine, a deity, but a slightly lesser deity than God. God had always existed as fully God, Arius said, and then God created Jesus as a slightly lower deity, and then together God the Father and Jesus the Son were involved in creating everything else that existed. In this way, Arius thought to preserve the uniqueness of God, but also describe Jesus as Creator. Major sections of the Roman Empire rallied in both support and opposition to Arius's position. The empire was threatened with division. Emperor Constantine convoked the council at Nicea in order to find a settlement that would keep his empire together.

In response to Arius, the Council of Nicea declared that Jesus was *homoousios* with God the Father. *Homoousios* was a Greek compound word. Its two parts are *homo*, which means "same," and *ousios*, which means "substance" or "being." With this term, the creed that emerged from the council declared that Jesus is the "same substance" or the "same in being" with the Father. At the Council of Constantinople in 381 CE, the creed was brought out again in a slightly revised form. Emperor Theodosius endorsed this version of the creed as the official imperial policy, and it is the version of the Nicene Creed still in use today. By declaring Jesus to be of the same substance or one in being with God, the Nicene Creed asserts the full deity of Jesus, his equality with God.[2]

---

2. For an exhaustive history of the development of the Nicene Creed, see Hanson, *Search for the Christian Doctrine of God*. An analysis that emphasizes change and context of Nicene doctrine is Burrus, *"Begotten Not Made."*

This equality of deity is also extended to the Holy Spirit, which produces the doctrine of the Trinity. This doctrine asserts that God the Father, Jesus the Son, and the Holy Spirit are all three equally God, even as they are also distinguishable. The traditional formula for distinguishing the Three-in-One is to say that they are "one God in three persons." This formula was proposed by three men from Cappadocia, the brothers Basil of Caesarea (c. 330–379) and Gregory of Nyssa (c. 330–c. 395) and their friend Gregory of Nazianzus (c. 330–389).

The term "person" is yet another development of language beyond categories of the New Testament. The word translated as "person" came from the context of the theater. In a one-person performance, an actor would wear or carry a mask that identified the particular role he was in on stage. The term translated as "person" was the name given to the mask as well as to the role indicated by the mask. The Cappadocians suggested that this term for mask could be used to designate the three roles in which God appeared to human beings. It was one God in three "roles," just as it was one actor in the several masks or roles in the theater performance. However, the church developed the term "person" far beyond its original meaning of a "role." Each of the three persons was much more than a mere role taken up by the divine actor. Each person was fully God, but nonetheless the three had one divine essence or being. When Emperor Theodosius declared the decision of Constantinople to be imperial policy, his action included the new language of Trinity, namely that Father, Son, and Holy Spirit are equal deity as three persons and one God.

The assertion that Jesus the Son is equal deity to God the Father raises other questions. How *human* was Jesus? How was his humanity related to his deity? After all, the Gospels portray Jesus in very human terms. He was born as a baby; he learned things and grew (Luke 2:52); he ate and drank; he got tired and slept; he felt sadness (John 11:35); and in the most human action of all, Jesus died.

The question of how to understand this human picture of Jesus alongside the assertion of his deity produced a lot of controversy. The final answer came from the Council of Chalcedon in 451 CE.

The council's answer attempted to satisfy the two major schools of thought at one time. One school wanted to safeguard the unity of Jesus' person. Their chosen language for recognizing humanity and deity in a unified person was to say that in Jesus the Word that was with God from the beginning had became flesh. The other school of thought was most concerned to assert Jesus' full humanity and to distinguish his humanity from his deity. This school preferred language which said that in Jesus the Word became human.

The key phrase in the formula proclaimed by the Council of Chalcedon was that Jesus was "fully human and fully divine" or "truly God and truly human." For this formula, the Council used the language from Nicea that proclaimed Jesus as "one substance" (*homoousios*) with God, and then said that Jesus was also *homoousios* with humanity. Along with this assertion that Jesus was both fully human and fully divine, they added that these two natures "undergo no confusion, no change, no division, no separation" and that both natures come together and are preserved "in a single person." This statement of "truly God and truly human" was not included in a creed, but the formula from Chalcedon has enjoyed creed-like status almost from its beginning.[3]

Changes in Christology?

Our question for Christology becomes, was there a change in the way Jesus is identified from a narrative in Acts and in the Gospels to the statements from the Councils of Nicea, Constantinople, and Chalcedon, and the Cappadocians' language of Trinity, which have come to define the inherited approach to Christology?

At one level, it is possible to argue that there was no change. The intent of the formula of Nicea and the accompanying doctrine of Trinity was to assert that Jesus is equal deity with God. That is one way of affirming a conclusion from chapter 2, where it was stated that the resurrection testifies that God was in the life of Jesus and that Jesus' life made present the reign of God. As far as stating that God is in the story of Jesus, depicting Jesus by a narrative agrees with the intent behind the formulas from Nicea and for the Trinity.

Looked at another way, however, there is a profound difference between the manner Jesus is depicted in Acts and the Gospels and in the classic formulas of Nicea, Trinity, and Chalcedon. In Acts and in the Gospels, Jesus was identified with a narrative, that is, by telling his story. In contrast, the classic formulas identify Jesus in terms translated variously as "essence" or "substance" or "being," which stated very crassly is the generic "stuff" or "essence" of his being. The classic categories assume

---

3. For a wide-ranging analysis of the events leading to the Council of Chalcedon, see Jenkins, *Jesus Wars*.

a philosophical system in which things can be reduced to their particular essence or being. Thus, these classic terms say that Jesus is of the same being or essence as God, and also that at the human level Jesus is of the same substance or being of all humanity. Further, there is an assumption about the cosmos behind the classic description. These descriptions assume a hierarchical universe, making a claim that the being of God in the upper realm is the same as the being of Jesus in the lower or earthly realm.

This way of identifying Jesus from Nicea, Chalcedon, and the Cappadocians's Trinity language is clearly different from how he is identified in the Gospels, but it is not intrinsically wrong. In fact, if one wants to know how Jesus relates to God with the answer given in terms of the philosophical system that assumes essence or being and within a hierarchical universe, then the classic answers are true answers.

But there is more involved here than merely changing the category for identifying Jesus from narrative to being or substance. When Christian ethics is the lived version of the story of Jesus, it is the narrative that identifies Jesus in a way that his actions become the basis for the behavior of Christians. The generic categories of "humanity" and "God" from the classic formulas say nothing that would guide the behaviors of Christians. In fact, there may be a different kind of correlation between behavior and theology that stems from the classic categories.

These formulas were affirmed as policy for the church and empire in the fourth and fifth centuries of the Christian era. By this epoch, the church had made peace with the sword of the emperor. Emperors pursued their aims with armies, and powerful bishops appealed to the emperors for support in the theological disputes that led up to the councils. Since the formulas lack mention of the narrative of Jesus, they provide no resources to challenge the emperors' use of the sword or to challenge the engagement of church officials in power politics backed by armies. Fourth- and fifth-century emperors would not have tolerated a formula that challenged their authority by identifying Jesus via his story.[4] In other words, the foundational identification of Jesus as "humanity" and "deity" allows emperors and others to profess faith in Jesus while plying the violence he rejected.

James Cone, founder of the Black Theology Movement, made a similar point with respect to racism. Parallel to the observation that the

---

4. For analysis that recognizes this problem but seeks to rehabilitate Nicene doctrine for ethics, see Rieger, *Christ and Empire*, 69–117.

classic terminology accommodated the sword, Cone wrote that the classic christological terms allowed profession of faith in Jesus while practicing slavery and accommodating racism. And parallel to my suggestion, Cone's beginning point for an alternative was the story of Jesus, whom he read as liberator.[5]

Recently, writings of J. Kameron Carter and Willie James Jennings have taken Cone's critique of the standard creedal formulas even further. Their work identifies the beginning of the accommodation of racism and the development of the idea of white supremacy in the separation of Jesus from his Jewishness by the early church fathers who developed the classic formulas that refer only to humanity and deity. With Jesus separated from his Jewishness and the covenant with Israel, Europeans could apply the concept of chosenness to their own agendas. Jesus was raised above racial identity, which allowed European whiteness to become the essence of what it meant to be human and people of color relegated to lesser degrees of.[6] This racist orientation was well in place when the Pope declared the Doctrine of Discovery in 1493, which gave Europeans the right to "discover," that is dominate, expel, or enslave the inhabitants, and exploit any territory not ruled by Christians, that is, by Europeans. This outlook and this doctrine were then used to justify slavery and the slave trade, and European colonial domination and exploitation of peoples of color around the world, including the settlement of North America by white Europeans and the "manifest destiny" for them to possess the land from coast to coast.[7]

These observations are important for the discussion of change in theology. There were changes from the New Testament to the emergence of the classic formulas three and four centuries later. There was a change in the category used to identify Jesus and how Jesus was related to God, and change in the way that Jesus could be confessed and applied. When the story was told, as in the accounts in Acts, the hearers asked to join in the story, with the implication that they began acting in line with the narrative of Jesus. Jesus' word about not responding to evil in kind was echoed by statements from Paul in Romans 12:17, 20, 21 and 1 Thessalonians

---

5. See Cone, *God of the Oppressed*.

6. Carter, *Race*; Jennings, *Christian Imagination*.

7. A Google search brings numerous hits on Doctrine of Discovery. In Recent years, church-related structures have begun to challenge this doctrine. For one to which I have contributed blog posts, see the "Dismantling the Doctrine of Discovery" website at https://dofdmenno.org/.

5:15 and in 1 Peter 3:9. There was an expectation that living with the story of Jesus meant turning away from the use of violence. Thus, identifying Jesus by his story clearly gives visibility to his rejection of violence. It is the disappearance of that dimension of Christian faith that is apparent in the embrace of Christian faith by emperors and the power politics of the church and the accommodation of slavery by Christians.

Posing an alternative to the inherited formulas does not disregard universal truth nor reject Jesus. Posing an alternative that makes visible Jesus' rejection of violence and his challenge to racism is a recovery of that which was lost for the majority of Christians for many centuries. In this light, posing an alternative is actually an assertion of greater faithfulness. It is a move that brings Christian practice, namely ethics based on Jesus, in line with theology, namely the words used to identify Jesus. Posing a narrative-based alternative is not an outright rejection of the classic formulas. In the context of the worldview and philosophical givens within which the formulas emerged, they are a correct answer. But since we have a different world picture and no longer define reality in terms of some universal essence or being, we are not bound to use their categories in our theologizing.

Thus, theology in our time can change, just as there was change visible in the New Testament itself, and then more change in the centuries after the New Testament. The change suggested here is of two kinds. On the one hand, suggesting that Jesus be identified by a narrative is a change from the received or inherited way of defining Jesus since the fourth or fifth century of the Christian era. This is a change that actually brings theology closer to the original New Testament orientation, even as we can identify the contemporary church as a continuation of the story that passes through Jesus.

However, another kind of change has even more significance. For centuries it was assumed that there was an absolute truth that could be determined and enforced. In the fourth and fifth centuries, imperial policy decreed the theology that was required of all Christians. Of course, conformity was never complete, and there were ongoing efforts by opponents to have another version enforced by imperial edict. But these actions assumed that there was an absolute truth that could be determined and enforced. Today, for the most part, we have abandoned the idea that there is an absolute truth that can be determined and then imposed on others. We live in a time of relativism and pluralism, with no norm of appeal recognized by everyone that can demonstrate the validity of one claim or another to know truth absolutely.

Nonetheless, the world religions do make claims to profess truth. For Christians, the claim is that God is revealed in Jesus, and that Jesus thus becomes the norm of truth in our world. However, there is no source of logical or rational appeal that can compel a Muslim or a Buddhist to accept the particular truth of Christians. But Christians are not left without a way to demonstrate their belief in the truth of Jesus Christ. To demonstrate their belief that universal truth resides with Jesus, Christians will live by the story of Jesus, even when it is costly or dangerous. Christians in every age have chosen to give the witness of martyrdom rather than surrender their faith. In tolerant North America, some Christians give such a witness by carrying out their vocations and professions in ways that work for social justice rather than pursing high earnings. I know a doctor, for example, who surrendered her comfortable practice in order to open a clinic that served poor people. Lawyers might do pro bono work and assist immigrants without documents rather than pursuing a lucrative corporate practice. A teacher might choose to work in an inner-city school faced with daily challenges of poverty and homelessness rather than an elite private school. The list of such choices could continue indefinitely. Of course, adherents of other faiths have the same opportunity to witness to the truth of their beliefs. The point here is that the means of validating the truth of Christian profession has changed markedly since the development of the creedal formulas in the fourth and fifth centuries. In our modern context when we recognize that all theology reflects a particular context, it is the narrative way of identifying Jesus and living in his story that fits with the professions of faith in our contemporary context of pluralism and relativism.

19

Does Theology Change? Atonement

THE BOOK ENDS WHERE it began, with atonement theology. For atonement theology change is just as real as it was for Christology. In the history of the church, a number of significant changes have occurred with atonement images.

Nonviolent Atonement in Revelation

The book of Revelation pictured Jesus and his church as they confronted the power of the Roman Empire. In Revelation 6, the seven seals correspond to imperial epochs. The first five seals and the first scene of seal six depict harm or threats of harm to the church by the empire. The second scene of seal six, which is the whole of Revelation 7, then depicted immense throngs that celebrated the victory of the reign of God over Rome through the resurrection of Jesus. These images depict a confrontation of church and empire, with victory on the side of church in the resurrection of Jesus. Revelation 12 featured the image of the heavenly battle between the forces of God and the forces of Satan represented by the dragon, with victory won by the resurrection of Jesus. But since the symbolic description of the dragon identified it as Rome, again it is a depiction of the earthly confrontation of church and empire, with victory by the reign of God in the resurrection of Jesus.

The Gospels presented Jesus and his followers as they confronted evil systems and ultimately the Roman empire, which killed him. Since the symbols in Revelation refer to Jesus, his church, and the empire, it is evident that the Gospels and Revelation are actually two ways to picture the same confrontation of Jesus, church, and empire.

In discussion of how Jesus is Savior, his story can be interpreted as a narrative atonement image called nonviolent atonement. We saw that already in chapter 2 of the book in hand. Since the book of Revelation pictures the same confrontation as the Gospels, readers can easily recognize the parallel between Revelation and the Gospels. Revelation has multiple representations of the confrontation of Jesus and church against the empire, which means that Revelation has multiple versions of the motif I called nonviolent atonement. It is another version of the motif visible in the narrative of Jesus from the Gospels. The nonviolent atonement motif bridges the New Testament, with a narrative version at the beginning, in the Gospels, and a symbolic version at the end in Revelation.

When the nonviolent atonement motif is articulated today, it is a way of reading the Gospels' story of Jesus as a saving story, and then reading the book of Revelation as another version of that same story. With this in mind, the question that must be asked is: What happened to this reading of the story? Why did the interpretation of the story disappear that pictures it as a confrontation of Jesus and the church against empire?

The Demise of Nonviolent Atonement

I believe that this interpretation of the story disappeared because of the changes that occurred within the church in the first several centuries of the Christian era. In the time of Jesus and for several centuries thereafter, Christianity was opposed by the Roman Empire. Many Christians became martyrs for their faith as the church stood against the empire. Both church and empire claimed the individual's highest loyalty. Church and empire were not separated geographically. That is, Christians were living in the midst of the empire, but the values and orientation of Christians were different from those of the empire. This situation of church confronting empire is visible in the book of Revelation. When we looked at Revelation, we saw Christians being encouraged to remember the resurrection of Jesus and to remember the previous hostility of the empire to Christians, and not to be deceived by a seemingly benevolent empire at the end of the first century.

The empire's hostility toward the church gradually changed. Over time Christians were tolerated, which is visible already in Revelation when Christians are warned about the true character of empire. As Christians became tolerated, the number of Christians increased. Early in the fourth century, Emperor Constantine embraced the God of Christians and used the cross as a symbol for his army. As we saw with the discussion of Christology, the church made peace with the emperor's sword. Emperors called councils to deal with divisive theological arguments, and church officials were comfortable seeking support when emperors sided with them and opposed emperors when they backed opponents of church authorities.

Church and empire were still two different entities and two different authorities that could come into conflict about ultimate control, but they saw themselves as structures that ruled over the same societies. Although these conflicts were never completely resolved, the church's status of being comfortable with empire is quite different from the hostile relationship of church and empire pictured in the book of Revelation. By the time of the councils in the fourth century, church and empire had become tacit allies.

Nonviolent atonement depicted the church in confrontation with empire. With empire no longer harassing the church, confrontation depicted in Revelation no longer reflected the reality that people were living. As time passed, it was easy for the references of the symbols to be forgotten. To grasp that reality, contemporary readers need only think about how quickly the meaning of political cartoons fades away or how political satire from earlier decades loses its meaning. Thus, for many early readers, the meaning of Revelation was lost as a book that depicted the church in confrontation with empire.

Nonviolent atonement, which is a name for a particular way of reading the narrative of Jesus in Revelation, lost its meaning because the church no longer confronted the empire. The image remained of a heavenly battle between the forces of Satan and God, but with the references to empire forgotten, that battle no longer seemed to touch the life on earth of Christians and the church.

A version of Christus Victor did remain for a number of centuries. The ransom version of Christus Victor was still around in the eleventh century. As was described in chapter 2, in this image Jesus' death was a ransom paid to the devil in exchange for the release of the souls of sinners. Satan was tricked in this exchange; he did not recognize Jesus' deity hidden under his humanity. As a result of the exchange, souls were ransomed from Satan's clutches, and Satan was defeated by the resurrection of Jesus, a Christus Victor motif. But this version concerned a cosmic exchange and did not touch earth and the church in the way of nonviolent atonement that uses the narrative of Jesus' life on earth.

The Advent of Satisfaction

Anselm of Canterbury rejected the ransom version of Christus Victor in his book *Cur Deus Homo* or *Why God Became Man*, published in 1098.[1] Anselm wrote that it was not fitting to picture God tricking Satan; and it was certainly inappropriate to feature God making a deal with Satan since Satan had no rights that God was bound to respect.

In place of this ransom motif, Anselm spelled out what has come to be called the satisfaction theory of atonement. As we have seen, in this image human sin had offended the honor of God, which meant that the order of the universe was disturbed. To restore order in the universe, God's honor had to be satisfied. Since human sin had disturbed the order, it was necessary for humans to repay or satisfy the offended honor. But this satisfaction required a sinless human to die. And to make satisfaction for all those to be saved, the sacrifice to God's honor needed to be infinite. Thus, God sent Jesus as the God-man, Chalcedon's "truly God and truly human," to die in order to make the sacrifice that would satisfy God's offended honor and thus restore order in the universe. As a human being, Jesus would be identified with humankind and as sinless he was qualified to die in their place to make satisfaction of God's offended honor. As deity, his sacrifice for all humankind would be infinite, and thus would cover the sins of all those who would be saved. After some initial opposition, Anselm's suggestion was eventually accepted and one version or another of it has been the dominant understanding of the saving work of Christ for perhaps the last eight centuries.

This shift from nonviolent atonement to satisfaction atonement is reflected in the church's iconography. Images in the early church featured a resurrected Jesus, and the cross was a symbol of resurrection. Belief in the resurrection was an act of defiance against the ultimate violence and authority of empire. Images of the crucifixion began to appear after the torture inflicted by Charlemagne (742–814), who coerced "correct" Christian belief among the Saxons. The first surviving crucifix, the Gero

---

1. Anselm of Canterbury, "Why God Became Man." For analysis of Anselm and his context, see Southern, *Saint Anselm* and Rieger, *Christ and Empire*, 19–58.

Cross, was produced in Saxony around 960–970. "Pressed by violence into Christian obedience, the Saxons produced art that bore the marks of their baptism in blood." Theologically, the culmination of the shift from emphasis on Jesus' resurrection to stress on his death is Anselm's *Cur Deus Homo*, which concentrates on the death of Jesus without mentioning resurrection.[2]

Anselm wrote that he was demonstrating by "reason alone" how the God-man produced the salvation of sinful humans. Of course, his view was based on what seemed to be common sense—reason alone—in his time and context. But today, we can describe Anselm's context, which was medieval feudalism. A feudal lord held power over all the people who lived on his land. His underlings owed him obedience and in return he protected them and could grant favors. This system depended on the authority of the ruler to command this obedience. When an underling offended the lord, either satisfaction was paid to the ruler, or the ruler punished the offense. If the ruler lacked the authority to demand satisfaction or to carry out punishment, the system was in turmoil, the social order broke down. Satisfaction was required to restore order.

Anselm inhabited this system of feudal order as a given. He believed that the archbishop and the king were the two rulers at the top of the order. As Archbishop of Canterbury, he could engage in struggle with the king for most control, but between them they were the feudal powers that exacted satisfaction for offenses. It was within the givens of this feudal order that Anselm could say that he was demonstrating the necessity of the God-man by "reason alone." With this description of Anselm's world, it is more than obvious that Anselm conceived of God as the ultimate feudal lord. Human sin offended God; order in the universe was disturbed. God had to be satisfied so that order could be restored. Jesus offered his death on behalf of sinful humankind to satisfy God's offended honor and thus restore order in the universe. The explanation for the God-man in Anselm's motif makes sense by "reason alone," only when one assumes the feudal order of his time as an unquestioned given.

It is quite evident that significant theological change occurred between the end of the New Testament and Anselm's *Cur Deus Homo*. Nonviolent atonement is a reading of the New Testament's story of Jesus. This motif made sense in the context of the church that confronted an empire that was potentially hostile to the church. The symbols in

---

2. For the description of the theological shift and the iconography involved in it, see Brock and Parker, *Saving Paradise*, 223–70, quote 232.

Revelation were correlated with imperial epochs. By Anselm's time, these references had been forgotten. Rather than standing against empire, the church now contended with empire to see whether secular or churchly leaders possessed the authority to anoint the other. Anselm's satisfaction motif, articulated in *Cur Deus Homo*, reflects this context, which differed markedly from that of the book of Revelation.

Further changes occurred with sixteenth-century reformers such as Martin Luther and John Calvin who shifted the imagery from satisfying God's honor to satisfying the penalty of death demanded by divine law. Now, beginning in the late twentieth-century, with the feudal backdrop outmoded and distaste growing for the harsh image of God in the penal substitutionary motif, some theologians have attempted to rescue the satisfaction motif by suggesting softer ways of understanding the target of Jesus' death. Instead of satisfying the death penalty demanded by divine law, theologians suggest that Jesus' death restores obedience or true worship to God, or becomes a means by which God identifies with humanity in order to take on the shame of their sin.

We no longer live in a feudal world. It seems obvious that we need not be beholden to an atonement motif that was written in and for a feudal world. Dislike for the harsh God of the penal-substitution motif underscores that conclusion. The recent suggestions for salvaging the satisfaction motif by softening or renaming the image may camouflage the death but cannot avoid the fact that these motifs still envision that the death of Jesus needs to impact God. As described in chapter 3, all satisfaction motifs, including the recent efforts to salvage it, still have the problem that Jesus poses an unhealthy model of passive submission to abuse and violence that impacts God. And these motifs still feature a God who employs violence, who sets up Jesus to die as the condition that enables God to grant salvation. Given these problems and their harmful impacts, the satisfaction motif in all its forms should be abandoned.

Reaching back to the narrative of Jesus for a new beginning, I suggest nonviolent atonement for a motif that can be adapted to our world. In North America as well as in much of the world, we live in a society where there is a separation of church and state. North American Christians do not face a hostile state. However, Christians who espouse nonviolence nonetheless encounter many places where the church confronts or witnesses against the violent practices of the state. Economic injustice and racism call for the church to challenge the structural violence of prevailing social norms. Nonviolent atonement, which pictures Jesus as a model of active nonviolence, fits within this social context.

The New Testament writings of the apostle Paul have figured prominently in the discussion of atonement theology. The idea of theological change applies to Paul's writings as well.

Paul on Atonement

For centuries, it has been assumed that the writings of Paul supported satisfaction atonement imagery associated with Anselm of Canterbury or the later penal substitutionary atonement. After all, Paul talked about the cross and about Jesus' death as a sacrifice and about the fact that Jesus "died for sin" or "died for us."

However, recent scholarship has challenged such interpretations of Paul. With better awareness of the feudal orientation of Anselm's satisfaction image, there has been a growing willingness to consider different ways of understanding the writings of Paul. One example is the book by David Brondos, *Paul on the Cross*. This book is an independent validation of the approach to Jesus' saving work that I have called nonviolent atonement.

The first edition of *The Nonviolent Atonement* was published in 2001. A few years later I began work on what became the revised and much-expanded second edition. In the midst of this work, David Brondos approached me at the annual meeting of American Academy of Religion. He had read *The Nonviolent Atonement* and suggested that since he was saying the same kind of thing that I was, I might want to read his new book. It so happened that I had purchased a copy and it was the first book I was planning to read when I returned home. Brondos showed that Paul did not support a satisfaction approach to atonement, and his way of reading Paul supported nonviolent atonement. Thus, in the revised version of my book, I included a major section on Brondos's understanding of Paul. The discussion of Paul in what follows comes from the scholarship of David Brondos.[3]

For Paul, it was the life, mission, death, and resurrection of Jesus as a unified whole that contributed to redemption, that is, to salvation. Paul expanded the narrative of Jesus that is visible in the statements in Acts and then filled out in the Gospels. Paul's theology expanded on this

---

3. Brondos, *Paul on the Cross*.

narrative. For example, in 1 Corinthians 15:3–7 Paul repeats the outline of the story from Acts as the basis of his argument for a general resurrection and extending redemption to all people, including gentiles, which had been God's intent from the beginning.

Paul's understanding of the role of Jesus' death is thus fundamentally different from the way it has been depicted in any of the inherited theories of atonement. In this new interpretation of Paul, the death of Jesus has no saving impact in and of itself. For Paul, just as for nonviolent atonement, Jesus' death does not impact God. As an isolated entity the death does not change God's attitude toward sinful humans. Jesus' death is rather the consequence of faithfully carrying out his mission to witness to the salvation of the reign of God.

The inherited atonement theories focus on the death of Jesus, while for Paul it is the whole event of Jesus that saves, the whole of his ministry, death, and resurrection through which God saves. By itself, the death does not produce any kind of change. Jesus died for the same thing for which he lived, namely to witness to the redemption of all people in the reign of God. Paul's repeated references to the cross are not a statement that the cross itself—that is, Jesus' death—is what accomplishes salvation. Rather, the cross represents everything for which Jesus lived and died; it is the ultimate expression of the grace and love of God manifested in all that God has done and continues to do through Jesus.

In this interpretation of Paul, some familiar phrases take on new meanings. When Jesus is "delivered up," that does not mean that Jesus' death satisfied a need in a cosmic equation as understood by Anselm. Rather, it means that God did not intervene and Jesus was allowed to die in fulfillment of his mission to bring redemption to all people, to make the reign of God visible and available to all people. When Paul says that Jesus gave himself up for others, it is not a reference to death as an isolated entity that impacted God; rather it means that Jesus was willing to give his life for the cause of his mission. When Paul said that Jesus died "for us," or "for our sins," these phrases should not be understood in terms of penal substitutionary atonement. That is, they do not mean that Jesus submitted to the punishment that sinners deserved in order to satisfy God's law as is stated in penal substitutionary atonement. To say that Jesus died "for us" means that it was "for us" that he was willing to carry out his mission of witness to God's salvation for all people, even when it cost him his life. Stated briefly, Jesus died carrying out his mission "for us."

For Paul, the ultimate purpose for which Jesus gave up his life in obedience to God was the redemption of God's people, which included both Jews and gentiles. But this redemption was the goal, not only of Jesus' death, but also of his life and his ministry before his death, and of his resurrection after his death. For Paul, Jesus' appearance, life, ministry, death, and resurrection are a unified whole, focused on the redemption of God's people, focused on making the reign of God present and immediately accessible. Because he was raised from the dead, Jesus will return some day to make that redemption a reality.

Conclusion: Atonement for Today

Nonviolent atonement is posed as a new atonement motif for today, but finding the image in the book of Revelation shows that it is also a return to an early understanding of the way that the church relates to the social order. For perhaps eight centuries, some version of satisfaction or penal substitutionary atonement has been the dominant motif, along with the assumption that this motif reflected the writing of Paul. This chapter has challenged satisfaction atonement on a broad front. The feudal context of satisfaction has been exposed, which opens wide the option to develop another motif not dependent on feudal assumptions. One such motif is nonviolent atonement, which reflects the Bible's story of Jesus, and which also fits within the current political and social context of North America and beyond. Its stance of witness to the reign of God and confronting injustice can be adapted to serve many contexts around the world.

When I was in Kenya in a school for ministers several years ago, I presented the story of Jesus so as to emphasize his confrontation of injustices and to invite them to join in that confrontation. These students had heard only that Jesus "died for their sins." The idea that Jesus confronted injustices was new for them. One told me, "You may have started a revolution!" Just a few years ago, I gave lectures on nonviolent atonement theology in the Democratic Republic of Congo. There were many questions about applying the insight of the Jesus who confronted injustice to their particular political situation. The Congolese are still working to confront the colonial legacy of learned helplessness, the idea learned from the colonial occupiers that only the Europeans knew how to do things. One pastor and Bible school principal told me that some missionaries told the Congolese "Blessed are the poor," and that now the people are still sitting and waiting for God to bless them in their poverty. Of course God blesses us, the pastor said, but we are teaching our people that they have to help God as well. Thus the idea that Jesus confronted injustice and that relating to Jesus means to join in that struggle, the pastor said, was for them a "real gift from God."

These brief anecdotes illustrate the way that nonviolent atonement can be adapted to contexts around the world.

Open-Ended Conclusion

THIS BOOK BEGAN WITH five-year old Zach's question: "A parent would never put their child to death on the cross, right?" In a sense, this book has been a multifaceted answer to Zach's question.

The book has displayed how theology has changed, including the appearance of some images that worried Zach. In the last two chapters we observed significant changes through history for the way Jesus has been identified (Christology) and in understanding of his saving work (atonement imagery). For both Christology and atonement images, there were changes in the language used. Changes in ethics accompanied the language developments. The new language of Christology in the fourth and fifth centuries allowed the church to profess Jesus while accommodating the sword that he rejected and then to accommodate slavery. The image of satisfaction atonement featured a God who needed the death of God's Son, and a Jesus who modeled passive submission to injustice, a model that was counter to Jesus' active confrontation of injustice.

As alternatives to these classic images, I suggested a narrative approach to defining who Jesus is and how his mission made the reign of God visible on earth. Thus, the Christology and narrative atonement image of this book point to the nonviolence of God who is revealed in the life and work of Jesus. The suggestion for a nonviolent atonement image with its nonviolent image of God addresses specifically the concern expressed by Zach's question. Other chapters covered a wide range of issues related to living in the life of Jesus, the practice of nonviolence, and in understanding the Bible from the perspective of the nonviolence of God—God without violence. This God without violence is Creator of all that is, and the Creator's imprint on that creation becomes visible to eyes of faith. This book used the metaphor "grain of the universe" to describe that nonviolent imprint.

Much of the material in these chapters was the result of a rereading of the story of Jesus from a new or contemporary context. Well into the nineteenth century, many Christians defended the practice of slavery as biblical. Now we read the Bible to oppose slavery, and show that living in the story of Jesus requires challenging the racism that is still present in our society. It was only in the twentieth century that large numbers of Christians have come to oppose patriarchy, to accept the equality of women, and to admit women to all of the leadership functions of the church, including ordination. This change is a result of rereading the Bible and particularly the narrative of Jesus. In the church of my youth, we were taught that Jesus' words "Resist not evil" in Matthew 5:39 meant nonresistance, a passive stance toward evil. In particular, this stance meant staying away from Civil Rights protests, since these protests were a kind of resistance. Now I believe that the meaning of Jesus' words is to resist without mirroring evil, and today I appeal to Jesus to support active nonviolence and even civil disobedience. Another change still underway and accompanied by significant controversy is acceptance of people who are gay and lesbian as full participants without restrictions in the church, including ordination and the possibility of marriage. This change is provoked in part by a rereading of the Bible to show Jesus' acceptance of people on the margins of society.

All such changes and more that we could mention have come about in part through rereading the Bible. Contexts change, which raises new and different questions. Reading the Bible with new questions in mind often leads to reinterpretations. The conclusions of this book are a testimony to such reinterpretations.

With this rereading and the subsequent reinterpretations, another facet of theology has emerged. This presentation of theology has been a book-length demonstration of the fact that theology's ultimate source is the narrative of Jesus as found in the New Testament. Theology is the words used to extend or draw meaning from that story, or to apply it to new situations or in new contexts. This approach then extends to the Old Testament so that the entire Bible is the book for Christians.

With this summary of content and methodology in mind, the book has come to a conclusion. It poses new motifs for Christology and atonement, and it highlights new versions of Christian practice; at least they are new with respect to early-twentieth-century practices.

However, the conclusions of this book can only be provisional. It is not as though we have finally figured out the content of true theology.

There are unforeseen changes to come. There is a conclusion still to be written by future generations of Christians. Recognizing the results of rereading the Bible and particularly the narrative of Jesus means becoming aware that the narrative itself is subject to reinterpretation. There is, or at least there should be, a continual return to or looping back to the narrative for new insight. And that new insight may then produce new theological formulations and changes in the practice of Christians who seek to live within the narrative of Jesus. The process of thinking theologically and of rereading the biblical text for new insight is thus a never-finished, open-ended process between the text and questions raised by the context in which we live.

The theology presented in this book is my current understanding of the meaning of the story of Jesus and what it means to live in it today. But these are not ultimately final words. We need always to be open to new insight from the story of Jesus in ways that we do not foresee at the moment, in the same way that many Christians a century ago had a hard time envisioning the ordination of women. We need to be open to ways that questions that arise in our society may send us back to the narrative of Jesus with new questions that produce different theological formulations. Theology is always subject to revision, based on a new reading of the story of Jesus, while questions raised by our changing society provoke that new reading.

Discussion Questions

Introduction

1) What were your childhood religious experiences?
2) What religious or faith questions did you have as a child? Have they been resolved, or do they remain with you to this day?
3) How does the definition of theology in this chapter differ from your understanding?
4) If you identify as a Christian, what was your path to this identity? If not Christian, how do you describe your religious identity?
5) What other identities do you hold? For example, professional identity, family relationships, regional or national affiliations, social or political outlook? How do these various identities fit with your religious identity?

Chapter 1: The Story of Jesus

1) What stories of Jesus are important to you?
2) What stories of Jesus did you hear in your childhood?
3) How would you characterize the description of Jesus in this chapter?
4) How does this chapter's description of Jesus align with your current understanding of Jesus?

5) How does this chapter's description of Jesus align with your previous understanding of Jesus?

6) What questions does this chapter's description of Jesus raise for you?

Chapter 2 The Story of Jesus and Atonement

1) Briefly describe each theory of atonement.

2) Which theory lines up with your congregation's teachings? With your denominational teachings? With the church of your childhood?

3) Which theory resonates with you now?

4) How does this discussion line up with other faith identities that you may hold?

5) What questions do you still have?

Chapter 3: Atonement and God

1) How does this chapter assess the various atonement images?

2) What messages, subtle or direct, accompany each of the atonement images?

3) What are applications of nonviolent atonement in your community? Country? The world?

Chapter 4: New Testament Teaching and Nonviolence

1) What do you find in this chapter that is new or compelling to you?

2) What do you still question?

3) With what do you resonate in this chapter?

4) When have you witnessed nonviolence in action?

Chapter 5: Active Nonviolence

1. What is new or surprising in this chapter?
2. What questions do you have now?
3. With what do you resonate in this chapter?
4. Can you add to the examples of successful nonviolence described in this chapter?
5. Can you add any examples of alternative actions that might have avoided a war or other major catastrophe?

Chapter 6: Atonement and Forgiveness

1) Reflect on a time when you have been wronged or have wronged someone else. Is it hard or easy to think about offering forgiveness or accepting forgiveness?
2) How does your experience fit with Robert Enright's description of situations for forgiveness?
3) How does that experience fit with atonement images offered here?
4) Consider these stories of forgiveness from the New Testament—Zacchaeus (Luke 19:1–10); the woman taken in adultery (John 8:3–11); healing a paralytic (Luke 5:17–26). How does the forgiveness in these stories correspond to the understanding of forgiveness outlined in this chapter?

Chapter 7: Jesus and Economics

1) What economic disparity do you see in your community?
2) What are ways to address this inequity?
3) How does addressing this inequity fit with the discussion in this chapter?
4) Oscar Romero, an Archbishop of San Salvador, was assassinated March 24, 1980, because of his support for poor people against their oppressors. Some lines from a poem written in his memory say,

> We accomplish in our lifetime only a fraction
> of the magnificent enterprise that is God's work.
> Nothing we do is complete, which is another way
> of saying that the kingdom always lies beyond us. . . .
> This is what we are about. We plant the seeds that one
> Day will grow. We water the seeds already planted
> Knowing that they hold future promise.

How do these words fit the discussion of injustice and economics?

Chapter 8: Racism, Ethnicity, and Gender

1) What identities would you use to describe yourself?
2) When and how do you interact with those who identify differently?
3) What stories of Jesus encourage people to cross boundaries of ethnicity? Economics? Gender?

Chapter 9: The Omnipotence of God

1) What are the inherited understandings of God and God's control of events?
2) How does this chapter challenge these inherited views?
3) What issues worry you concerning God's control?
4) Does reading this chapter give you a different perspective?
5) What did you learn about early American history in your childhood? In school? Does this chapter offer a different perspective than you have heard before?
6) What questions do you still have? Or, what questions were raised by this chapter?

Chapter 10: The Nonviolence of God's Creation

1) What have you observed or been taught about the violence in nature?
2) With what world news do you have the most experience?

3) In what ways do you assess the world around you? Emotional? Theological? Spiritual? Biological? Psychological?

4) What shift in your thinking occurred, if any, after reading this chapter?

Chapter 11: God of the Biblical Narrative: Violent?

1) What Old Testament stories did you learn as a child?

2) What were your thoughts and reactions to these stories then?

3) What are your thoughts and reactions to these stories now?

Chapter 12: God of the Biblical Narrative: Nonviolent?

1) What stories from this chapter give you hope?

2) Did you already know some of the nonviolent stories in this chapter? If so, did you link them the way this chapter does?

3) Do you resonate with the way this chapter links these stories together? What questions or challenges do you still have for this viewpoint?

4) How does this chapter affect how you read the Old Testament?

Chapter 13: God of the Biblical Narrative: A Resolution

1) What parables and stories of Jesus resonate with you?

2) Which stories or parables give examples that you can follow for living?

3) What conversations of faith and social justice are taking place in your church today? In your community today? How can the descriptions of Jesus and the Bible outlined in this chapter assist these discussions?

Chapter 14: Reading the Bible Again

1) Describe some of the "messiness" of the Bible (such as contradictions, disagreements with today's science, different versions of the same event).

2) How might discovering the "messiness" of the Bible cause you distress or offer you comfort?

3) Over what issues have you changed your mind over the years?

4) Over what biblical issues has your perspective shifted?

5) In what areas of life, learning, or profession are you an expert? How did you arrive at that point? Does recognizing this expertise impact how you view the Bible?

6) With whom do you read or discuss the Bible?

Chapter 15: Interpreting Revelation

1) Before reading this chapter, what was your understanding of Revelation?

2) Do you think it makes more sense to look for the meaning of Revelation's symbols in the first century or in our world today?

Chapter 16: Looking at the Past in Revelation

1) What interpretations of Revelation from this chapter are new to you?

2) Can learning about previous history help the world today?

3) If Revelation were written today, what symbols might the author use to show evil and destruction in the world? To show the victory of the reign of God?

4) What history does Revelation make you want to study now?

Chapter 17: Looking Ahead in Revelation

1) What interpretations of Revelation from this chapter are new to you?

2) Would you like to live in the cube city?

3) What applications from Revelation would you make for the church today?

4) What would you say about Revelation to someone, either a Christian or a non-Christian, who claimed that God was violent and that Jesus will exercise violent judgment?

Chapter 18: Does Theology Change? Christology

1) What is the traditional or inherited understanding of Christology?

2) How has the understanding of Christology changed over the centuries? What alternatives does this chapter offer?

3) What is your experience with different kinds of Christology or different ways to identify Jesus:? How did you think about Jesus before reading this chapter? Did anything surprise you?

4) Do you see the author's description as more a return to an earlier way of identifying Jesus, or as a new idea?

6) How does your life reflect your belief systems, religious or otherwise? If you are a Christian, what is important about Jesus for you? If you are not a Christian, is anything about Jesus of interest or important for you?

Chapter 19: Does Theology Change? Atonement

1) What are the inherited or traditional theories of atonement?

2) Does the description of the developmental stages of atonement imagery in this chapter make sense to you?

3) What experiences have you had with different atonement motifs or their applications?

4) Where do you still have questions?

Open-ended Conclusion

1) What new thoughts have arisen for you with the reading of this book?
2) What questions do you have now?
3) What does the reading of this book make you want to read or discuss next?

Bibliography

"About CPT at-Tuwani." https://cpt.org/work/palestine/tuwani/about.
Ackerman, Peter, and Jack DuVall. *A Force More Powerful: A Century of Nonviolent Conflict*. New York: Palgrave, 2000.
Alexander, Michelle. *The New Jim Crow: Mass Incarceration in the Age of Colorblindness*. Rev. ed. Foreword by Cornel West. New York: New Press, 2012.
Anselm of Canterbury. "Why God Became Man." In *Anselm of Canterbury: The Major Works*, edited and with an introduction by Brian Davies and G. R. Evans, 260–356. Oxford: Oxford University Press, 1998.
"At-Tuwani." https://en.wikipedia.org/wiki/At-Tuwani.
Aulén, Gustaf. *Christus Victor: A Historical Study of the Three Main Types of the Idea of Atonement*. Translated by A. G. Herbert. New York: Macmillan, 1969.
Bellah, Robert N. "Civil Religion in America." In *American Civil Religion*, edited by Russell E. Richey and Donald G. Jones, 21–44. New York: Harper & Row, 1974.
Boersma, Hans. "Response to J. Denny Weaver." In *Atonement and Violence: A Theological Conversation*, edited by John Sanders, 33–36. Nashville: Abingdon, 2006.
———. *Violence, Hospitality and the Cross: Reappropriating the Atonement Tradition*. Grand Rapids: Baker, 2004.
———. "Violence, the Cross, and Divine Intentionality: A Modified Reformed View." In *Atonement and Violence: A Theological Conversation*, edited by John Sanders, 47–69. Nashville: Abingdon, 2006.
Boring, M. Eugene. *Revelation*. Interpretation. Louisville: John Knox, 1989.
Bowley, James E. *Introduction to Hebrew Bible: A Guided Tour of Israel's Sacred Library*. Upper Saddle River, NJ: Pearson Prentice Hall, 2008.
Boyarin, Daniel. *Border Lines: The Partition of Judaeo-Christianity*. Philadelphia: University of Pennsylvania Press, 2004.
Bright, John. *A History of Israel*. 4th ed. Introduction and appendix by William P. Brown. Louisville: Westminster John Knox, 2000.
Brock, Rita Nakashima. *Journeys by Heart: A Christology of Erotic Power*. New York: Crossroad, 1988.
Brock, Rita Nakashima, and Rebecca Ann Parker. *Saving Paradise: How Christianity Traded Love of This World for Crucifixion and Empire*. Boston: Beacon, 2008.
Brondos, David A. *Paul on the Cross: Reconstructing the Apostle's Story of Redemption*. Minneapolis: Fortress, 2006.

Brown, Joanne Carlson, and Rebecca Parker. "For God So Loved the World?" In *Christianity, Patriarchy and Abuse: A Feminist Critique*, edited by Joanne Carlson Brown and Carole R. Bohn, 1–30. New York: Pilgrim, 1989.

Brueggemann, Walter. *The Theology of the Old Testament: Testimony, Dispute, Advocacy.* Minneapolis: Fortress, 1997.

Burkholder, J. Lawrence. "The Limits of Perfection: Autobiographical Reflections." In *The Limits of Perfection: A Conversation with J. Lawrence Burkholder*, edited by Rodney J. Sawatsky and Scott Holland, 1–54. 2nd ed. Waterloo, Ontario: Institute of Anabaptist and Mennonite Studies, 1993.

Burrus, Virginia. *"Begotten, Not Made": Conceiving Manhood in Late Antiquity.* Stanford: Stanford University Press, 2000.

Cahill, Lisa Sowle. *Love Your Enemies: Discipleship, Pacifism, and Just War Theory.* Minneapolis: Fortress, 1994.

Calvin, John. *Calvin: Institutes of the Christian Religion.* Edited by John T. McNeill. Translated by Ford Lewis Battles. The Library of Christian Classics 20. Philadelphia: Westminster, 1960.

Carter, J. Kameron. *Race: A Theological Account.* New York: Oxford University Press, 2008.

Cherry, Conrad, ed. *God's New Israel: Religious Interpretations of American Destiny.* Rev. ed. Chapel Hill, NC: University of North Carolina Press, 1998.

Cone, James H. *The Cross and the Lynching Tree.* Maryknoll: Orbis, 2011.

———. *God of the Oppressed.* Rev. ed. Maryknoll: Orbis, 1997.

Crossan, John Dominic. *God and Empire: Jesus Against Rome, Then and Now.* New York: HarperCollins, 2007.

Easwaran, Eknath. *Nonviolent Soldier of Islam: Badshah Khan, a Man to Match His Mountains.* Tomales, CA: Nilgiri, 1999.

Eller, Vernard. *The Most Revealing Book in the Bible: Making Sense of Revelation.* Grand Rapids: Eerdmans, 1974.

Enright, Robert D. *Forgiveness Is a Choice: A Step-by-Step Process for Resolving Anger and Restoring Hope.* Washington, DC: American Psychological Association, 2001.

Epp, Charles R., et al. *Pulled Over: How Police Stops Define Race and Citizenship.* Chicago: The University of Chicago Press, 2014.

Federal Bureau of Investigation. "A Study of Active Shooter Incidents in the United States Between 2000 and 2013." https://www.fbi.gov/file-repository/active-shooter-study-2000-2013-1.pdf/view.

"Florida Women Disarm Intruder with Food, Rum." *Dayton Daily News*, October 31, 2003.

Follman, Mark. "More Guns, More Mass Shootings—Coincidence?" *Mother Jones*, December 15, 2012. https://www.motherjones.com/politics/2012/09/mass-shootings-investigation/.

Grimsrud, Ted. *The Good War That Wasn't—and Why It Matters: The Moral Legacy of World War II.* Eugene, OR: Cascade, 2014.

Gushee, David. *Changing Our Mind.* 2nd ed. Canton, MI: Read the Spirit, 2015.

Hanson, R. P. C. *The Search for the Christian Doctrine of God: The Arian Controversy 318–381 AD.* Edinburgh: T. & T. Clark, 1988.

Harder, James M. "The Violence of Global Marketization." In *Teaching Peace: Nonviolence and the Liberal Arts*, edited by J. Denny Weaver and Gerald Biesecker-Mast, 179–93. Lanham: Rowman & Littlefield, 2003.

Hart, Drew G. I. *Trouble I've Seen: Changing the Way the Church Views Racism.* Harrisonburg, VA: Herald, 2016.
Harvey, Jennifer. *Dear White Christians: For Those Still Longing for Racial Reconciliation.* Grand Rapids: Eerdmans, 2014.
Howard-Brook, Wes, and Anthony Gwyther. *Unveiling Empire: Reading Revelation Then and Now.* Maryknoll: Orbis, 1999.
Jenkins, Philip. *Jesus Wars: How Four Patriarchs, Three Queens, and Two Emperors Decided What Christians Would Believe for the Next 1,500 Years.* New York: HarperOne, 2010.
Jennings, Willie James. *The Christian Imagination: Theology and the Origins of Race.* New Haven: Yale University Press, 2010.
Kraybill, Donald B., et al. *Amish Grace: How Forgiveness Transcended Tragedy.* San Francisco: Jossey-Bass, 2007.
Lindsey, Hal. *The Late Great Planet Earth.* Grand Rapids: Zondervan, 1970.
Machinist, Peter. "Nahum." In *The Harper Collins Bible Commentary*, edited by James L. Mays, 665–67. Rev. ed. New York: HarperCollins, 2000.
Mast, Gerald J. *Go to Church, Change the World: Christian Community as Calling.* Harrisonburg: Herald, 2012.
McDonald, H. D. *The Atonement of the Death of Christ in Faith, Revelation, and History.* Grand Rapids: Baker, 1985.
McGovern, George. "Calling a Time Out." *Washington Post*, January 22, 2009. http://www.washingtonpost.com/wp-dyn/content/article/2009/01/21/AR2009012102489.html.
McLoughlin, William G. *Revivals, Awakenings, and Reform: An Essay on Religion and Social Change in America, 1607–1977.* Chicago History of American Religion. Chicago: University of Chicago Press, 1978.
Montel, Angela Horn. "Violent Images in Cell Biology." In *Teaching Peace: Nonviolence and the Liberal Arts*, edited by J. Denny Weaver and Gerald Biesecker-Mast, 223–34. Lanham: Rowman & Littlefield, 2003.
Murphy, Nancey, and George F. R. Ellis. *On the Moral Nature of the Universe: Theology, Cosmology, and Ethics.* Minneapolis: Fortress, 1996.
Murphy, Nancey C. *Reconciling Theology and Science: A Radical Reformation Perspective.* Scottdale, PA: Pandora, 1997.
Nelson-Pallmeyer, Jack. *Jesus Against Christianity: Reclaiming the Missing Jesus.* Harrisburg: Trinity, 2001.
Pal, Amitabh. *"Islam" Means Peace: Understanding the Muslim Principle of Nonviolence Today.* Santa Barbara: Praeger, 2011.
Paul, Robert S. *The Atonement and the Sacraments: The Relation of the Atonement to the Sacraments of Baptism and the Lord's Supper.* New York: Abingdon, 1960.
Pitts, Leonard, Jr. "Helping Fox's Bill O'Reilly Understand White Privilege." *Wisconsin State Journal*, December 8, 2014.
Rainey, W. Todd. "Nature's Tooth-and-Claw Conflict Resolution." In *Teaching Peace: Nonviolence and the Liberal Arts*, edited by J. Denny Weaver and Gerald Biesecker-Mast, 235–45. Lanham: Rowman & Littlefield, 2003.
Reddish, Mitchell G. *Revelation.* Smyth and Helwys Bible Commentary. Macon, GA: Smyth & Helwys, 2001.
Rieger, Joerg. *Christ and Empire: From Paul to Postcolonial Times.* Minneapolis: Fortress, 2007.

Sanders, John. *The God Who Risks: A Theology of Providence*. Downers Grove: InterVarsity 1998.
Seibert, Eric A. *Disturbing Divine Behavior: Troubling Old Testament Images of God*. Minneapolis: Fortress, 2009.
Sharp, Gene. *The Methods of Nonviolent Action*. The Politics of Nonviolent Action 2. Boston: Porter Sargent, 1973.
———. *Waging Nonviolent Struggle: 20th Century Practice and 21st Century Potential*. Boston: Porter Sargent, 2005.
"Singing Revolution." https://en.wikipedia.org/wiki/Singing_Revolution.
Smith, H. Shelton, et al. *American Christianity: An Historical Interpretation with Representative Documents*. Vol. 1, *1607–1820*. New York: Scribner's, 1960.
Southern, R. W. *Saint Anselm: A Portrait in a Landscape*. Cambridge: Cambridge University Press, 1990.
Spronk, Klaas. *Nahum*. Historical Commentary on the Old Testament. Kampen: Kok Pharos, 1997.
Stassen, Glen H., and Michael L. Westmoreland-White. "Defining Violence and Nonviolence." In *Teaching Peace: Nonviolence and the Liberal Arts*, edited by J. Denny Weaver and Gerald Biesecker-Mast, 17–36. Lanham: Rowman & Littlefield, 2003.
Swoboda, Jörg. *The Revolution of the Candles: Christians in the Revolution in the German Democratic Republic*. Macon, GA: Mercer University Press, 1996.
Thomas, Steve. "Martial Arts as a Model for Nonviolence: Resisting Interpersonal Violence with Assertive Force." *The Conrad Grebel Review* 33.1 (Winter 2013) 72–91.
Untener, Ken. "Prophets of a Future Not Our Own." http://www.usccb.org/prayer-and-worship/prayers-and-devotions/prayers/archbishop_romero_prayer.cfm.
Van Voorst, Robert E. *Reading the New Testament Today*. Belmont, CA: Thomson/Wadsworth, 2005.
Waal, Frans B. M. de. *The Age of Empathy: Nature's Lessons for a Kinder Society*. New York: Harmony, 2009.
Walker, Williston. *The Creeds and Platforms of Congregationalism*. Boston: Pilgrim, 1963.
Weaver, J. Denny. *The Nonviolent Atonement*. 2nd ed. Grand Rapids: Eerdmans, 2011.
———. *The Nonviolent God*. Grand Rapids: Eerdmans, 2013.
———. "Responding to September 11—and October 7 and January 29: Which Religion Shall We Follow?" *The Conrad Grebel Review* 20.2 (Spring 2002) 79–100.
Weaver, J. Denny, and Gerald J. Mast. *Nonviolent Word: Anabaptism, the Bible, and the Grain of the Universe*. Eugene, OR: Pickwick, 2020.
Whisenant, Edgar C. *88 Reasons Why the Rapture Will Be in 1988*. Nashville: World Bible Society, 1988.
Williams, Delores S. *Sisters in the Wilderness: The Challenge of Womanist God-Talk*. Maryknoll: Orbis, 1993.
Willimon, William H. "Bless You, Mrs. Degrafinried." *Christian Century* 101.9 (14 March 1984) 269–70.
Wink, Walter. *Engaging the Powers: Discernment and Resistance in a World of Domination*. The Powers 3. Minneapolis: Fortress, 1992.
———. *Jesus and Nonviolence: A Third Way*. Minneapolis: Fortress, 2003.

Wise, Tim. *Dear White America: Letter to a New Minority*. San Francisco: City Lights, 2012.

Wright, N. T. *The Resurrection of the Son of God*. Christian Origins and the Question of God 3. Minneapolis: Fortress, 2003.

Yoder, John Howard. "Armaments and Eschatology." *Studies in Christian Ethics* 1 (1988) 43–61.

———. *The Jewish-Christian Schism Revisited*. Edited by Michael G. Cartwright and Peter Ochs. Grand Rapids: Eerdmans, 2003.

———. *Preface to Theology: Christology and Theological Method*. Introduction by Stanley Hauerwas and Alex Sider. Grand Rapids: Brazos, 2002.

Yoder, John Howard, et al. *What Would You Do? A Serious Answer to a Standard Question*. Expanded ed. Scottdale, PA: Herald, 1992.

Subject Index

A

Abelard, Peter, 39–41. *See also*
    Atonement, moral influence
Abraham (Patriarch), 21, 88, 133,
    136–37, 147, 155–57, 162
activism. *See* Nonviolence, active
Afghanistan, 69, 71
Age of Empathy, 119
Alexander, Michelle, 96
Amish, Old Order, 64, 67n8, 76
Anselm of Canterbury. *See also*,
    Atonement, satisfaction.
    atonement doctrine, 38
    Cur Deus Homo, 38, 209–11
    death of Jesus aimed Godward,
        40
    removed Satan from atonement,
        38, 40
    feudal context, 210
    not Pauline, 212–14
    rejected ransom theory, 38, 41
    restored order in creation, 38,
        209–11
    Why God Became man, 38, 209
Arius, 199
atonement, definition of, 6
atonement, Christus Victor, classic,
    37–38
    as cosmic battle, 37, 40
    death of Jesus aimed at Satan, 40
    image of God, 46
    image of Jesus, 43
    as ransom, 37, 38–39, 43, 208

atonement, moral influence. 39. *See
    also*, Abelard, Peter
    death of Jesus aimed at
        humankind, 39, 40
    rejected ransom atonement,
        39, 41
    rejected satisfaction atonement,
        39, 40, 41
    image of God in, 39, 40, 46
    model of Jesus, 43
atonement, nonviolent, xi
    climax, 42
    confronts evil, 45, 48–49, 50–51,
        206–9
    death does not impact God, 44
    fits the Bible, 38–39, 206–7
    definition, 36
    demise of, 207–9
    distinguished from classic
        Christus Victor, 37–38, 41
    and ecclesiology, 206–12
    forgiveness in, 79–81
    as lived faith, 44, 46
    model of Jesus, 43
    as narrative of Jesus, 32, 33–36,
        44
    as narrative Christus Victor, 42
    and nonviolent God, 46–47, 69,
        100, 113
    and Paul, 35–36, 212–14
    and Prodigal Son, 82–83
    in Revelation, 206–7
    as saving story, 35–36
    See also Resurrection

atonement, penal/substitutionary,
  definition of, 6, 33, 39
  forgiveness in, 79–80
  image of God in, 42–44
  model of Jesus, 43, 45
  in Protestant Reformers, 39
  Jesus' death pays divine law, 40
  as surrogacy, 48, 97
  and womanist theology, 48, 96–97
atonement, satisfaction, 38
  abusive imagery in, 46–48
  advent of, 38, 209–11
  agent of Jesus' death, 43–44
  and black theology, 48
  Jesus' death aimed Godward, 40, 45
  defenses of, 49
  feudal context, 209–11
  forgiveness in, 79–80
  image of God in, 42–44
  model of Jesus, 43
  as surrogacy, 48, 97
  and womanist theology, 48, 96–97
At-Tuwani, x, 71

B
bananas, 90–91
Barak, 127–28
Basil of Caesarea, 200
Bible
  character of, 154–59, 162, 166–67
  as narrative, 157–59
black theology, 48, 202–3. *See also* Cone, James; Carter, J. Kameron; Jennings, Willie James
Brondos, David, 212–14
Brueggemann, Walter, 118
bus boycott, 69

C
Caligula, 176, 181
Calvin, John, 39, 105, 211. *See also* Atonement, penal/substitutionary, in Protestant Reformers
Cappadocians, 200–202
Carter, J. Kameron, 203
Chalcedon. *See* Christology. Chalcedon
Charlemagne, 209
Christian Peacemaker Teams, x, 12, 72, 109
Christology,
  changes in, ix, 192, 193–94, 201–5
  classic, 199–201
  Chalcedon, 200–202, 209
  Constantinople, 193, 199–201
  definition of, 6, 32
  life of Jesus, separated from, 58
  narrative, 32, 194–96, 201–4
  Nicea/Nicene Creed, 193, 199, 201–2
Christus Victor. *See* Atonement, Christus Victor, classic; Atonement, Christus Victor, narrative
civil religion, 60
Civil Rights movement, 67n8, 68, 70, 96–97, 218
Civil War, 73, 96, 103, 131
Claudius, 176, 181
Cone, James H., 48, 202–3
The Congo, 109, 214
Connecticut Yankee in King Arthur's Court, 167
conquest of Canaan, 127, 138, 155, 158
Constantine, 199, 208
Constantinople. *See* Christology, Constantinople.
Copernicus, Nicolaus, 11
cosmos/cosmology, 10–11, 36, 45, 111, 113, 121–23, 134, 168, 172, 197–98
creation, 28n1, 112, 116, 117–18, 123–24, 132–35, 155, 157, 197, 217
crusades, 102

D

Deborah, 127
de Gaulle, Charles, 13–14
Degrafinried, Mrs., 71, 74
David (King), 21, 128–29, 139, 142, 173–74
Devil. *See* Satan
de Waal, Frans, 119
Doctrine of Discovery, 203

E

economic issues, 50, 63, 84–92, 97, 113, 147, 211
Elisha, xii, 139
Enuma Elish, 133–34, 161
England, Martin and Mabel, 99
Epp, Charles R., 96
Estonia, 70–71
Eucharist. *See* Lord's Supper
exile, 142–44, 147
exodus (from Egypt), 60, 126, 130–31, 137

F

feminist theology, 46–47
feudalism. *See* Anselm, feudal context; Atonement, satisfaction, feudal context.
Flood, Great, 28n1, 125–26, 131, 135–36
football, 61, 106, 112–13, 166, 169
Force More Powerful, A, 70
forgiveness,
    in atonement images, 39, 55, 79–81
    by God, 25, 55, 82–83
    by Jesus, 34
    and love of enemies, 78–79
    Prodigal Son, 82–83
    in psychology, 76–78
    and restorative justice, 77, 81–83
freedom
    human (free will), 112–13, 123–24
    linked to war, 59–60

G

Gandhi, Mahatma, 71–72, 75, 79

gay, 28n1, 99, 103, 107, 160, 218
Gero Cross, 209–10
Gideon, 138–39
God
    anger/punishment by, 2, 38–39, 80, 101–4, 108–9, 125–26, 128–31, 144–45, 148–50, 213
    modeled on humankind, 106–7
    nonviolence of, 1, 30, 46–47, 69, 71–72, 123–24, 132–45, 150–52
    omnipotence of, 101–14
    omnipotence, definition of, 107–8
    revealed in Jesus, 1, 3–6, 9 12, 14–15, 23, 31, 46, 50–52, 58, 69, 74–75, 79, 82, 88, 95, 99–100, 101, 106–8, 113–14, 116–17, 119, 122, 124, 125, 147, 150, 153, 163, 168, 180, 186–88, 192, 205
    violence of, 59–62, 101–6
    See also Jesus, reveals God.
grain of the universe, ix, 31, 52, 63–64, 68–69, 73, 75m 78–80, 82, 99, 113, 116, 124, 217
    definition, 31
Gregory of Nazianzus, 200
Gregory of Nyssa, 200
Gulliver's Travels, 166

H

Habitat for Humanity, 12
Haider-Markel, Donald, 96
Hurricane Katrina, 103, 108–9, 121, 131
Hurricane Sandy, 102

I

immigrants/immigration, 12, 64, 94, 205
Iraq, 69, 103
Isaac (Patriarch), 137, 155
Islam. *See* Muslim, 31, 64

J

Jennings, Willie James, 203

Jesus,
    birth, 20–21
    continuing Israel's history, 146–47
    death, 27–29, 33
    and economics, 84–87
    identified by narrative, 12–14, 152–53
    healing withered hand, 24
    healings and restorations, 23–24
    lived narrative of, 14–15
    mission of, 21–22
    narrative as atonement, 34–36, 209
    and nature, 116–17
    nonviolence of, ix, 53–56, 74–75, 123, 150–52
    "proved," 10–12
    reveals God, 1, 9–10, 30, 36, 58
    resurrection, 29–31, 33–34
    and Samaritans, 24, 30, 34, 45, 56, 93–95, 97, 99, 107, 150, 160
    as saving story, 30–31, 35–36
    sayings, 25–27
    as surrogate, 48, 97
    temple cleansing, 24–25, 27, 34, 55,
    and women, 24, 26, 31, 34, 45, 95–96, 99, 107, 147, 150, 160
    See also Resurrection
Jordan, Clarence and Florence, 98–99
judges of Israel, 127–28, 138–39, 142–43

K
Kenya, 214
Khan, Badshan, 71–72, 75, 79
Koinonia Farm, 98

L
Late Great Planet Earth, 166
law codes, 24–27, 55, 93, 126, 155–56
Leipzig, 70
lesbians, 99, 103, 107, 160, 218
LGBTQ. *See* gay; lesbian

Lincoln, Abraham, 103–4, 131
Lindsey, Hal, 166
Lord's Supper, 27, 63
love of enemies, 55–57, 78
Luther, Martin, 39, 211

M
Maynard-Moody, Steven, 96
McGovern, George, 69
Mennonite Central Committee, 12m4, 13
Mennonites, x, xii, 12n4, 64, 67n8, 72, 109, 155
Mexico, 89
Montel, Angela Horn, 120
moral influence atonement. *See* Atonement, moral influence theory
Murphy, Nancey, 121–23
Muslim, 31, 64, 71–72, 102, 205

N
NAFTA, 89
nature/natural world, 115–24
    red in tooth and claw, 118–21
narrative Christus Victor. *See* Atonement, narrative Christus Victor
Native Americans, 48, 73, 102, 203
Nero, 176–77, 179, 181, 185–86
New Jim Crow, The, 96
Nicea. *See* Christology, Nicea/Nicene Creed.
Nicene Creed. *See* Christology, Nicea/Nicene Creed.
nonviolence, 53–75
    active, 53–56, 63–66, 68–75
    by Jesus, 53–56, 68–69
    continuum of, 66–68
    defined, 8
    nonresistant, 54, 64, 67n8, 68, 218
    as resistance, 53–56, 63–75
    and nonretaliation, 8, 56–57
    Sermon on the Mount, 53–56
    Paul, 56
    See also, God, nonviolence of.
Nonviolent Atonement, The, xi, 212

SUBJECT INDEX 239

Nonviolent God, The, xi

O
Old Testament, 5, 14, 84, 156, 162, 195, 198, 218
   and civil religion, 60
   violent imagery, 3, 59, 61, 125–31, 146, 148–51, 155
   nonviolent imagery, 132–45, 146–47, 151–52
Operation Dove, 72

P
pacifist dilemma, 74
Penn, William, 72
Pitts, Leonard, 98
Prodigal Son. *See* Forgiveness, Prodigal Son.
Pulled Over, 96
Puritans, 102, 104–5, 131

Q
Quakers, 72

R
racism, 45, 48–50, 58, 93–97, 107, 113, 150, 211, 218
   in theology, 202–4
Rainey, Todd, 118–20
Reformation, Protestant, x, 39, 105, 154, 211
restorative justice, 64, 73, 81–83, 87
resurrection,
   absent Anselm/satisfaction atonement. 210
   identifies/validates Jesus with God, 14, 30, 32, 35, 51, 171, 194, 201
   explains saving story, 30, 32, 36, 213
   omnipotence of God revealed, 107–8, 113
   reign of God present in the world, 44, 80, 111
   symbol of resistance, 48, 182, 206
   ultimate power of God displayed, 35, 111, 168
   as victory over death/Satan, 36. 37, 112–13, 116–17, 123–24, 169, 172, 179–80, 182, 188–89, 191–92, 198, 208
Revelation, book of, 3, 59, 156–57, 161–62, 163–92, 198, 206–8, 211, 214
   anti-Christ, 184–87
   cosmic battle, 145, 180–83, 189
   dragon/Satan, 180–82
   ecclesiology of, 181–83, 191–92
   heavenly throne room, 171–75
   about Jesus, 168, 173–75, 186, 192
   Jesus linked to God, 173–75
   martyrs, 177–79, 181, 183
   millennium, 188–89
   New Jerusalem, 189–91
   as nonviolent atonement, 206–7
   and nonviolent God, 163, 168, 180, 182, 186, 188, 190, 192
   not predictive, 164–67, 168, 170, 177, 183, 186
   principles of interpretation, 163–70
   and resurrection, 168, 179–80, 182, 189, 191
   rider on white horse, 187–89
   seven seals, 172, 175–80
   slain lamb, 173–74, 178, 198
   and violent God, 3, 163
Revolution of the Candles, 70
Revolutionary War, 59–60
Romero, Oscar, 109–10

S
Samaritans, 24, 30, 34, 45, 56, 93–95, 97, 99, 107, 150, 160
   Good Samaritan, 94–95
satisfaction atonement. *See* Atonement, satisfaction theory
Satan,
   in classic Christus Victor, 37–38, 40, 43, 45, 208
   as dragon/empire, 181–83, 185–86, 189, 206

Satan (*continued*),
    removed from atonement, 8–41, 209
Saul (King), 128
science, branches of, 121–23
"Scripture alone," 154–55
"secret plan," 105, 111
September 11, 69–71
Sermon on the Mount, 53–55, 58, 78, 85
Singing Revolution, 70
Sisera, 127–28
Sisters in the Wilderness, 97
slave, slavery
    biblical, 28, 54, 60, 126, 137, 148–50, 160, 177, 185
    United States, 48, 60, 73, 96–97, 103, 131, 160, 203–4, 217–18
Soccer, 151
Stassen, Glen H., 7
substitutionary atonement. *See* Atonement, substitutionary theory
surrogacy, 58, 97
Swift, Jonathan, 166–67
Syrophoenician woman, 94, 136

T
Tallinn, 70
theology
    reflections on narrative, ix, 4–8, 32, 52, 58, 158–59, 194, 218–19
    linked to ethics, 2, 6, 30–31, 58–59, 202–3
    specific to Jesus, 8–9, 58
Tiberius, 176, 181
Titus, 177, 180, 181
Trinity, 9, 193, 200–202

V

Vespasian, 177–81
violence,
    in atonement, 1, 7–8, 37–41, 43–49, 50–51, 80, 209
    continuum of, 66–68
    is cyclical, 56–57, 72, 75, 78
    defined, 7–8, 58–59
    national, 59–60
    New Testament, 3, 148–50
    Old Testament, 3, 60, 125–31, 146
    in popular media, 60–61
    structural/systemic, 7–8, 34, 50–51, 58–59, 88–92, 95–96, 98–99, 113, 150, 211–12
    See also God, violence of

W
West Nickel Mines, 76
What Would You Do?, 71n15
Whisenant, Edgar C., 166
white privilege, 97–100
Williams, Delores, 48, 97
Witness for Peace, 12
womanist theology, 48, 96–97, 193
women, 8, 24, 26, 29–30, 34, 45–46, 48–49, 61, 93–97, 99, 102, 104, 107, 118, 147, 150, 155, 160, 218–19. *See also* Jesus, and women.
    In atonement images, 45–49, 95, 96–97
World War I, 13, 60, 73
World War II, 13, 60, 73

Y
Yoder, John Howard, 71n15, 74,

Z
Zacchaeus, 87–88
Zach, xii, 1–4, 6, 42, 44, 46, 217

Scripture Index

OLD TESTAMENT

Genesis
1 and 2	117, 131–35
1:27	117

Exodus
14:25	126
22:25–27	55

Leviticus
19:18	25
19:27	155

Deuteronomy
6:5	25
13:1–5	126
13:6–11	126, 155
14:3–21	155
17:2–7	126
21:18–21	126, 155
22:5	155
22:13–22	126
22:22–24	155
23:9, 11	155
24:10–13	55

Joshua
1–12	127, 155
6:21	127
7:24	127
13:1	138

Judges
4:23	128
7	138–39

1 Samuel
	128
15:3	128
15:10	128
16	128

2 Samuel
	128
7:13	128
7:16	128
8:14	129

1 Kings
1–2	128

2 Kings
6	139

1 Chronicles
11–29	128

Psalms
78:11–16, 43–48	130
106:40–41	130
118:22	149
135:10–12	131

Isaiah

10:5–19	129
10:5–11	129
10:16–17	130
42:1–4	140
49:1–6	140
50:4–9	140
52:13—53:12	140
53:4–6	140
56:7	25
61:2b	22

Jeremiah

5:26–28	85
7:11	25

Daniel

1	143
3	143
6:22	144

Amos

2:6	84
5:11–12	84
6:1–7	84

Jonah

4:2	141
4:10–11	141

Nahum

1:2	130
1:3	141
1:14	130
2:2	130
2:10	130
2:13	130

NEW TESTAMENT

Matthew

	20–21
5:39	218
5:38–42	54
5:44	55, 78
6:19–21	85
9:35–10:15	22
13:3–9, 24–30	116
15:21–28	136
16:4	151
18:18–30	151
18:23–35	148
18:35	148
19:16–30	151
19:21	86, 151
21:33–46	148
21:41	149
21:42	149
21:43–44	149
22:1–14	149
22:9	149
22:13	149
22:36–38	26
23	26
25:14–30	149
26:3–5, 14–16	27
26:47	27

Mark

1:18	25
7:24–30	136
10:6–12	155
10:17–31	151
12:1–12	148

Luke

	20–21
4:16–39	21
5:17–26	23
6:43–44	116
7:11–17	23, 116
8:1	22
8:40–56	23, 116
10:1–16	22
10:25–28	26
10:29–37	94
12:6, 22–28	116
12:24, 27–31	86
13:6–9	116
14:12–14	85
15:11–32	82, 151
14:21, 23–24	150

18:18–30	151
19:1–10	87
19:12–27	149
19:46	25
19:47–48	25
20:9–19	148
20:25	25

John

1	139, 197
2:15	25
4:1–39	93
11:38–44	116
12:6	86
13:26–30	27
18:3	27
18:10	28
18:36	28, 152

Acts

2	36
2:14–39	35, 159, 195
3:13–26	35, 159, 195
4:10–12	35, 159, 195
5:30–32	35, 159, 195
10:36–43	35, 159, 195
11:28–29	176
13:17–41	36, 159, 195
13:28	195

Romans

1:4	30
12:17, 20, 21	56, 78, 203

1 Corinthians

11	155
15	35, 36, 159, 196, 197
15:3–7	213

Ephesians

6:17	188

Philippians

2	159

Colossians

1	159

1 Thessalonians

5:15	56, 78, 203

1 Timothy

6:15	187

Hebrews

1:1	9
4:2	188

1 Peter

3:4	155
3:9	56, 78, 204

Revelation

1:1	168
4 and 5	159
4:11	172
5 and 6	198
5:9	173
5:13	173
6	175–80
6:1	173
7	178–79, 208
12	180–83
12:10	181
13	184–87
17:14	187
19:21	190
20	188–89
21	189–91

www.ingramcontent.com/pod-product-compliance
Lightning Source LLC
Chambersburg PA
CBHW031731230426
43669CB00007B/316